Back Page Football

A CENTURY OF NEWSPAPER COVERAGE

For Judith, Nicholas and Emma

Back Page Football

A CENTURY OF NEWSPAPER COVERAGE

STEPHEN F. KELLY

Aurora Publishing

A QUEEN ANNE PRESS BOOK
for Aurora Publishing

First published in Great Britain in 1988
by Queen Anne Press, a division of
Lennard Associates Limited
Mackerye End
Harpenden
Hertfordshire AL5 5DR

Revised Edition 1995

ISBN 1 85926 067 5

British Library Cataloguing in Publication Data is available

Cover photographs
Front: Stanley Matthews (left) and members of the
England side after winning the World Cup in 1966 (Colorsport)
Back: Blackburn, the 1995 Premier League champions (Colorsport)

Printed and bound in Great Britain by
Butler and Tanner Ltd, Frome

Errata page 211 The text should end with the words 'credit and style.'
page 215 The text should end with the words 'able to attend.'

CONTENTS

INTRODUCTION

As the twentieth century dawned, football was still in its infancy. The FA Cup had been launched in 1871 but the League had been born only twelve years earlier in 1888. Formed with only a dozen clubs it had, by 1900, multiplied to 36 members divided into two divisions. All of the original clubs had come from the Midlands and the North-West, but the new additions brought recruits from Yorkshire, the North-East and even London. The turn of the century saw an era of enterprise and municipalism, which had thrived under Queen Victoria, draw to a close. The growth of local authorities and public utilities, the increase in leisure time, improved cheap rail links and the advent of community identity all helped encourage the development of sport, and in particular football. The aristocratic roots of the game had already ended when as far back as 1883 Blackburn Olympic overpowered the élitist Old Etonians to not only bring the Cup north for the first time but to give it a new working class identity. From that moment on the game became the preserve of the working classes and began to centre around the churches and organisations that lay at the heart of their communities. Spurred on by an emphasis on sport as a spiritual and moral cleanser of the mind and body, competition quickly spread. Rugby, which for so long had been the dominant winter sport, suddenly found itself challenged by the new game and as spectator interest heightened, rugby was forced into second place.

Attendances at matches were still low in 1900. The Cup Final could attract crowds of 70,000 but few league games attracted more than 20,000. Stadiums were still small with usually no more than one stand and a couple of cinder bankings, and administrators were only just beginning to realise that there was money to be made from the sport. The game needed more widespread publicity to excite interest and there was only one place that that could come from – the newspapers.

The press had not ignored the development of football. The *Athletic News*, founded in 1875, along with other sporting papers such as the *Sporting Life*, *Sporting Sketches*, the *Sportsman*, the *Sporting Clipper* and the *Sporting Chronicle*, had given extensive coverage to the game long before the turn of the century. Although some of the more 'quality' newspapers continued to ignore it, the popular newspapers featured soccer alongside other sports. Local newspapers, particularly in the north showed more interest and in Liverpool a Saturday evening *Football Echo* had been launched to coincide with the opening of the Football League. There was no radio in those days and information came only through newspapers. If there was no local football echo published on a Saturday evening, then it was often a case of waiting until the following morning when the Sunday newspapers arrived before the results could be gleaned, or in some cases waiting even until the Monday morning for the weekly edition of the *Athletic News*, the *Sporting Chronicle* or one of the many other sporting newspapers or dailies.

In 1900 a number of factors suddenly emerged to spur the press's interest. The first was a breakthrough in photography which allowed fast action shots to be captured without the usual blurring. At the same time, newspaper technology improved sufficiently to allow the speedy reproduction and printing of photographs on pages. Out went the posed player portrait and the wide distant match photograph, and in came the action shot and touchline photography. Suddenly names became faces and description was turned into action. The second development was the spread of education, with wide sections of the working classes learning to read. It meant that newspapers became more accessible. Finally, a new brand of newspapers such as the *Daily Mirror* – which relied heavily on photographs, large headlines and short simple sentences – were launched, aimed at a wide, popular market. The tabloid which let the pictures tell the story had arrived, and reached out to many thousands who before would never have bought or even read a paper.

Sport became an essential ingredient of these

newspapers with football leading the assault. Football had already hit the front page on one occasion when, in 1902, a disaster at Ibrox Park in which 25 died was splashed across the front, but that was a rare occasion with football incidental to the tragedy. Coverage was still fairly basic, relying heavily on results, although the first £1,000 transfer in 1905 brought a new departure with the sports pages giving more space to transfer news as well as introducing speculation. By the time the next big transfer barrier was smashed in 1928, when David Jack signed for Arsenal for £10,000, the headlines were even bigger and the story had been promoted from the back page to the front.

Having helped soccer become the most popular sport in England, the newspapers continued unchallenged in their reporting of the game for thirty years or more. In the early 1920s, the arrival of a third division north and south meant even more space had to be devoted to the sport. Radio did not arrive seriously until the 1930s, with the first broadcast from Highbury in 1927. But once regular football coverage was adopted by the BBC, newspapers had to begin the painful process of change. Radio could provide results cheaply and quickly. Many of the small specialised footballing newspapers and magazines had disappeared as far back as 1910, when the popular dailies increased their coverage of the game, and even the most famous of them all, the *Athletic News*, was forced to merge with the *Sporting Chronicle* in July 1931. By then, even the quality newspapers had been forced to give coverage of the game.

For a brief time the Second World War interrupted sport, with football relegated to the occasional corner and given little prominence. Paper was in short supply and there were far more serious matters to be reported than events at Ashton Gate, Roker Park or Maine Road. But once the war had ended, football rose to new peaks as crowds flocked to matches in the new climate of peacetime leisure and fun. There were record attendances, and international club football arrived in the shape of Moscow Dynamo and then Honved and Real Madrid, and with it floodlit football. And in 1950 England participated in the World Cup for the first time.

All of this was welcomed enthusiastically by Fleet Street who were as excited and fascinated as the average fan. But after world domination of the game, the English press – which had adopted a coarse jingoistic attitude – suddenly learnt that England and many of its club sides were no match for some continental teams. The USA knocked England out of the 1950 World Cup, causing the *Daily Express* to dub it English sport's 'worst day', and when Hungary thrashed England at Wembley three years later, the *News Chronicle* reckoned that 'the world is really upside down'.

Patriotism has always been a hallmark of Fleet Street, whether describing war, diplomatic negotiations or sport. There was, and remains, an assumption that Britain – or England – is the best. As far back as 1930 both the *Guardian* and the *Athletic News* wondered how the first ever World Cup could possibly be described as such when England were not participating. At least they mentioned it, however; the rest of Fleet Street simply ignored the event. Again, when the European Cup was launched in 1955, the British press paid no attention to events on the Continent. Even more recently, the back pages recklessly predicted an English triumph in the 1988 European Nations' Cup, only to then turn on Bobby Robson and his team when they returned home humiliated after three defeats.

But if England's dominance of the world game was a dilemma the papers had to confront during the post-war years, the greater problem came during the 1960s and '70s when the challenge of television and falling circulations along Fleet Street led to a catastrophic re-evaluation of the back pages. Newspapers could not compete with TV. Nobody wanted to read match reports of a game already seen on the small screen and nor could the back pages match slow motion replays and the carefully crafted analysis of soccer commentators. As a result, the back-pages of the popular papers assumed a more magazine-like quality. Sensational transfer stories, the odd brief match report and player interviews were soon sitting comfortably side by side.

Newspapers may have been able to make Stanley Matthews, Tommy Lawton and Billy Wright into household names, but television could turn them into stars. The abolition of the maximum wage had catapulted players into a new salary bracket, helping to create the image of well-heeled sporting heroes. Players like George Best, Rodney Marsh and Bobby Moore suddenly found themselves the equal of film stars, appearing not just on TV sports programmes but on chat shows and in commercials. In the newspapers, too, they were now to be found not only on the back pages but on the front pages and in the gossip columns as well.

Managers, too, with their 'rentaquotes' and champagne personalities became just as important as the players. Prior to 1960, probably only Herbert Chapman, Stan Cullis, Matt Busby and Walter Winterbottom were well known, but with the 1960s came Bill Shankly, Tommy Docherty, Alf Ramsey, Don Revie and a host of quickly to be forgotten names. The manager assumed a new importance. Some encouraged the trend with their exuberant lifestyles, but as the manager grew more important, so he would become the scapegoat for defeats.

Players were frequently encouraged to give their opinions – the more forthright, the higher the payment – and even managers today blast away at each other across the trenches of Fleet Street. Any famous name nearing the end of his career can be guaranteed a lucrative pay-off if he will reveal locker-room secrets or slam manager and chairman alike. Others like George Best with their good looks, girlfriends and drinking habits, not only found their way on to the front pages of the tabloids but have had their sexual exploits graphically detailed for all to read. It has not always been for the good of the game, leading to players being labelled arrogant, greedy and irresponsible.

If players have had their sex lives splashed across the papers, then at least the manager might have reckoned he was immune. But not so. In 1977 Tommy Docherty, then manager of Manchester United, found his love life splattered across the front pages and was quickly hounded out of Old Trafford. Other managers followed in his wake. John Bond, Malcolm Macdonald and David Pleat all suffered the same fate as the tabloids revealed their dark secrets.

This is not to say that the back pages have not produced some splendid journalism. Over the years fine writers such as Ivan Sharpe, Charles Buchan, J. P. W. Mallalieu, Geoffrey Green, Michael Parkinson, Brian Glanville and Hugh McIlvanney, to name but a few, have added to the richness of the game through their dedicated prose, while others have toiled to uncover the seamier side of the sport. The *Sunday People*, for instance, in 1964 unearthed a massive betting scandal which, had it continued much longer, could have had dire consequences.

More recently – though it undoubtedly should have happened much earlier – the popular press has campaigned against racial chants on the terraces and the religious bigotry of Glasgow football. Still more rich pickings must surely remain for the investigative reporter, while the campaigns against hooliganism and racism will continue for many more years, until they are driven away from the terraces.

Football journalists work under enormous pressures. The daily grind of producing news to fill the back pages is never easy, but sometimes leads to excesses with over-familiar clichés, unnecessary speculation and a reluctance to expose the humbug of players, managers and chairmen. The lobby which has grown up where newspapers and clubs mutually feed off each other for news and exclusives has reached an unhealthy level. Journalists may not always feel free to criticise when they rely so much on clubs for access and information. Indeed, reporters and newspapers continue to be threatened by some clubs who are oversensitive to criticism.

Yet despite the declining standards of some newspapers, the back pages have remained a triumphal record of the history of football. From the earliest match reports which often ran to as much as 2,000 words, to the sensational banner headlines of today's tabloids, the papers provide the excitement, the results and the glamour of what has become the world's most popular sport. No doubt many favourite moments have been omitted from this book or important events neglected such as Cup Finals, championship deciders and World Cup games. I apologise if they have, but space unfortunately permits only a select choice.

At least three-quarters of the nation's male population begin reading their daily newspaper at the sports page, and more often than not that page will be dominated by football. Cricket may have its column inches in the summer, rugby may regularly capture space in the quality papers and athletics may occasionally have its moments, but it is soccer which nearly always dominates the headlines. What follows is not so much a book about journalism but more a history of football through the eyes of the papers and the journalists who recorded the great events in the game. Today's newspapers are tomorrow's history books, and there can be no more exciting a way to discover history than through newspapers. Long may football continue to dominate the back pages.

Acknowledgements

My parents never bought a morning newspaper. It was a luxury we could ill afford, but every summer and Christmas when I was young we would visit my grandparents in Huddersfield, where I would spend at least a day devouring the huge neat stack of *Daily Heralds* which had been collecting on the kitchen cabinet for the best part of six months. It was the 1950s and the back pages were filled with names like Billy Wright, John Charles, Di Stefano and Duncan Edwards. It whetted my appetite not just for football and the sports pages but for newspapers in general. To find myself years later not only working as a journalist but to be writing a history of the back pages is therefore something of a privilege. So perhaps first and foremost I owe a great debt to my grandfather who, for some reason or another, devotedly kept all those *Daily Heralds* which fortuitously excited my interest in newspapers.

This book however could not have been written without the help of many others who gave valuable time and advice during its conception. In particular I would like to thank Maurice Golesworthy who spotted and corrected various errors and Stephen Boulton whose checking of the manuscript and pursuit of the misrelated participle knew no bounds. I would also like to thank the staff of the Liverpool Central Library and the British Newspaper Library at Colindale, but in particular I owe special appreciation to the staff of the Manchester Central Library who must have grown weary of my continual demands each day for more newspapers. Credit should also go to Tony Fabiani who unearthed newspaper cuttings on Scottish football, George Highman for his many suggestions, Simon Inglis, Ray Spiller, Ian Ridley, Jack Rollin, the National Museum of Photography, the Association of Football Statisticians, the staff of the Football League and the Football Association, Sports Programmes of Coventry and to the many journalists and newspapers which have been quoted liberally in my text. Thanks are due most, though, to my wife Judith Rowe Jones who gave unrelenting support and constructive criticism throughout the many long hours of writing, and even managed to time the arrival of young Nicholas to the day I completed the manuscript. Finally, but not least, I am indebted to my publishers Queen Anne Press and in particular my editor Christine Davis, Alan Samson, picture researcher Donna Thynne, and designer Jane Warring for their professionalism and hard work in helping to make this such a worthwhile endeavour.

Stephen F. Kelly
Manchester, August 1988

ABOVE: *Aston Villa displaying the League Championship Trophy, 1900*

1900

THERE IS no doubt that, at the turn of the century, Aston Villa were the team of the moment. In April 1900 they clinched the league championship with a 1–0 win at Molineux that gave them a record number of first division points. Formed in 1874 they had been founder members of the Football League in 1888, and over the next dozen years won the championship on no less than five occasions, also winning the FA Cup twice while losing the 1892 Final. Seven trophies were captured in as many years, and in 1897 they achieved the Double following in the footsteps of the great 1889 Preston team, the Invincibles.

During their heyday Villa boasted a team of outstanding internationals, the most famous pair being half-back James Crabtree, a one-time Burnley player who won 14 England caps, and Charlie Athersmith, a prince among wingers. Athersmith had joined the Villa in February 1891 and collected a dozen caps for England during his Villa period. Right-back Howard Spencer was another England international who was capped 6 times and went on to become a distinguished director of the club. Behind him was goalkeeper and three-times England international William George who finished his days as a trainer with Birmingham City. Upfront there was left-winger Stephen Smith who won just one England honour before joining Portsmouth, and inside-left Fred Wheldon who made four appearances for England while at the Villa but left in the summer of 1900 to join their neighbours West Bromwich Albion.

Top scorer in the 1900 championship team was centre-forward Billy Garratty who netted 27 goals and won one England cap before leaving for Leicester Fosse in 1908. Another stalwart who had seen all the action throughout the 1900s was inside-right John Devey who had joined Villa in 1891. He collected two England caps and served as a club director until 1934. Yet another player from that side who would become a Villa director was half-back Bertie Wilkes who won five England caps. On an average Saturday Villa could muster at least half a dozen England internationals. And all this was to ignore James Cowan, a towering centre-half who won three Scottish caps. In their 6–2 defeat of Notts County – a win which clearly signalled their claim to the championship – Villa fielded no less than nine players who either were or would become internationals. It was little wonder that they should capture the first league championship of the twentieth century, pipping Sheffield United, who had made the running for most of the season, at the post.

A BRILLIANT GAME BY ASTON VILLA.

[BY BRUM.]

VISITORS to the Villa's headquarters on Saturday, and they must have numbered upwards of twenty thousand, had splendid value for their money, for they were treated to a superb exhibition of football such as no club in the country to-day could have excelled. This may seem extravagant praise, but it would be safe to say, and it would be the verdict of the vast majority of those who witnessed the match. For the first time since the season opened Aston Villa can boast of a clean bill of health, and with the Cup team all fit and well, no alterations were dreamt of. Except that Fletcher took the place of Goss in the forward line, Notts County were at full strength. The weather was decidedly more genial than what has lately been experienced, but the ground was dreadfully heavy and holding after the thaw, and thoroughly tested the staying powers of the players. Mr. Strawson was master of the ceremonies, and had charge of the following—

Aston Villa.—George, goal; Evans and Spencer, backs; Crabtree, Cowan, and Bowman, half-backs; Smith, Wheldon, Garratty, Devey, and Athersmith, forwards.

Notts County.—Suter, goal; Montgomery and Lewis, backs; Macdonald, Bull, and Ball, half-backs; Chalmers, Fletcher, M'Main, Maconnachie, and Hadley, forwards.

Athletic News, 19 February 1900

1901

LEAGUE CHAMPIONS Liverpool advertising for players in the situations vacant columns of the *Athletic News*. It sounds bizarre but that was precisely what happened at the end of the 1900/1901 season. And they were not alone. Leicester Fosse, Aston Villa, Grimsby, Sheffield Wednesday, Bristol Rovers and Southampton were among the many other clubs searching for talent. The advert appeared in the *Athletic News* on the day Liverpool clinched their first League title by defeating West Bromwich at the Hawthorns and simply read: 'Wanted players for all positions for next season: maximum wage paid to class men.'

The explanation was simple. On April Fool's Day 1901 the Football League had introduced a new maximum wage of £4 a week but with many first division players earning as much as £10 in a good week, a number of players decided to turn their backs on the game and seek employment elsewhere. For Liverpool, where high wages had been the policy, the maximum wage had disastrous consequences. Liverpool's chairman, John McKenna, a future president of the Football League, was a fierce critic of the scheme, yet he had to stand by and watch many of his most talented players leave. McKenna told the *Athletic News* that the club could not retain all 18 of its players because of the £4 limit and that many were refusing to re-sign. But one man Liverpool did hang on to was Alex Raisbeck, their Scottish international defender who was given the job of bill inspector. It was his task to check all the advertisements around the ground and for this he was given an extra wage. But there was a limit to how many other jobs could be found for the rest of the team. With many players gone Liverpool finished the next season only two points from relegation.

Two other interesting adverts appeared in that same issue of the *Athletic News*. One was from an unknown footballer advertising his skills. 'First league half-back. Age 24, 5′ 11″, nearly 12 st,' read the advert, no doubt penned by a disatisfied player seeking more lucrative pay at another club. The second advert simply read, 'The Football League – clubs desirous of applying for a position in the second division must make written application on or before May 7 to H. Lockett, Secretary, Parker's Terrace, Stoke-on-Trent'. The advert certainly worked for two clubs. Out went New Brighton Tower and Walsall and in came Bristol City and Doncaster.

SITUATIONS WANTED AND VACANT.

PRESTON NORTH END F.C. Want First-class PLAYERS, all positions, for next season.—Apply by letter, stating age, height, weight, and present club, CHARNLEY, 17, Cannon-street.

SHEFFIELD UNITED FOOTBALL CLUB.—Wanted PLAYERS for all positions; class men need only apply.—J. NICHOLSON, Secretary, Bramall-lane Ground, Sheffield.

WANTED, PLAYERS for all positions, 1901-2.—Apply, at once, RALPH ECCLES, Sec. Darwen Football Club.

SHEFFIELD WEDNESDAY FOOTBALL CLUB open for First Class PLAYERS for next season.—Apply by letter, to A. J. DICKINSON, 5, Pool-square, Sheffield.

FIRST DIVISION, Second Division, Southern League players desirous of change, state age, height, weight, and probable amount of transfer to E. HIGSON, Atherton, Manchester.

SOUTHAMPTON F.C. require PLAYERS (all positions) for next season, on May 1 next. Applicants to state last club played for, age, height, and weight, to E. ARNFIELD, 25, Derby-road, Southampton.

KETTERING FOOTBALL CLUB WANT PLAYERS for all positions for next season; Southern League.—Application to T. MOORE, 20, Lower Duke-st., Kettering.

BRISTOL ROVERS' F.C., LTD., Require First-class PLAYERS for next season.—Full particulars as to age, height, weight, and lowest terms to A. G. HOMER, Black Swan Hotel, Eastville, Bristol.

PLAYERS FOR ALL POSITIONS.

WANTED, by a Second Division club for next season, Reliable PLAYERS for all positions.—Address O 67, Athletic News, Manchester.

LIVERPOOL F.C.—PLAYERS Wanted for next Season; all positions.—Apply, by letter, to Mr. TOM WATSON, Anfield-road, Liverpool.

FIRST LEAGUE HALF-BACK open for next season; age 24, 5ft. 11in., nearly 12 stone.—Address, "SOCKER," "Athletic News."

LIVERPOOL FOOTBALL CLUB. Wanted PLAYERS for all positions for next season; maximum wages paid to class men.—Apply by letter to TOM WATSON, Sec., Anfield-road, Liverpool.

Athletic News, 29 April 1901

ABOVE: *Alex Raisbeck, one player Liverpool were not going to part with*

In 1901 Spurs became the only non-league side to win the FA Cup when they defeated Sheffield United in a replay at Burnden Park. The final at the Crystal Palace in front of 114,000 had resulted in a 2–2 draw, but a week later in front of only 20,000, Spurs won 3–1 after being a goal behind. It was the first triumph by a professional team from the south.

Most newspapers reported the game with as many as two or three thousand words, for it was not uncommon even then for journalists to be paid according to the amount of copy written. Photographs were still rare. The *Athletic News,* like others, carried only posed portraits and the occasional team photo and did not introduce action shots until later. The problem was that when early telephoto lenses were used the shutter speed had to be reduced and much of the action became blurred. Equipment was also cumbersome and hardly suited for erecting on the touchline. It was not until after 1886 when more sophisticated lenses, faster shutters and the roll film camera had been invented that sports photography improved. In the meantime most shots were taken some distance from the subject with a standard lens. By 1897 *Sporting Sketches* was using the new equipment, and had positioned a cameraman on the sidelines, but most papers continued to use artists and even when photographs were published, they rarely showed exciting action.

Some of the first quality pictures were taken at the 1901 final and published in *Sporting Sketches*, which continued to lead the field until the *Daily Mirror* appeared in 1904. The *Mirror* forged a new journalism committed to photographs, simple words and short paragraphs aimed at the increasingly literate industrial class. The next improvement was in 1907 when a system for transmitting photographs by telegraph wires was devised.

ASSOCIATION CUP.

RE-PLAYED FINAL TIE.

THE SOUTHERN SUN SHINES AT BOLTON.

TOTTENHAM HOTSPUR VICTORIOUS.

A SQUALLY DAY AND A DISAPPOINTING CROWD.

SIDE LIGHTS ON THE GAME AND A FEW ODDS-AND-ENDS.

[BY NONDESCRIPT.]

"FOR 'TWAS A FAMOUS VICTORY."

Yes, I think it will go down to history that Tottenham Hotspur's triumph over Sheffield United on Saturday by three goals to one was one of the very best performances ever accomplished in a Cup final. Their superiority over their opponents was not so early made manifest as was the case when Bury ran Southampton off their legs in the first 20 minutes of the corresponding game a twelve month back, but it had been demonstrated with almost equal force before the end of the afternoon, and there was no doubt as to which was the better side. Just for a moment I bid you glance at the table

which is set forth elsewhere at the doughty deeds of the "Spurs," or the "Hottentots," as I love to call them, from the days of the first round.

Athletic News, 29 April 1901

[Photo by the Standard Photo Co.

Tottenham Hotspur v. Sheffield United at Burnden: Clawley effects a save.

ABOVE: *The photograph as it appeared in* Sporting Sketches

1901

ABOVE: *The New Brighton Tower ground*

THE EARLY years of league soccer saw many romantic teams rise and fall. Gainsborough, Glossop, Darwen and Burton Swifts were just a few of the names that appeared out of the northern mists and then as quietly vanished. New Brighton Tower was another such side, a short-lived dream, which died in 1901.

Regular holidays for industrial workers and increased leisure time in Victorian England had led to a boom in holiday resorts and Blackpool, further up the coast from New Brighton, was leading the race to become Britain's premier seaside town. The Fylde resort had built a huge tower and boasted a second division football club. To compete with Blackpool, the burghers of New Brighton decided to construct a similar tower, only bigger and better. They also built amusement parks, zoos and a fairground in their audacious challenge to outstrip Blackpool. Visitors meant money and someone hit upon the idea of forming a football club and building a stadium that would cater not just for soccer but a host of other sporting events. First division football, it was argued, would help attract thousands to the expanding resort. So, New Brighton Tower became the first football club to be set up as a business venture in October 1896 when they were formed as an offshoot of the New Brighton Tower and Recreation Company. Their stadium also boasted the first cycle track in the land. It was a daring scheme.

FOOTBALL.

THE ASSOCIATION GAME.

COLLAPSE OF NEW BRIGHTON TOWER CLUB.

A considerable sensation has been caused in Liverpool football circles by the unexpected decision of the directors of New Brighton Tower, one of the leading Second Division clubs, to disband the organisation. The club was admittedly founded with the view of obtaining a First Division team as a winter attraction for the noted Cheshire resort, and their three failures in this respect, together with the heavy financial loss that must have been sustained, have evidently discouraged the management. Several of last season's players have been transferred to other League clubs, or gone south, but such well-known men as Barratt, Hulse, Farrell, Holmes, Petrie, and Hargreaves are still disengaged. Not only had the Tower's League fixtures been arranged, but the club had been excused participating in the early stages of the English Cup competition.

Sporting Chronicle, 2 September 1901

Because the club was starting from scratch and was not a member of any league, it did not have to pay transfer fees and was not restricted in the wages it could pay. It could attract the best and set out to hire some of the finest players in the land. They signed the Welsh international full-back Smart Arridge, and the great England international Alfred Milward, both from Everton, as well as the England goalkeeper, Jack Robinson of Derby County. It was a talented team, packed with internationals. The Football League however was not impressed and when Tower applied to join in their first season, permission was refused. Instead, they were forced to join the Lancashire League but with so many outstanding stars it was not surprising that they were runaway champions and drawing record crowds. The following season, they again applied to join the Football League and this time were duly elected.

They began well and soon topped the second division. At the end of the season they were vying with Glossop for promotion but lost a vital game at Leicester and wound up in fifth place. Now that they were a league side however, the Football League ruled that all the players they had signed were liable to a transfer fee. It cost New Brighton dearly. With some of their stars also rebelling at the restricted wages which the club was now forced to pay, a number of them decided to move back into the higher division and the following season with a much depleted team they finished in tenth place. A year later they were again challenging for promotion, coming within a whisker to end the season in fourth place. Two weeks later the owners decided that they had had enough and the club folded.

Another New Brighton reappeared in 1923, shortly after the third division north had been formed. They played at Sandhey Park until 1941, then moved back to the Tower ground. In 1951, bottom of the third division north, they failed to be re-elected. Yet another New Brighton team had ended its league career.

FOOTBALL CATASTROPHE.

TERRACE COLLAPSES AT GLASGOW.

20 KILLED, 217 INJURED.

FEARFUL SCENES OF DEATH AND SUFFERING.

IN THE HOSPITALS.

The most terrible disaster in the history of football occurred at Ibrox Park, Glasgow, on Saturday afternoon, on the occasion of the international match between England and Scotland.

Considerably over 80,000 spectators were present.

Before play commenced the crowd invaded the ground, and in the rush back from the charge of mounted police many were injured.

When the game had progressed but a few minutes the iron stanchions of one of the enormous stands snapped, and, the crowd swaying forward and backward, the back of the structure collapsed, precipitating hundreds below.

Heartrending scenes followed as the dead, dying, and injured were carried away on improvised stretchers to the pavilion.

The greatest confusion prevailed in the vicinity of the accident, but the game was allowed to proceed to prevent further panic and a possible greater disaster.

Hastily cabs and other conveyances were filled with the injured, who were conveyed to the infirmaries, which soon commenced to fill up.

Daily Express, 7 April 1902

ABOVE: *Sketch by an eye-witness*

BELOW: *The collapsed terracing which left 25 dead*

1902

FOOTBALL HIT the front pages for the first time in 1902 when disaster struck at Ibrox Park, Glasgow. The occasion was the annual Scotland v England international, when what had promised to be a memorable match turned into a scene of devastation as 25 lay dead while hundreds more were injured.

The Sunday papers had all gone to press too early to report the full extent of the tragedy and with all communication restricted to the telegraph, news was slow to filter back to Fleet Street. By Monday morning, however, the full horror had become apparent and news of more than 170 casualties in the Boer War that weekend was forced onto the inside pages.

It was the first time for ten years that the Scotland–England fixture had been played at Ibrox and more than 80,000 were crammed into the ground as the two teams appeared. But even before kick-off, there was a near disaster as mounted police quelled a pitch invasion by charging with batons drawn. Dozens lay injured as the fans retreated in panic but the pitch was quickly cleared and the two teams kicked off on time. But within minutes a loud, ominous sound reverberated around the stadium. The main stand had collapsed, spilling hundreds of spectators onto those packed beneath.

Although most reporters reckoned a stanchion had snapped, the inquest revealed that it was in fact the wooden planks which had given way. Yet despite the tragedy, the game continued and the match eventually ended in a 1–1 draw. As a result of the tragedy high wooden stands of the kind that had existed at Ibrox were banned and more solid structures were introduced.

1903

SPORTS PHOTOGRAPHY was still in its early infancy when Bury met Derby County to contest the 1903 Cup Final. The only photographs which ever appeared had been shot from some distance in order to eliminate the blur which would occur from fast moving players. Most newspapers relied on artists to speedily draw their interpretation of events and the weekly sports paper *Athletic News,* was among the foremost exponents of the line drawing. Each Monday's edition usually carried a front page sketch from the previous Saturday's principal fixture often along with caricatures of the game's leading players.

Bury's 6–0 thrashing of Derby was to go down in the history books as the biggest margin of victory in a final while the Lancashire side had also emulated Preston North End in not conceding a goal throughout the tournament. They had begun their campaign with a 1–0 win over Wolverhampton, followed by another single goal victory at Sheffield United. In the third round they scraped home 1–0 against Notts County but in the semi-final hit three goals without reply against the Villa. Unfashionable Bury, in the middle of the first division, were clearly improving but could hardly have anticipated such an emphatic victory over their more famous rivals in the Final. It was probably explained by the absence of County's England international forward, Steve Bloomer, who was forced to cry off through injury, leaving Derby with a selection problem and no proven goalscorer. But excuses aside, Bury who had already won the trophy in 1900 with a 4–0 victory over Southampton, totally outplayed Derby in what the papers reckoned a disappointing and one-sided game. Yet, the 63,000 crowd at the Crystal Palace had been forced to wait until the twentieth minute before Bury captain George Ross opened the scoring. At half time the score still stood at 1–0 but in a sudden flurry of excitement in the second half, Bury added four more goals in the opening eleven minutes to leave Derby reeling. The football writers may have been disappointed but at least the artists had plenty to capture – as the *Athletic News* of the time shows.

LEFT: *Bury Football Club, 1903 – Cup-winners without conceding a goal*

EN PASSANT.

DERBY'S DISAPPOINTMENT.

[Speaking to a reporter before Saturday's final on the prospects of his team, Mr. Newbould, the Derby County secretary, said:—"The players themselves are all confident about winning. They are not afraid of Bury. You take the teams man for man, and you will find that we are the better side. We are strong in the half-back division, but, in addition to this, we have some good and smart young forwards." Archie Goodall added:—"If you come down to-morrow night, you will very likely see us drinking a bumber out of the Cup. 'Going to win?' What do you think?"]

Flip flop, kicketty hop!
Derby's gone down, and Bury's on top;
Never, 't'would seem,
Came such a gay team
So flipperty, flipperty, flipperty flop.

Down, down, high derry down!
Fortune on Derby has looked with a frown;
Six goals to nix!
Like cartloads of bricks,
Came calamity down, high derry down.

Squeak, squeak, squicketty squeak!
Poor old "Peak County" (they're spelling it "pique"),
Their gloom can't be "loomer"
(Where were you, O Bloomer?)
Squeak, squeak, squicketty squeak.

Quack, quack, alas and alack!
Once their proud colours were red, white, and black;
Red and white now don't matter,
But leave 'em the latter—
That's black—quack, quacketty quack!

Tip, tup, tipperty tup!
Didn't they thirst for a drink from THE Cup?
But sour was the chalice
They quaffed at the Palace,
Tip, tup, tipperty tup!

* * *

Although only 63,102 people passed through the turnstiles at the Crystal Palace on Saturday when the Final Tie for the Association Cup was brought to issue, this gathering is quite up to the average if we omit 1901 and 1902, when the South had a special interest in the direct destination of the trophy. The figures may appear small compared with these annual reunions, but they are nevertheless convincing of the tremendous grip the Association game has upon the public, for the vast majority of the sightseers were travellers from the provinces. We are more inclined to cavil at the exhibition of football than at the dimensions of the crowd, for many seasons have passed since such a one-sided game was seen. The hollow victory of Bury made the match appear poorer in quality than it really was.

Athletic News, 20 April 1903

ABOVE: *Bury v Derby County – from a distance. The limitations of early photography meant that newspapers relied on line drawings to capture the action of a match*

1904

FOOTBALL WAS rapidly becoming the favourite pastime of Edwardian Britain, with crowds flocking to grounds all over the country each Saturday. In the north the game had been firmly rooted for some years, but it was also growing in popularity in the south – even though their only league representatives were Woolwich Arsenal of the first division and Bristol City of the second. Nevertheless, a professional Southern League had been thriving since 1894, with Tottenham and Southampton sharing the glory during its early years. Both clubs had enjoyed fine runs in the FA Cup, with Tottenham becoming the only non-league side this century to have captured the trophy, when they defeated Sheffield United in the replayed 1901 Final.

Tottenham's Cup triumphs over the masters of the Football League brought the crowds pouring into White Hart Lane whenever there was the prospect of another giant-killing act. And when Spurs found themselves with a plum draw for a second round Cup tie on February 20th 1904 – against five-times league champions and three-times Cup winners Aston Villa – it was inevitable that a huge crowd would be attracted to their north London ground. But nobody had anticipated anything like the numbers who arrived, especially as the admission charge had been raised to one shilling. Within half an hour of the gates being opened it was estimated that 30,000 were inside the ground, and as the two teams kicked off as many as 50,000 were crammed into the

RUCTIONS AT TOTTENHAM.

In the 'Spurs v. Aston Villa Cup-tie the Crowd Broke Into the Field of Play, and the Game had to be Abandoned.

Daily Illustrated Mirror, 22 February 1904

ABOVE: *The crowd spills over the goal line*

stadium. It was far too many, and long before the teams had appeared, the crowd had spilled onto the pitch.

The first serious encroachment occurred after 20 minutes' play, and the referee was forced to halt proceedings while stewards urged everyone back onto the terraces. Nothing quite like it had been seen since the 1899 semi-final replay between Sheffield United and Liverpool at Fallowfield, when the referee had been forced to abandon the match after the crowd had flooded uncontrollably onto the pitch.

But it did not take long for the crowd at Spurs to overflow onto the pitch once more, and after three further encroachments and further stoppages the referee called the two teams together and abandoned the game as a cup tie. Instead, they would continue to play a friendly in order to avoid any possible crowd trouble. Villa quickly took the lead but after only 35 minutes' play, the referee blew for half time. The second half was a mere five minutes old when the crowd again poured onto the pitch and, sensing the obvious danger if the game continued, the referee bravely called a halt and abandoned the tie.

Approving his decision, the newspapers all agreed that in the circumstances the spectators had behaved commendably although there was much criticism of Tottenham's crowd control. The FA concurred and fined the club £350, ordering the tie to be replayed at Villa Park on the following Thursday evening. That turned out to be fortuitous for Spurs, who won 1–0 to earn themselves a third

1904

round tie against The Wednesday at White Hart Lane two weeks later. Fearful of another huge gate, Tottenham erected a 5-foot iron fence around the playing area and more police were drafted in, but they need not have worried as most of those who had attended the Villa crush sensibly stayed away. Spurs could only manage a draw and in the replay went down by two goals to nil.

BELOW: *Spurs on the defensive, watched by 50,000 spectators*

Trouble at Tottenham.

On Saturday it was estimated that close upon 50,000 people were desirous of entering the Tottenham Hotspur ground, and unfortunately too many of them succeeded. It is possible, by making special arrangements, to get a crowd of 30,000 into the enclosure, but it is a very tight fit. As it was, nearly 2,000 over that number were admitted, although the gates were closed to all but ticket-holders three-quarters of an hour before the kick-off. Thus the capacity of the ground was overtaxed, and it was early apparent to the practised eye that trouble was brewing.

Five minutes before the start the crowd invaded the playing pitch. They were with difficulty forced back over the touch-line. But the relief was only temporary, and throughout the first half the breaking-in was intermittent. However, this part of the game was disposed of in some sort of a fashion. But the second portion had hardly been in progress a minute before a mass of people swarmed across the field. The referee, Mr. J. T. Howcroft, gave the players a hurried intimation; they scampered pell-mell to the dressing-room, and the day's play was over.

Daily Illustrated Mirror, 22 February 1904

1904

ON THE EVE of the 1904 all-Lancashire Cup Final between Manchester City and Bolton Wanderers, the *Umpire* ran a competition to discover the most popular player in the Football League. It was always obvious who would win.

Billy Meredith, the Manchester City right-winger, topped the poll easily with 17,526 votes, well ahead of Derby County's Steve Bloomer. In third place was Bob Crompton of Blackburn Rovers followed by 'Nudger' Needham of Sheffield United. It hardly needed a poll to ascertain the popularity of Meredith who was the most talked about player in soccer.

As football grew more popular, so the back pages took more interest in the personalities of the game. The Victorian stalwarts such as Edgar Chadwick, John Goodall and Charlie Athersmith had been recognised for their playing skills alone with the lack of photographs limiting any wider fame. But as photographic processes improved, so newspapers began to publish action close-ups instead of the traditional posed portrait. The result was that players suddenly emerged as personalities and Meredith, always a controversial character, soon became the pin-up of the terraces. With an ever-present toothpick gripped between his teeth, and with his fine stylish Edwardian moustache, Meredith was easily recognisable. What's more, he was also an outstanding player.

Born in Chirk on the Welsh borders in July 1874, he joined Ardwick as an amateur in 1894 and in his first season played 18 games for the second division side, scoring 12 goals. In 1899 he helped Ardwick, soon to become Manchester City, to the second division championship. But it was in 1904 with Meredith at his best that City became a force in the land. After winning the Cup with a 1–0 victory over Bolton at the Crystal Palace, they almost clinched the Double but could only finish as runners up in the league. City's success led to even greater popularity for the Welsh international. His fame helped to sell Oxo while the Great Central Railway Company produced a famous poster offering excursions to the Crystal Palace to 'see Billy Meredith secure the Cup'. Meredith was the most famous footballer in the land, known not just to soccer fans but to newspaper readers everywhere.

A year later, however, he was sensationally suspended by the Football League, accused of attempting to bribe an Aston Villa player. Meredith always maintained his innocence and indeed it is hard to understand what possible motive he could have had. With little support from his own club, however, Meredith decided to try his luck elsewhere, and made the short move across the city to Manchester United. In 339 appearances for City the 'Welsh Wizard', as he was now known, had scored 146 goals, proving himself as much a goalscorer as a winger. United, newly promoted to the first division, looked to Meredith to work the same miracle. They would not be disappointed. In 1908 they were league champions; a year later they won the Cup and in 1911 they were champions again. Meredith meanwhile had won further notoriety by helping to found the Players' Union (later to become the PFA) and had agitated vehemently against the maximum wage and transfer fees, making himself hugely popular with supporters and players but even more unpopular with the game's administrators.

He played for City during the war but, still contracted to United, he returned to Old Trafford for two seasons when hostilities ended. At the end of a United career that had spanned just over 300 games, he sensationally re-signed for his old club and played three more seasons before retiring in 1924 at the age of 50 after almost taking City to a Wembley Cup Final. At the end of his playing days he could count 670 league games with 181 goals as well as 48 appearances for Wales. He settled down to run a pub in Manchester and died at the age of 83 in April 1958, just two months after the Munich air disaster.

ABOVE: *Billy Meredith the legendary 'Welsh Wizard', has been described as 'a Matthews, Finney and Best of his day rolled into one'*

FOOTBALL COMPETITION

RESULT.

MEREDITH, BLOOMER, AND CROMPTON CAPTURE THE ·PLAYERS' PRIZES.

W. MEREDITH. S. BLOOMER. R. CROMPTON.

The Umpire, 13 March 1904

After many weeks of hard work in connection with our Football Competition, we are pleased to be in a position to announce the result. The process of recording votes has entailed a vast amount of labour, as we have previously hinted; but we are now convinced that every vote has been carefully and accurately recorded. The result thus obtained places the following players in the order set forth in the proud position of being, in the estimation of our readers, the TWELVE MOST POPULAR FOOTBALLERS of the present season:—

Name.	No. of Votes.
1. W. MEREDITH (Manchester City)	17,526
2. S. BLOOMER (Derby County)	15,006
3. R. CROMPTON (Blackburn Rovers)	13,518
4. E. NEEDHAM (Sheffield United)	12,630
5. T. BADDELEY (Wolverhampton Wanderers)	10,551
6. J. LOMAS (Salford)	9269
7. W. FOULKE (Sheffield United)	7734
8. S. FROST (Manchester City)	7563
9. J. SHARP (Everton)	7194
10. R. WILSON (Broughton Rangers)	7005
11. J. SETTLE (Everton)	6867
12. G. ROSS (Bury)	6768

PLAYER' PRIZES.

W. Meredith, S. Bloomer, and R. Crompton are therefore the lucky winners of the Players' Prizes, Meredith taking the first prize of £10, and Bloomer and Crompton £5 each for the second and third prizes.

RIGHT: *Bob Crompton, whose third place won him £5 through the* Umpire's *competition*

BELOW: *Billy Meredith (centre) with the Manchester City team in 1904*

1904

FEW CLUBS can boast Arsenal's proud and pioneering record in international competition – a record which goes back to 1904 when the Plumstead club met a Parisian eleven at the Manor Ground. History may show that this was not the first visit of a continental side to England, but it must certainly rank as one of the first international games between a Football League club and European visitors.

The fixture was played on a dreary Monday afternoon in December before a mediocre crowd of just over 3,000. The French team was made up of players from Club Athlétique Parisien, Club Athlétique Grenellors and Club Sporting Français plus Hodges, the Arsenal reserve. The result was an overwhelming victory for Arsenal who ran up an astonishing 26 goals with only one against. Most newspapers ignored the match and the *Daily Express* showed its contempt under the headline 'Farce At Plumstead'.

'To give a description is quite unnecessary,' wrote their correspondent brusquely. He added somewhat savagely that 'any one of our school elevens could easily have given the Paris team of yesterday a beating'. It was probably the earliest example of jingoism among the football writers.

For the record Arsenal were 8–1 ahead at half time and owed their 26–1 win to goals from Watson (7), Hunter (5), Briercliffe (4), Coleman (4), Buchan (2), Linward (2), Blackman (1) and Ransome (1). And by all accounts the French goal could easily have been saved by the Arsenal goalkeeper Ashcroft, who seemed to have taken pity on the inept French forwards.

BELOW: *Arsenal FC, 1904*

FARCE AT PLUMSTEAD.

ARSENAL BEAT FRENCH TEAM BY 26 GOALS TO 1!

Football as played at Plumstead yesterday, although highly amusing, serves no good purpose beyond the fact that it proves to our friends from across the Channel that they have still a lot to learn before they can hope to compete with our best Association clubs. Twenty-six goals to 1! This was the astounding result of the friendly between the Woolwich Arsenal and a French eleven playing under the title of the Club Athletique Parisien.

Only four of the players really belonged to this club, the eleven being completed by four players from the Club Athletique Grenellors, two from the Club Sporting Francais, and Hodges, an Arsenal reserve.

To give a description of the game is quite unnecessary. They were hopelessly outplayed from start to finish, and the one point scored by them was practically a gift by Ashcroft, who could no doubt have easily saved if he had so willed.

Suffice it to say that the success of the Arsenal afforded plenty of opportunity for hilarity to the three thousand spectators and excellent shooting practice for the "Reds'" team, eight of whom shared between them the honour of scoring the goals.

Such farces are seldom seen on English grounds, and it is to be hoped that in future fixtures of this kind will not be encouraged. Any one of our school elevens could easily have given the Paris team of yesterday a beating.

Daily Express, 6 December 1904

ABOVE: *Alf Common in Sheffield Utd shirt*

1905

IT WAS RARE in 1905 for transfer news to hit the headlines. Few deals ever involved more than a couple of hundred pounds and with most transfers it was rare for any money to change hands at all. So when Sunderland's English international Alf Common moved to Middlesbrough for £1,000 in February that year, it caused a sensation. It was far and away the biggest transfer deal in British football and marked the beginning of a spiral that would eventually lead to seven-figure transfers.

Common had been born in Sunderland in 1880 and played as a young lad with Hilton and Jarrow before joining his home team. In 1901 he was transferred to Sheffield United for £325 and then rejoined Sunderland at the beginning of the 1904/05 season. By that time he had won a couple of England caps, playing against Wales and Northern Ireland, and scoring in both games. A skilful inside-right, he was one of the highest scorers in the League in 1905 which made it even more bizarre that Sunderland should be prepared to consider offers. But money talked even then and Middlesbrough, lying in the relegation zone, were desperate. The press were clearly shocked by the size of the deal. Most carried a paragraph or two, calling it a 'sensation', with the *Daily Dispatch* featuring the deal more prominently than any other newspaper. A week later the *Daily Mirror* was linking Middlesbrough with Derby County's Steve Bloomer but no deal ever transpired. But it demonstrated that transfer stories and, above all, speculation were now big news. As for Alf Common, he worked wonders, helping to keep Middlesbrough in the First Division and winning another international cap. It was certainly money well spent.

The event of the week in the North of England has been the transfer of Alfred Common to Middlesbrough! It seems only the other day that Common returned to Sunderland from Sheffield United, and it is curious that he has not yet played a full season with the Sunderland League team. When he was first promoted to the senior eleven a few seasons ago he was transferred to Sheffield United before the completion of the season. Last summer he went back to Wearside, and is now going to finish this campaign on Teesside. At his best Common is a fine player, and we have no doubt he will prove a help to Middlesbrough.

* * *

The Teessiders paid £1,000 for the transfer! This fee also included a friendly match at Middlesbrough on Saturday, in which the home club took all the receipts, and the visitors paid their own expenses. The cheque will afford Sunderland some consolation, but we can hardly conceive that their treasury needed any repletion. We rather fancy that Sunderland, who were approached on this matter by Middlesbrough early in January, have been actuated by a desire to help their neighbours—at a price. Seemingly every club has its price. But what a price? The transfer fee may be justified as expedient and useful, but whether the principle is perfectly sound and legitimate is very open to question. We believe that £1,000 is a record for a player, and we are tempted to wonder whether there is to be a limit, and if Association football players will eventually rival thoroughbred yearling racehorses in the market. But fancy a young club like Middlesbrough with their resources paying £1,000 for a single player. As a matter of commerce ten young recruits at £100 apiece might have paid better, and as a matter of sport the Second Division would be more honourable than retention of place by purchase.

* * *

The position of Sheffield United in this matter ought not to be overlooked. Originally the United secured Common for £325, but they refused an offer of £700 from Aston Villa for this player. After this they were compelled to re-transfer Common to his old club at something like the original figure, although they had offered him the maximum wages, simply because the international wished to return to Sunderland, his home, to conduct a private business. At least that was what was generally understood. And now Sunderland make a bargain for Common for a cool £1,000.

Athletic News, 20 February 1905

1906

THE GROWING popularity of football was recognised by the press in September 1888 when Liverpool became the first city to introduce a football edition of its local newspaper, the *Echo*. There was no radio 'Sports Report' in those days and the only way to learn the football results was through newspapers. Often it was a case of waiting until Sunday – or even Monday morning when the *Athletic News* appeared – to learn Saturday's results. And so in order to bring the scores to fans as early as possible local newspapers intro-

ENGLISH CUP FINAL.

EVERTON v. NEWCASTLE UNITED.

CRYSTAL PALACE BESIEGED.

AN IMMENSE CROWD OF SPECTATORS.

SANDY YOUNG SCORES THE WINNING GOAL.

CUP COMES TO LIVERPOOL AT LAST.

[From Our Own Reporters by Special Wire from the Crystal Palace.]

Liverpool Football Echo, 21 April 1906

BELOW: *The Everton goal through the eyes of the* Illustrated Sporting and Dramatic News. *4.55 pm, and the* Liverpool Football Echo *reporter was prompted to wire back to his office: 'Sandy Young a hero'*

duced the special football edition. It was appropriate that Liverpool should be the first city to boast a *Football Echo*, for as early as 1901 the city's two teams, Everton and Liverpool, had both won the league championship, and first division football flourished with 40,000 spectators regularly attending games.

But the technology was hardly equipped to bring news out so quickly and ingenious schemes had to be devised to satisfy the hungry punter. The inside pages would be set and printed well in advance of Saturday afternoon so that only the outside page with its crucial reports and scores needed to be printed late. And each Saturday evening as soon as the scores and reports had been telegraphed to the *Echo*'s office, the race would begin to set the outside page, print it and rush copies onto the streets as soon as possible.

In 1906 the city of Liverpool crowned their footballing achievements by becoming the first city to clinch both the FA Cup and league title in the same season. Liverpool won the title from Preston while neighbours Everton marched to the Cup Final after beating Liverpool in the semi-final at Villa Park. It was the beginning of the Merseyside monopoly of football.

Everton's victory over Newcastle United in the final at the Crystal Palace served as a perfect example of how the reports were wired back to the office. The fact that Everton had actually won the Cup came some way down the headlines, because the main headline would have been typeset earlier. The report of the game was also written minute by minute in order to hasten publication. Messengers would then rush each minute's report to the nearest wire where it would be telegraphed back to the *Echo*'s office. On receiving the wire, compositors would begin to typeset the one sentence text onto the page so that immediately the final whistle had blown and the last wire received, printing could begin.

"ECHO" CLOCK.

TIMED AND REGULATED.

BY JAY CEE.

3.29.—Veitch starts palpitation of the heart [illegible] round. One hundred and one kodaks fixed simultaneously, and the cinematograph man grinds away the film, which is almost as important as the match nowadays.

Off we go.

3.30.—Brave efforts on the part of both even that early.

3.31.—First danger comes from the Blues. Balmer lobs the ball in from a free kick, and the Newcastle goal is almost captured. Young's "header," however, is put over the bar by Lawrance. Corner proved useless.

3.32.—Everton giving the Geordies beans hereabouts.

3.33.—The much-vaunted Newcastle halves absolutely in Queer-street, but M'Combie and Carr defend like fury.

3.34.—The players show some heat already, and Mr. Kirkham called them together, and said a few words.

3.35.—Everton all over the other people. Bolton shoots. His idea is good; his execution rotten.

3.36.—Play quieter, but still in favour of the Blues. United seem very much untried just now.

3.37.—Ditto.

3.38.—Everton forwards having a field-day, but they seldom shoot—the importance of the occasion too great, I suppose.

3.39.—Newcastle can't get out of their own half, and Lawrance is on tenter-hooks.

3.40.—Sandy Young gets in a lovely header, and it was worth a goal, but did not come off.

3.41.—Young is giving great satisfaction.

3.42.—John Rutherford at last changes the venue, and Newcastle get a corner.

3.43.—Poor play in midfield.

3.44.—The same.

3.45.—Worse.

3.46.—Sharp and Bolton scintillate and fairly walk round M'William.

3.47.—Jimmy Settle has half a chance, but fails to improve it. It was only half a chance, anyhow.

3.48.—Everton seem to be able to do anything but score. What a pity! Not half!

3.49.—Another minute without incident.

3.50.—At last Newcastle show the stuff they are made of. It was bound to come.

3.51.—Orr sails through and flashes a hurricane shot just past the post. Scott tiptoes to save and gets rid of impending trouble.

3.53.—Thousands of eyes are on him as he rubs his hands in dirt. Thousands of eyes are on him as he wipes them on his shirt.

3.54.—Newcastle bucking up wonderfully well, and Everton now seriously on the defence.

3.55.—High faluting play vetoed by honest Jock.

3.56.—Everton redivides.

3.57.—Goals are mighty scarce.

3.58.—Exertions and alarms.

3.59.—Nothing between them just now.

4.0.—Crowd wants a goal badly, and fairly howled at every miss.

4.1.—Howie has a chance, but shoots too soon, and Balmer clears with plenty of room.

4.2.—Everton not nearly so cocky, but still on the job.

4.3.—Wonderful shot from Rutherford, but still more wonderful save b Scott.

4.4—United busy as bees now, but the Everton defence holds them up.

4.5.—Pressure by the Blues hot and strong.

4.6—More pressure.

4.7.—And still more.

4.8.—Yet no goal. Buck up Sandy.

4.9.—Newcastle press again, but no good. Balmer and Crelly on their best behaviour, likewise Scott.

4.10.—Mutual work in midfield.

4.11.—Ditto.

4.12.—Referee Kirkham a great success.

4.13.—Nil.

4.14.—Half-time, no score.

4.25—Off again.

4.26—Everton first away; John Sharp send bobby-dazzler over the bar.

4.27—Corner to the Blues.

4.28—Everton giving other people socks.

4.30—Everton still top dog, and visions of the precious bauble loomed in my eye.

4.31—Brave work by Newcastle spoilt by Everton halves.

4.32—Makepeace glorious.

4.33 [illegible] out 30 yards to save. Which he does—and well.

4.34.—Linesman Whittaker stops the game and examines the ball. He thinks it has gone soft, but it is all right.

4.35.—Everton press like demons.

4.36.—Young scores, but Kirkham declares him offside. Great snakes! No matter. Our withers are unwrung.

4.37—Takes the whole of this minute to recover from the shock.

4.38—And the next.

4.39—Only one team in it just now. The other team is Newcastle.

4.40—Typical Cup-tie play. Either side attempting to settle down to their usual methods.

4.41.—Things quiet hereabouts, even the crowd.

4.42.—Nothing to enthuse over from either lot.

4.43.—Finest bit of play in the match from the Georgies' whole line participates and foot it right up to Scott, who saves grandly from Rutherford.

4.44—Everton at it again, but Young offside.

4.45—But Jack is as good as his master all the time.

4.47—Further visions.

4.48—Exciting attack on Scott's charge.

4.49—Frantic efforts by Newcastle to settle the issue. They do not want to be bothered going to Sheffield.

4.50—Promising play by the Blues right in front of Lawrence.

4.51—Settle nearly does the trick, hooks the ball into the corner, but Lawrence just reaches it.

4.52—Everton fairly racing round M'Combie and Coy.

4.53—Nothing eventual.

4.54—Newcastle still being pressed.

4.55—At last a goal. Sandy Young a hero. Fireworks and minature earthquakes in galore—shades of San Francisco.

4.56.—The big glasshouse still shakes at its foundations.

4.57.—Everton still keeping up in good style.

4.59.—Newcastle somewhat disjointed.

5 o'clock—Game looks as good as finished, but Everton must be wary of a final rush.

5.6.—Everton declared winners.

5.11.—The Cup is ours. Huroo!

Liverpool Football Echo, 21 April 1906

The only drawback was that details of the goal were often buried deep in the text. Mention of Sandy Young's winning goal for instance did not occur until near the end of the report when at 4.55: 'At last a goal. Sandy Young a hero. Fireworks and minature earthquakes in galore – shades of San Franscisco,' a reference to the tragic earthquake in the American city which had happened only that week. All in all, it was a clever and efficient system and although it did not make for fine writing or fascinating reading, it served the purpose of getting the news and all the results on to the streets as quickly as possible.

1907

ABOVE: *The famous 'Outcasts' who refused to give up the union. All but one were Manchester United players*

THE PLAYERS' Union, later to be known as the Professional Footballers' Association, was founded on December 2nd 1907 in Manchester. The driving force behind it was Billy Meredith, the Manchester United winger who chaired the inaugural meeting at the Imperial Hotel. But it was not the first attempt at forming a players' union. Back in December 1897 a union had been set up in Liverpool by two Everton players, John Bell and John Cameron, but the organisation had never gained a foothold and had soon been abandoned. Yet it had always remained an ideal of John Bell's and ten years later, now playing with Preston, the Scottish international discovered in Billy Meredith a like-minded colleague, equally determined to fight injustice in the game.

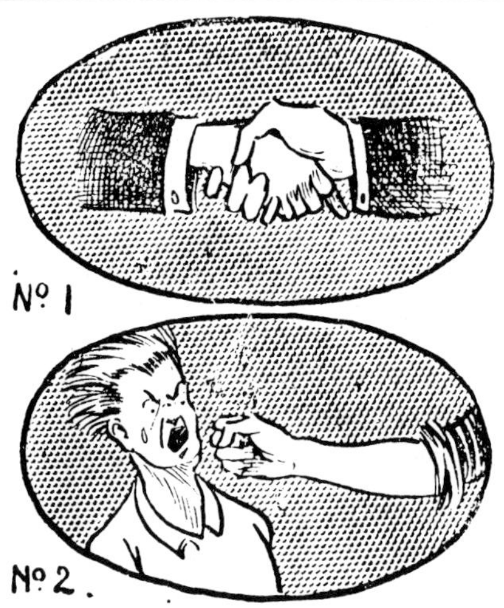

(1) The Players' Union badge as it is.
(2) The badge as it appears to some people.

ABOVE: *Today's PFA logo (bottom) has its origins in the tumultuous beginnings of the Player's Union*

More than 500 league players were represented at the first meeting. They came mainly from clubs in the north and midlands and it was clear that the new body would need to attract players from elsewhere if it was ever to have any chance of success. Along with four others, Meredith and Bell were elected to a subcommittee to draw up the rules and constitution of the union. The others were Craig of Bradford, Evans of West Brom, M'Combie of Newcastle and Lipsham of Sheffield. The six travelled south to meet the southern representatives in London the following weekend to enrol them in the new trade union.

The impetus behind this attempt to organise a union was the £4 a week maximum wage which had been introduced in 1900. Seven years later, the wage remained the same and the maximum had now become the standard. Meanwhile the popularity of the game had increased considerably with bigger gates and higher admission charges. It was well known that many clubs were secretly paying above the maximum rate and although their wages were still higher than those of the average industrial worker, the footballers felt it was time for everyone to 'come clean'.

FOOTBALLERS' UNION.

NORTHERN PLAYERS STRONGLY IN FAVOUR.

Enthusiastic Meeting in Manchester.

Sporting Chronicle, 3 December 1907

The other grievances were the maximum transfer fee of £350, which was to be introduced at the beginning of the new year, and freedom of contract. The players had argued strongly against the continuation of a maximum wage but without an effective organisation to co-ordinate their campaign, they were losing the battle. The League had some sympathy but the problem was the Southern League which refused to budge from its rigid stance, arguing that liberalising the wage structure would be too costly for many of its members.

The players were determined to fight the League and the first step was to set up an organisation. The Labour Party had recently been formed and trade union militancy was beginning to sweep through industry. Meredith may not have been a staunch socialist but he had Liberal leanings and as most players came from ordinary working class backgrounds, they had seen how collective action could defeat even the most stubborn of employers.

INTERNATIONAL ASSOCIATION PLAYER: Come along, boys; it's an easy jump from here.

When Meredith and Bell met the southern footballers in London there was unanimous agreement, and a month later in January 1908 the Players' Union was officially born at the King's Arms in Sheffield. The Manchester United chairman J. H. Davies was elected President and the vice-chairmen included John Cameron of Spurs, John McKenna of Liverpool and Jimmy Catton of the *Athletic News*. Although some of these men were employers, they had been elected because they sympathised with the abolition of the maximum wage and were seen as useful allies. An office was also opened in St Peter's Square, Manchester, close to Meredith's own sports shop, and the Manchester United Reserve goalkeeper Herbert Broomfield, was elected secretary.

ABOVE: *John Bell, whose early attempts at a players' union foundered in 1897*

In March its constitution and rules were published and players were invited to sign up with the new organisation. Growth was rapid and membership soon spread among the players, but its ambitions were not so successful. Against continuing intransigence, the campaign to defeat the maximum wage failed miserably. In 1908 there was talk of a 'super league', led by Manchester United and the richer clubs who wanted to break away and introduce a more flexible wage structure. The FA were furious but offered an amnesty to the clubs provided they introduced a loyalty clause in all contracts and disowned the Players' Union. It was eagerly accepted. A year later those Manchester United players refusing to sign the loyalty contract organised a strike but it was a disappointing failure. By now the administrators had the upper hand and the maximum wage continued for another fifty years until 1961 when Jimmy Hill as chairman of the PFA led the battle that finally realised the ambitions of the union's founding fathers.

THE RESURRECTION.
Willie Meredith is endeavouring to revive the Players' Union.

1908

ASSOCIATION FOOTBALL.

ENGLISH FOOTBALL TEAM IN VIENNA.

VIENNA, JUNE 6.

The English football team which is now on tour defeated an Austrian team composed of players from Vienna and Prague this afternoon by six goals to one.—*Reuter.*

The Times, 8 June 1908

ENGLAND FIRST journeyed abroad in June 1908 when a party of thirteen players visited the Continent for a series of fixtures against Austria, Hungary and Bohemia. A number of club sides had already toured Europe and some foreign teams had even travelled to Britain, but no international side had either visited our shores or played against the national team. The tour therefore not only pioneered close season international trips but also allowed England their first glimpse of foreign opposition.

They began their campaign with a game against Austria in Vienna on June 6th and romped home with a 6–1 victory. But the English press paid little attention and given that Reuters were credited with providing the reports, it is clear that no pressmen had bothered to travel with the team. Just a short paragraph appeared in *The Times* with even the

BELOW: *No photographs were taken of the England tour but a month later Arsenal also visited the Austro-Hungarian Empire where they beat Slavia of Prague 5–1*

ABOVE: *Bob Crompton of Blackburn Rovers and England*

ABOVE: *Billy Wedlock*

LEFT: *Vivian Woodward*

Athletic News virtually ignoring the encounter. Two days later England played the Austrians again and this time went even better, scoring eleven goals while conceding just one. They then travelled to Hungary and in Budapest on June 10th defeated the host nation 7–0. On June 13th they concluded their brief tour with a 4–0 win over Bohemia in Prague which resulted in the referee being attacked by the crowd as the game ended.

The stars of the tour were the forwards whose 28 goals underlined the gulf between English and continental soccer. Vivian Woodward hit six goals, while two Chelsea players, Hilsdon and Windridge, scored eight and five respectively. The tour allowed Woodward, the Tottenham and England centre forward, to take a close look at the kind of opposition Great Britain would be facing in the forthcoming London Olympics. Woodward, an amateur, was also eligible to play for Great Britain and went on to captain them to gold medals in both the 1908 and 1912 Olympics. Behind these goalscoring forwards were some skilful defenders including the veteran full-back Bob Crompton of Blackburn Rovers, Jesse Pennington, the WBA left-back who continued to play for England until 1920, Ben Warren the Derby County half-back and Billy 'Fatty' Wedlock the fine Bristol City half-back. A year later England returned once more to Austria and Hungary, only to discover that little had been learnt by their continental friends as they easily rattled in another 20 goals in three games.

1908

THE MODERN Olympic games were only 12 years old when they were hosted by Britain in 1908. The first games in Athens in 1896 had been a quiet success, but the 1900 games in Paris had been overshadowed by the World Exhibition while the distance to the St Louis games four years later had discouraged most foreign competitors from making the long and difficult voyage. But the London games heralded the true birth of the Olympics with all the accompanying razzamatazz, publicity and public interest. They began with only skimp coverage in the press but once the royal family had officially declared the athletic events at the White City stadium open, interest mushroomed. Yet it still took a moment of unparalleled drama to force the Olympics into the headlines and onto the front pages when the Italian marathon runner Pietri staggered across the White City finishing line, with assistance from officials and spectators. It was a gallant effort which won the hearts of the vast crowd but the rules quite explicitly did not permit assistance and poor Pietri was disqualified. The memorable photograph of Pietri crossing the line filled the front page of the following morning's *Daily Mirror*. The Olympic games had arrived as a media event.

While the majority of events took place in July, the football tournament, strangely, did not begin until October. By then interest in the Olympics had waned and a new League season had begun. It was also the first time football had been officially included in the Games and the British team was strictly amateur. Six teams took part, the United Kingdom, France A, France B, Sweden, Denmark, and Holland. The British side powered its way to the final, beating Sweden 12–1 and then Holland 4–0 in the semi-final. The Dutch side was coached by Edgar Chadwick, the former Blackburn

BELOW: *The Danish goalkeeper saves, but the UK still win 2–0*

OLYMPIC FINAL TIE.

UNITED KINGDOM DEFEAT DENMARK

After a really hard game at the Stadium yesterday United Kingdom beat Denmark in the final of the Association football Olympic Games by 2 goals to 0. It was a keen struggle, and only the superior shooting of the forwards enabled England to win, as quite as many openings fell to Denmark, but they were not taken advantage of. A feature of the play was the splendid work of Buchwald, the Danes' left back. He was the best back on the field, although opposed to such fliers as Woodward and Berry, he more than held his own. The English eleven was by no means so good as they were expected to be, and there will probably be some changes before the Internationals come along. The match attracted some 5,000 spectators, and the weather was delightfully fine.

Play opened with Denmark attacking, but the ground was very slippery and the forwards on both sides experienced great difficulty in controlling the ball, and there was not much to choose from in the first few minutes. The game was fast, but not particularly clever—certainly the English amateurs did not display their proper form. Denmark had the first real chance of scoring, a smart passing run by the inside forwards leaving N. Neilsen in possession close in, but his shot went wide. Denmark continued to have a trifle the best of matters, and Bailey had to kick away a shot from Rasmussen. N. Neilsen forced a corner, which Smith headed out. Then England took up the attack, and the ball was kept close to the Danes' goal for some few minutes. Drescher fisted out a shot from Purnell, but Chapman fastened on the ball and scored a rather soft goal ten minutes from start. England continued to attack, but the forwards were time and again bustled off the ball by the sturdy Danish halves, and with Buchwald and Hansen showing capital determination at back, scoring was by no means easy. Indeed, England did not get another goal before the interval, and in one case at least they were lucky in not having a score registered against them, Wolfhagen missing a grand chance close in. Stapley once got the ball into the net from a pass by Hunt, but he was obviously off-side, and half-time came with England leading by 1 goal to 0. The second half opened ominously for England. The Danes now had the wind, and kept up a pretty sharp attack on the English goal. Smith and Corbett, however, defended well, and the anxious period passed away. The English forwards came away in a body, and after Purnell and Hardman had taken the ball down, a nice square centre to Woodward enabled the Hotspur man to score with a swift low shot after a quarter of an hour's play. The Danes broke away, Lindgren going through with a magnificent dribble, and Bailey only saved his shot at the expense of a corner. It was the finest piece of individual work in the match, and was cheered to the echo. Just afterwards Wolfhagen shot just over the bar with a fine drive. He ought to have scored, and probably would but for slipping. The English goal had further narrow escapes, Bailey being kept very busy by Lindgren and S. Neilsen. At the other end Purnell shot an off-side goal. Just on the close S. Neilsen missed an open goal from a centre by Rasmussen.

United Kingdom, 2 ; Denmark, 0.

Sunday Times, 25 October 1908

Olympic, Blackburn Rovers and Everton star who in his playing days had been one of the most outstanding names in soccer. In their opening fixture Denmark thrashed France B 9–0 and in the semi-final faced what was supposed to be the stronger French side, France A, yet won by seventeen goals to one with Neilsen, the Danish centre forward, scoring ten of his side's tally.

The final was played in front of 5,000 at the White City on Saturday October 26th in delightfully fine weather. By half time Britain were a goal up after Chapman had slammed home a poor clearance by the Danish keeper. In the second half they quickly shot into a two goal lead and although Denmark pressed hard they could not overcome the stubborn defensive work of their opponents. Starring in the British attack was Harold Hardman, formerly of Everton and recently transferred to Manchester United. Hardman, a solicitor, was one of the last great amateurs and was listed in the papers as a member of Northern Nomads. A full England international, he later served United as a director and chairman. Also in the team was Vivian Woodward of Tottenham who later played for Chelsea and won 23 full England caps. Like Hardman, he too became a director, serving on the board of Spurs and Chelsea for many years. Woodward captained the victorious England team and led them to further Olympic honours in 1912.

ABOVE: *Chapman about to score the United Kingdom's first goal after a poor clearance by the Danish keeper, ten minutes into the game*

BELOW: *A crowd of only 5,000 at the White City watched the United Kingdom take the first Olympic soccer gold medal*

The play-off for the bronze medals was held between Holland and Sweden with the latter standing in for France A who had returned home early. The trophy and gold medals were duly presented to the winning British team by the Lord Mayor but the event roused little interest in the British press who were more concerned with League happenings at St James' Park and Villa Park. Only *The Times*, the paper of record, carried anything like a full report of Britain's victory. And it remains much the same today with Olympic football still lagging well behind league soccer.

1909

ABOVE: *Old Trafford, 1910*

THE GROWING popularity of football in Edwardian England demanded bigger and better grounds for the swelling army of supporters that were now watching soccer regularly. Increased leisure time, the five-and-a-half day week and improved wages all helped boost attendances at football matches. Cup Finals at the Crystal Palace were annually drawing crowds in excess of 70,000 although the largest attendances at league fixtures were still around 40,000. This was primarily because few grounds could comfortably hold many more spectators. The stadiums were basic, usually with just one stand, a paddock and a cinder banked Kop behind the goals. As the crowds flocked to football, so the clubs grew wealthier on the proceeds and money became available to invest in more facilities. These would usually include a new stand, improved offices and club amenities or even a second stand. But for some clubs it meant a new opportunity to leave old decrepit stadiums behind and construct ambitious new grounds, capable of holding many more spectators. One such club was Manchester United.

Since 1892, Manchester United – or as it was previously known, Newton Heath – had played at Bank Street, Clayton. Declared bankrupt in 1902 after a miserable season in the second division, they had been rescued by a local brewer, J. H. Davies, who invested £500 to help build a new stand. His involvement dramatically changed the fortunes of the club, which not only altered its name but won promotion back to the first division and its first league title in 1908. These were also the days of Billy Meredith, and a year later United were in the Cup Final. Just six weeks before the great game, Davies, already counting the proceeds from a rich Cup run, was able to proudly announce that he was donating £60,000 to purchase a site in Old Trafford – near the headquarters of Lancashire County Cricket Club – for the club to build a new home. And on March 8th the *Athletic News* carried the first account and plan for the new ground. The stadium would be the largest in the North, capable of holding 100,000 spectators with 12,000 of those seated. More than 36,000 would be under cover with facilities such as tea rooms, a gymnasium, a billiard room and laundry. It would be the most magnificent ground in the country. The plans were drawn up by Archibald Leitch, a young Scottish architect who over the years would become well known for the many soccer stadiums he designed. The cost of constructing the ground itself was reckoned to be £30,000 but for United and their rich benefactor, money at first was no object. The stadium was finally opened on February 19th 1910 when United lost by four goals to three against Lancashire rivals, Liverpool. A year later Old Trafford would be bulging with fans as United climbed towards another league championship. But although Leitch's original design had promised a capacity of 100,000, plans had to be scaled down as costs began to rise. The ground's biggest gate was nearly 77,000 for the FA Cup semi-final between Wolverhampton Wanderers and Grimsby in 1939. Today, virtually no trace of the original design stands although Old Trafford remains one of the most exciting and dramatic stadiums in the land.

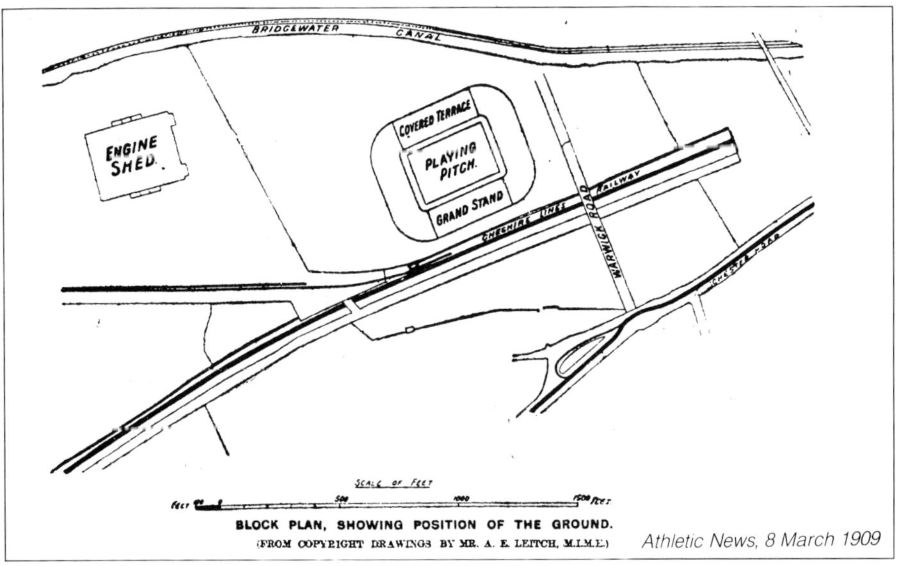

Athletic News, 8 March 1909

LEFT: *Leitch's plan of the new ground*

1909

ALTHOUGH CROWD trouble at football matches is considered to be the social disease of the 1970s and 80s, it has not been entirely restricted to recent years. Even before the turn of the century there had been serious trouble at Goodison Park when fans rioted and smashed club windows after the referee had abandoned a game, while at Villa Park in 1905 angry Aston Villa supporters stoned the Manchester City coach as it left the ground. But the worst trouble was in Scotland where poor refereeing, sectarianism and overcrowding frequently led to problems. Yet none of these skirmishes compared with the riot that followed the drawn Cup Final replay between Rangers and Celtic in April 1909.

The first clash between the two Glasgow giants had attracted more than 70,000 to Hampden Park to witness an exciting 2–2 draw. A week later another 61,000 turned up, this time fully expecting a positive result. At the end of ninety minutes however the scores stood level at one goal apiece and the two teams remained on the field, clearly unsure what might happen next. Celtic wanted to play an extra half hour but the Scottish FA had not had the foresight to arrange for extra time. Rangers, realising this, refused to play on and for a few minutes there was total confusion.

The newspapers had partly inflamed the situation with the *Daily Record and Mail* having reported that extra time would be played. A plethora of recently drawn Cup matches had also led to a suspicion that the draws were a deliberate ploy to raise extra cash. Tension mounted and when an official finally walked towards the corner flag, picked it up and strolled away, it was the signal for a pitch invasion. Thousands flooded over the walls as the two teams stalked off the field, with goalposts and nets being torn down and burned while the pay boxes were also set alight. Eight fire engines were immediately dispatched to deal with the blaze and the 94 policemen on duty were joined by a further 141 reinforcements. Battles raged over the next three hours with hosepipes slashed and many injured. In all 81 policemen were treated in hospital, six of them with serious injuries, but only three arrests were recorded. No third match was ever played with the Scottish FA refusing to award the trophy for that year.

The Glasgow papers laid the blame on just about everyone, including criminals, professional thieves and young ruffians, but exonerated the Scottish FA. The *Glasgow News* carried a fearsome cartoon showing a rampaging crowd and imaginatively linked the hooliganism seen at the match with recent political troubles at the trades council and town council. If the invading crowd really looked as savage as the cartoon depicted, then perhaps it can at least be said that football hooliganism must have mellowed with the years!

FOOTBALL RIOT.

MOB LAW AT HAMPDEN.

DISGRACEFUL SCENES.

PROPERTY DESTROYED AND BURNED.

SERIOUS ASSAULTS ON THE POLICE.

FIREMEN STONED: MANY PEOPLE INJURED.

Glasgow News, 19 April 1909

"SEEING RED."

[The spirit of disorder manifested at the Trades Council and Town Council meetings last week culminated in the disgraceful riot at Hampden on Saturday evening.]

KING HOOLIGAN.—"Red ruin and the breaking up of laws!"

Glasgow News, 19 April 1909

LEFT: *Pay boxes in flames, set alight by the rioters*

1909

FOOTBALL AND ADVERTISING go hand in hand in today's game, with companies sponsoring teams and players endorsing a whole range of products from television sets to fashionable men's wear. Precisely when the two interests coincided will always remain in doubt but 1909 seems as close as we are ever likely to come in pinpointing a date. In that year Manchester United won the FA Cup for the first time in their history, beating Bristol City by a goal to nil at the Crystal Palace. And in the Sunday newspaper the *Umpire*, the occasion was marked by an advert featuring the victorious name of Manchester United. The advert was for the popular tonic, Wincarnis, which had allegedly increased United's powers of endurance when training. It must have worked that April afternoon!

BELOW: *Manchester United in 1909*

The Umpire, 25 April 1909

1910

WHEN THE DRAW for the first round of the FA Cup was made in December 1909, Notts County were drawn at home to Bradford City. But with Nottingham Forest also drawn at home, another game in the city of Nottingham hardly suited County. So they came up with the novel idea of selling their home rights to Bradford for £1,000.

County were an impoverished club, desperately in need of ground improvements, and with Forest certain to steal considerable support from them with their attractive tie against Sheffield United, the likelihood was that the gate for the County v Bradford game would produce little more than £200 in receipts. So a deal was struck with the Yorkshire club: in return for the home rights, Bradford would guarantee County £1,000 from the gate receipts at Valley Parade. The *Athletic News* hailed the idea as sensible with obvious benefits to all sides, and given County's fine away record that season, there was every chance that they could still win the tie.

It was rated as the game of the round, but to raise the £1,000 they had promised Bradford were forced to increase their admission charges, with one shilling the cheapest price on the terraces. Indeed, the game nearly did not kick off, as a sudden snap of cold weather led to a frozen pitch and further cost for Bradford who had to spread 20 tons of hay over Valley Parade to protect it from further damage.

When the game did begin the pitch was surrounded with hay and only 18,000 had turned up, many no doubt discouraged by the high admission charges and cold weather. Selling their home rights may have been a cunning plan by Notts County but that was not the way it worked out. Not only did they lose their centre forward Cantrell – sent off for retaliating after a foul by Chaplin – but they also lost the tie, going down by four goals to two. And to rub salt into their wounds Forest slammed Sheffield United 3–2.

Bradford City hardly gained either. The game had not produced the receipts they had anticipated and they were obliged to dip into their coffers to settle the deal. What's more, in the second round Bradford faced Blackburn Rovers at the Valley Parade and went down by two goals to one. It had certainly been a costly campaign.

ABOVE: *Notts may have been impoverished but that did not diminish the achievements of their 6 ft 6 in goalkeeper Albert Iremonger, seen here v Chelsea in September 1909*

NOTTS PAY THE PENALTY.

**Bradford City.... 4 Notts County 2*

[BY HARRICUS.]

APART from the fact that the tie between Bradford City and Notts County was looked upon as the best of the bunch, if only by reason of their positions in the League table, public interest had been centred in the match perhaps more than any other owing to the reason that Notts County, the second club in the League table, had accepted the offer of Bradford City to give up their choice of ground. But I suppose it was a commercial transaction which concerns only the two clubs, even if distasteful to some people, and that the directors of the Yorkshire club were not acting in a philanthropic spirit is evidenced in the charges for admission to the contest.

The lowest price to the ground was one shilling, and stands were correspondingly raised, with the result that there were many seats vacant, and instead of there being the record attendance for the day there were not more than 18,000 spectators. Evidently the public resented the penalty imposed on them, though there is a weak sort of apology in the official programme.

There is no doubt that the two clubs were likely to produce a great game under ordinary conditions, but unfortunately the playing pitch at Valley Parade was in a deplorable condition. Some twenty tons of straw had been put down, though, as it happens, it did no good, and the piles of straw round the touch lines reminded one of a Rugby ground after a frost. Under the circumstances an exhibition of football of the highest standard was not expected, but nevertheless the game was most vigorously contested.

CANTRELL ORDERED OFF

Indeed, the vigour developed to such an extent that after eighteen minutes of the second half Cantrell, the centre-forward of Notts, was ordered off the field by the referee. It was certainly getting time that some drastic action was taken, though I do not wish it to be inferred that Cantrell was a greater offender than the other players.

He was the one who suffered, and I cannot say that any excuse can be made for him. True it is that he was tackled in a forcible manner by Chaplin, but that fact did not justify Cantrell turning round and kicking the full back, who in consequence had to retire to the touch-line for a few moments. I was sat next to a member of the Council of the Football Association, Mr. R. P. Gregson, who was of the opinion that the referee had no other alternative but to dismiss Cantrell from the field.

After this the Notts men got "narky," as we say in Lancashire, if, indeed, they had not previously displayed evidence of this complaint, and I am afraid that the Notts men took their defeat in a very bad spirit. Perhaps their disappointment was all the greater because they looked like winning during the first half-hour of the game, and when at half-time, with the score 1—1, they were just as likely to win as not.

Athletic News, 17 January 1910

1911

THE FOOTBALL pools are not unique to modern soccer. By the turn of the century the Sunday newspaper the *Umpire* was regularly carrying a football forecasting game. The rules were straightforward: you simply had to guess the results of a number of league fixtures each week. At one stage, it was a case of forecasting the result of every game in the first division but by 1911 it had become somewhat easier – presumably because predicting every game was virtually impossible. Instead, it was narrowed down to just six games each week. But rather than simply give the result, you now had to predict the score. Entry was free and the prize for anyone guessing right was £300.

Even in 1911 there were some unusual names on the coupon in the *Umpire*, including Woolwich Arsenal, Clapton Orient and Leicester Fosse. For the record, Manchester City drew 3–3 with Arsenal, Everton beat Bradford City 1–0, Notts County lost 1–0, Clapton Orient lost 4–1 to Chelsea, Blackpool and Leicester drew 1–1 and Plymouth beat Coventry 4–1 in a Southern League fixture.

Other newspapers were quick to follow suit with a variety of competitions, the most successful being Spot-the-Ball which has remained in much the same format since it was first introduced. There was another novel competition called 'Spot the Ground' where you had to identify a soccer stadium from an aerial photograph. But it was always the forecasting of results which was the most popular and the idea was later successfully taken up by John Moores, who introduced his own pools in 1923 with the Littlewoods coupon. That was followed a few years later by a succession of similar coupons including Vernons, Copes and Zetters.

BELOW: *Football pool checking in the thirties – by then forecasting the results had become big business*

FREE COMPETITION!

£300 PRIZE

FOR FOOTBALL FORECAST.

CONSOLATION £25.

(In conjunction with the "Athletic News.")

NO ENTRANCE FEE.

We give below a list of six Association matches, and invite our readers to estimate according to the form of the clubs and their ideas of the merit (individual and collective) of the players, what the result of the matches will be, specifying the scores.

A prize of £300 will be awarded to the competitor who displays skill sufficient to make a forecast accurate in every score.

In the event of no competitor being accurate in every score, £25 will be given to the one who shows the most skill.

Should two or more successful competitors be equal in merit, the prize will be divided

Should any of the matches not take place on the day named, or be postponed or abandoned at or before half-time the consolation prize will be awarded on the results of the remaining games. Where any play takes place after half-time the state of the game at the time of abandonment will be regarded as the result

No responsibility will be accepted by the Editor for the loss or non-delivery of any coupon.

We cannot enter into correspondence regarding this competition.

The decision of the Football Editor will be final and legally binding in all matters pertaining to this skill competition.

All replies should be addressed

FOOTBALL,
"UMPIRE" OFFICE,
MANCHESTER.

and must be received not later than WEDNESDAY NEXT.

Envelopes sent by post must have one penny stamp affixed. A box has been provided at the "Umpire" office for those able to deliver by hand, not later than 10 a.m. each Wednesday.

Any number of competitors may enclose their coupons in the same envelope, providing of course, that the proper postage is paid

Employees of the Firm are not allowed to compete.

Any Competitor who sends in more than ONE Competition Form will be disqualified.

.... CUT HERE ....

MATCHES PLAYED ON SATURDAY, OCT.

	Number of Goals		Number of Goals
Manchester City	....	v. Woolwich A.	......
Everton	....	v. Bradford City	......
Notts. County	....	v. Manchester U.	......
Clapton Orient	....	v. Chelsea	......
Blackpool	....	v. Leicester Fosse	......
Plymouth Argyle	....	v. Coventry City	......

I enter "Umpire" Football Competition in accordance with the rules announced above, and agree to accept the published decision as final and legally binding.

Name ....

Address ....

The Umpire, 22 October 1911

1912

BY 1908 SPONSORSHIP had crept into football, with the season's Cup finalists usually to be found in the advertising columns of the *Sporting Chronicle* or the *Athletic News* every April lending their support to products from Ovaltine to Oxo. But generally such endorsements were confined to teams rather than individuals. A few years later, personalities had taken over the game and the advertisers soon looked to them to sponsor their wares, though often as not they never even bothered to seek their permission let alone pay them. Billy Meredith of Manchester United and Bob Crompton of Blackburn Rovers were among the first league stars to endorse products, but perhaps the most influential was the legendary Derby County centre forward, Steve Bloomer.

In 1912 Bloomer could be found lending his name to the Sugg Football. 'Frank Sugg's football has been played with in more international matches in which I have taken part than any other football,' attested the England international, adding that it 'has always given entire satisfaction. Its perfect shape ensures good shooting. It always keeps a nice weight.' The reference to weight was very important as soccer balls at this time were made of leather and contained a rubber bladder which had to be regularly blown up. When the ball became wet, it also became heavier, making shooting and heading particularly difficult.

Athletic News, 4 November 1912

Born in 1874, Bloomer spanned two eras of football. He began his career with Derby County in 1892, when dribbling was the vogue, but by the turn of the century when passing was the new style Bloomer had adapted his game with equal effect. He had two spells with Derby County, scoring 292 goals in 473 appearances. Sandwiched in between were 125 games and 61 goals for Middlesbrough, creating a record career total of 353 goals in 593 appearances. He also won 23 England caps, and established a record which would stand for 50 years by scoring 28 goals. The dashing, handsome Bloomer, sometimes known as 'paleface', even scored five in one match for England in 1896 as they notched up a 9–1 win over Wales. Unquestionably the finest English forward of his day, Bloomer was much in demand as a sponsor though it is unlikely that he ever made much financial gain out of his various endorsements.

ABOVE: *Steve Bloomer of Derby County, Middlesbrough and England*

1913

WAR CLOUDS may have been gathering somewhere in Serbia but Edwardian England frolicked in its new-found leisure time. Everywhere crowds flocked to the music halls, the seaside resorts and to football. Everywhere that is except Plumstead, where Woolwich Arsenal, languishing at the foot of the first division, could barely raise more than £200 a week in gate receipts. For some reason football fans would not travel to Plumstead. The future looked decidedly grim and Woolwich Arsenal, with an undistinguished record, looked set to go the same way as defunct New Brighton Tower, Burton United and Gainsborough. There was only one solution – move lock, stock and barrel to an area that would guarantee larger support.

On March 5th at the luxurious Connaught Rooms, near Covent Garden in London, the then Arsenal chairman Henry Norris told a gathering of shareholders that the club was heading for disaster and that to ward off bankruptcy they were negotiating a move to north London, to a site owned by the London College of Divinity in Highbury. 'It would be a thousand pities if a club like the Arsenal had to put up its shutters for lack of support,' commented the *Daily Mirror* which recalled that for 12 years Arsenal had been the only London club in the Football League. But Arsenal's possible move was not greeted with enthusiasm everywhere. Over at White Hart Lane and at Clapton Orient there were furious grumblings at the prospect of competition. Both clubs issued a joint circular opposing Arsenal's plan. 'No club will be safe,' they argued, urging Arsenal to continue their search south of the river Thames. Although north London had a catchment area of two-and-a-half million, Tottenham

ABOVE: *The last game played at Plumstead – Arsenal v Manchester United, September 2nd 1913*

and Clapton did not relish the thought of a third club infringing and stealing their support.

The row brewed for weeks but it was a battle Spurs and Clapton were doomed to lose. The lease was negotiated and Arsenal kicked off at their new Highbury home on September 6th 1913 with a new name, The Arsenal, and in a new division, the second. But it was a move, given the nature of their landlords, which at least could be said to have been Divinely inspired.

1913

ABOVE: *Six days before the first Highbury match, and the ground still resembles a building site*

THE FUTURE OF WOOLWICH ARSENAL.

Statement by Mr. Norris on the Reasons for the Removal of the Club to Highbury.

THE GLASGOW MEETING.

Last night, at the Connaught Rooms, Mr. G. H. Norris, the chairman of the Woolwich Arsenal club, made a statement regarding the future of the club, and more particularly with regard to their proposed removal to Islington next season.

Mr. Norris pointed out that it was impossible for the club to pay its way any longer in the district. There was a time, he said, when there were no other attractions of the same kind in London, and in those days the club had a prosperous time. But it was impossible to get people to go to Plumstead nowadays, with other League clubs in the metropolis.

The following are the gates for the home matches this season: Sunderland £248, Manchester City £228, Everton £198, Blackburn Rovers £195, Notts County (Christmas Day) £235, Liverpool £234, Sheffield United £200, Oldham Athletic £227, Bradford City £247, and in the second round of the English Cup, against Liverpool, £343. On those gates, said Mr. Norris, it was impossible to make both ends meet.

They proposed, said Mr. Norris, to go to Highbury, which he described as the apex of an equilateral triangle, with a line drawn from Clapton Orient and Tottenham Hotspur grounds as the base. Highbury was four miles from Tottenham and four miles from Homerton, and Homerton was four and a half miles from Tottenham.

Going on to point out what Woolwich had done for League football in London, Mr. Norris said that they had been twenty years in the Football League, and they hoped to get back some of the patronage of the football public which had been transferred from Woolwich Arsenal to other clubs.

The Woolwich club had voted for Chelsea, Fulham, Clapton Orient and Tottenham being admitted to the League, when they applied for membership. He also said that, they had no knowledge or intimation that any protest would be raised at the Glasgow meeting to their proposed scheme.

Mr. Norris pointed out that the 'Spurs' ground is situated in the County of Middlesex, and in the area governed by the Edmonton Board of Guardians, the population being 500,000. The new ground of the Arsenal Club is in the County of London, and the population tapped by the three clubs would be some two and a half millions.

Mr. Norris also denied that Mr. T. A. Deacock had promised to join the board of directors, but he was understood to say that Mr. Deacock would be welcome as a colleague if he cared to throw in his lot with the Arsenal.

In endorsing the remarks of Mr. Norris, Mr. W. Hall, a director of the Woolwich club and a member of the Management Committee of the League, said that he took no part in the debate at the meeting of the Management Committee, whose decision was come to simply after the ex parte statements of the gentlemen who represented the Tottenham and Clapton clubs at the Glasgow meeting.

Without giving anything away in his speech, Mr. Norris made out a strong case for the removal of the club. In a way it is difficult to see how it will affect the other bodies. It has been the experience when professional football has been establishd in any quarter that a new public has been created for the game. Chelsea is a case in point.

It would be a thousand pities if a club like the Arsenal had to put up its shutters for lack of support, seeing that for twelve years they were the only members in town of the Football League, and most people will wish the Arsenal good luck in their plucky endeavour to keep the flag flying under the most disastrous conditions in recent years.

Daily Mirror, 5 March 1913

1914

THE 1914 Cup Final was marked by the first appearance of a reigning monarch at a Final. It was not the first football match royalty had attended but King George's appearance at the Crystal Palace gave not only public recognition to the growing popularity of the sport but also lent it the royal seal of approval. And once the King had presented the trophy to the winning side, a new tradition was inevitably born.

The presence of royalty also attracted Fleet Street and their cameras. And the *Daily Mirror*, which continued to boast more photographs than any other newspaper, did football proud with both a front page and back page splash. On the sports pages, the headline summed it up: 'The King Sees Burnley Win The Cup, Remarkable Demonstration of Loyalty From Final Tie Crowd at The Crystal Palace.'

The King had arrived late at the Crystal Palace, delayed by the heavy traffic and excited crowds that blocked the way. Sporting the red rose of Lancashire in his buttonhole in recognition of finalists, Burnley and Liverpool, he took his place in a makeshift royal box alongside dignitaries from the Football Association. Sadly the two finalists failed to serve up a match fit for a King with the game by all accounts a rather dour affair. Burnley eventually ran out 1–0 winners, thanks to a goal from their ex-Evertonian centre-forward, Bertie Freeman.

With Britain at war, the following season's final was shifted to Old Trafford, and the FA consequently had to make do with the Earl of Derby as guest of honour. But with the return to London as the venue for the Final after the war, royalty was again on hand to present the trophy. A precedent had been set which has remained almost unbroken ever since. But it was the presence of George V at the 1914 Final and the press's respectful coverage that helped turn the Cup Final into a national sporting occasion.

ABOVE: *Seeing more of the crowd than of the game – soldiers seated on posts*

BELOW LEFT: *The King, wearing the red rose of Lancashire, watches the match*

BELOW: *A dramatic header from Purcell of Liverpool*

THE KING SEES BURNLEY WIN THE CUP.

Remarkable Demonstration of Loyalty from Final Tie Crowd at the Crystal Palace.

UNEVENTFUL CONTEST.

Shot by Freeman Scores the Only Goal of the Match—Liverpool's Missed Chances

The King wound-up the football season of 1913-14, so far as general interest is concerned, when he presented the English Football Cup to T. Boyle, the Burnley captain, at the Crystal Palace on Saturday. Burnley had beaten Liverpool by a goal to nothing, and had secured the highest honours of the year.

His Majesty has never had a greater reception. When he arrived the hoarse cheers of the 74,000 people massed round the playing arena were most impressive, and when he was leaving after presenting the cup and medals the vast assemblage, which seemed to be concentrated in front of the pavilion, once sang "God Save the King" in a manner which testified to their loyalty.

And there was another demonstration of affection and loyalty. Outside the pavilion at the rear of the stands another great crowd began to assemble just before the end of the match, and when his Majesty came out he received another ovation from this army of football enthusiasts.

That the King was pleased was obvious from his smile, and as the motor-car took him away from his first final he repeatedly raised his hat to the cheering multitude. There was no mistaking the heartiness of the greeting football gave his Majesty.

Burnley played in their usual club colours of claret and light blue, and on the left breast wore the royal coat of arms. In the 'eighties the late Duke of Clarence, the King's elder brother, visited Burnley to open the Victoria Hospital, and in the afternoon saw Burnley play Bolton Wanderers. It was after that match that Burnley received permission to wear the royal arms.

Both teams had to make changes at the last moment. Dawson, the Burnley goalkeeper, had to cry off, and Sewell took his place between the posts. Liverpool's loss was a more serious one, for Lowe, their captain, broke down in a trial on Saturday morning and had to stand down. Ferguson went from left half into the centre, and McKinley took the vacant place on the left.

When the teams came out they lined up with the referee, Mr. H. S. Bamlett, and the linesmen and gave three cheers for the King. The captains, Boyle and Ferguson, were presented to his Majesty and the match started.

Burnley had the wind behind them at the start and came away with a rush, Lindley skimming the bar with a great shot. After that Liverpool were generally the aggressors in the first half, and once Taylor was knocked out temporarily with a shot from Nicholl which would have gone through had not Burnley's left back got his head in the way.

GREAT SAVE BY SEWELL.

Lacey did a lot of very clever things, and with Nicholl formed the most effective wing. Lacey tested Sewell once with a tremendous shot, which Burnley's reserve goalkeeper saved splendidly, and then Miller had the Burnley goal at his mercy, but shot just wide of the post. Generally speaking, Liverpool dominated the game in this half, and the Burnley defence could not be described as great. They got the ball away somehow or other, and Liverpool missed many grand openings.

It was expected that Liverpool would do better in the second half, but somehow or other they fell away and not until they were a goal down did they approach their play of the first half.

Daily Mirror, 27 April 1914

ABOVE: *King George shakes hands with Cup-winners after the game*

BELOW: *Bertie Freeman's shot was the only one that found the net*

1915

ABOVE: *Oldham Athletic 1915. Billy Cook is back row, far left*

FOOTBALL'S DISCIPLINE problems do not belong wholly to the social climate of recent years or to overpaid superstars, but can be traced back as far as 1915. On Easter Monday of that year, referee Mr H. Smith of Nottingham was forced to abandon the first division fixture between Middlesbrough and Oldham Athletic when the visiting left-back refused to leave the field after being sent off.

The incident occurred when fourth-placed Oldham faced middle-of-the-table Middlesbrough at Ayresome Park on Easter Monday. Oldham, challenging for the title, were just two points adrift of leaders Manchester City and desperately needed both points to keep in touch with the front-runners. But it was one of those days for the Lancashire side when nothing seemed to go right. They quickly fell behind to a Middlesbrough goal, and within 20 minutes were three goals down. One of those goals had arisen from a dubious refereeing decision and when Oldham were refused a penalty, some of their players naturally felt that referee Smith was not going to give any decisions their way.

Shortly into the second half with the score at 3–1 the Oldham left-back, William Cook, fouled the Middlesbrough forward, Carr, in the penalty area. Up to this point the game had been robust but not unruly. Nevertheless, the referee pointed firmly to the spot, and Middlesbrough's Tinsley easily converted the kick to make it 4–1. As if Oldham were not suffering enough, Mr Smith then decided to send Cook off. This led to an unseemly protest as players swarmed around the referee. The 7,000 crowd also became vocal and for a few moments nobody was quite sure what was happening.

'Eventually the referee ... was seen to take his watch out,' reported the *Athletic News*, 'and after looking at it a little while walked off the ground, the players of both sides following.' The *Athletic News* later interviewed the referee and were informed that he had ordered Cook off but that the Oldham man had refused to go. He had then told the player that he had a minute to obey his order. When he refused to leave, the referee felt he had no option but to abandon the game.

There was uproar. Never before had a match been abandoned because a player refused to leave the field. The *Athletic News* claimed that it was 'without precedent in the history of the premier combination of the country'. Most other papers agreed, urging stern action to be taken

WHO IS TO RULE: REFEREE OR OLDHAM ATHLETIC?

Athletic News, 5 April 1915

against the culprit, although because of the war few actually carried any football news.

The problem however was further compounded when Oldham selected Cook to play in a fixture at Manchester City a week later. Some of the Oldham directors had met after the Cook incident and had decided that he should not play again until the Football League had decided what action to take. Unfortunately when Oldham arrived at Hyde Road, two other directors were in charge of the team. They later claimed to be unaware of the decision not to play Cook, and consequently chose him to play at left-back. The Football League were furious and not only was Cook heavily punished but Oldham were also severely reprimanded and fined £350. Cook was suspended for a year although with football about to draw to a close, it proved to be of little hardship and he reappeared at Boundary Park for one season following the war. But even more damaging for Oldham – by now on the brink of capturing the title – was the decision that the game should not be replayed and that the result should stand. They ended the season as runners-up, just one point behind the champions Everton, and must have deeply regretted the indiscipline of their left-back who may well have cost them the league championship.

OLDHAM'S EXTRAORDINARY CONDUCT

Middlesbrough .. 4 *Oldham Athletic* .. 1
Tinsley (3), Urwin. Kemp.

[BY VULCAN.]

MIDDLESBROUGH has been the scene of some remarkable incidents, but the latest is without precedent in the history of the premier combination of the country. Oldham Athletic came to Tees-side full of confidence in their ability, if not to repeat [illegible] Middlesbrough [illegible] Oldham, to at least make the return journey in secure possession of the full complement of points. The weather was wet, and the ground in a slippery and holding condition. The attendance did not number more than 7,000 spectators, but those present had their reward for braving the elements by witnessing as fiercely contested a game as had been played on the Ayresome Park ground.

Both clubs paraded representative elevens, there being only one absentee of note on either side—Elliott, the home centre forward, and Donnachie, the Oldham outside left. A. N. Wilson substituted the Middlesbrough international, and Walters took the vacant place at outside left for the Athletic.

Middlesbrough had had a heavy engagement at Roker Park, and suffered their usual defeat there the previous day. The Oldham players, however, came on to the field fresh and full of dash. The home players started a surprisingly promising style. Adapting themselves splendidly to the ground conditions, they swung the ball about to excellent purpose, and so completely outclassed their opponents that they were leading by the decisive margin of four goals to one when the incident referred to happened.

COOK DEFIES THE REFEREE.

It followed upon the scoring of a penalty goal by Tinsley some ten minutes after the resumption from a foul by Cook on Carr. The trouble was accentuated, Cook again fouling Carr, with the result that the referee at once stopped play and ordered Cook off the field. The Oldham left back appeared loth to go, and the visiting players assembled round the referee. The crowd became intensely interested, and watched the movements of the official and players amid great excitement. Eventually the referee, Mr H. Smith, of Nottingham, was seen to take his watch out, and after looking at it a little while walked off the ground, the players of both sides following.

The spectators were amazed when they found that the game had been brought to an abrupt close with half an hour still to go. The action of the referee was freely criticised, some arguing that the police should have been called to remove Cook, others that the official should have continued the game with Cook still playing. The situation was a most extraordinary one, and under the peculiar circumstances I interviewed Mr. Smith in his room.

THE OFFICIAL VERSION.

On explaining the nature of my errand Mr. Smith very promptly and courteously stated that he had ordered Cook off the field for fouling Carr. Cook refused to leave the ground, and he (Mr. Smith) then gave him a minute to do so. On Cook remaining obdurate, Mr. Smith said his only course was to himself leave the field. This he did as stated, and the whole matter will come before the League in due course.

Such an ending to what had been as spirited and robust a contest as has been witnessed at Middlesbrough for a very long time is a matter for general regret. Although fought at a fast pace, with plenty of heavy charging and tackling, there were few incidents of a questionable character.

Athletic News, 5 April 1915

1915

BRITAIN DECLARED war on Germany on 4th August 1914, but at first there was little concern at home. Soldiers packed their bags and marched towards the ports with everyone expecting them back by Christmas. Theatres and music halls carried on regardless with their entertainment. Only the cricketers saw fit to bring their game to a halt while for football it was a new season as normal.

As the war dragged on and the news from France and Belgium brought untold horrors of trench warfare, so the footballing authorities grew more concerned. Adverts appeared in match programmes every week urging young men to enlist with Lord Kitchener's army but it was obvious to most that the game could not go on indefinitely while thousands of loyal soldiers were dying across the fields of Europe. Yet there were still those who

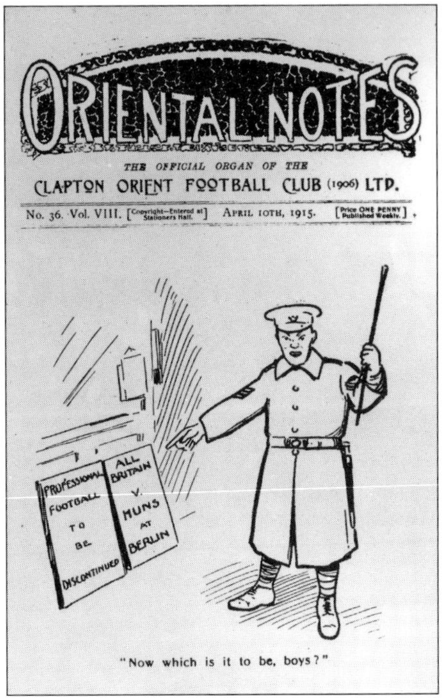

ABOVE *and* BELOW LEFT: Oriental Notes, *the Clapton Orient official magazine, with topical comment*

believed that it should. In April 1915 the Manchester City goalkeeper, Walter Smith, was urging in the *Umpire* that football should continue and even at the Football Association, one councillor, Mr Tillotson, argued that 'there has been a great outcry by silly sentimentalists and people who never took kindly to football.'

In March 1915 the FA reluctantly decided not to fix dates for the Cup competition, and once that decision had been made it was clear that the Football League would soon follow suit. The final game of the 1914/15 season took place on April 26th and a 2–2 draw between Everton and Chelsea at Goodison was enough to give the Merseysiders their second league title. But there was little rejoicing. Even the *Liverpool Football Echo* could hardly raise any enthusiasm, with Everton's win relegated to the inside pages while the front page was dominated by events at Ypres.

In early July representatives from all four British leagues met in the Winter Gardens at Blackpool, and with most clubs reporting a decline in revenue as crowds stayed away and players enlisted, it was decided to cancel the approaching season. In place of the league system it was agreed that ad hoc regional leagues would be set up, players would not be paid, no medals would be struck, and no internationals or inter-league games would be held. But with no games allowed during mid-week or when people were working, the new leagues were of little consequence. The terraces remained deserted as more men trekked to the battlefront while the shipyards and munitions factories raced against the clock to produce more battleships and weapons. Nobody was very interested in soccer.

SATURDAY SEPTEMBER 19th, 1914
Price One Penny. Copyright. Entered at Stationers Hall.

THE
Queen's Park Rangers' F.C.
Programme
OFFICIAL.

HANBURY, TOMSETT & CO.,
All communications to "ELECTRIC PRESS," KENSAL RISE.

Young Men of the Nation,
Your King and Country Need You
JOIN THE ARMY TO-DAY
Local Recruiting Station:
158, High Street, Harlesden.

ABOVE: *'Your King and Country Need You!' A plea to football fans*

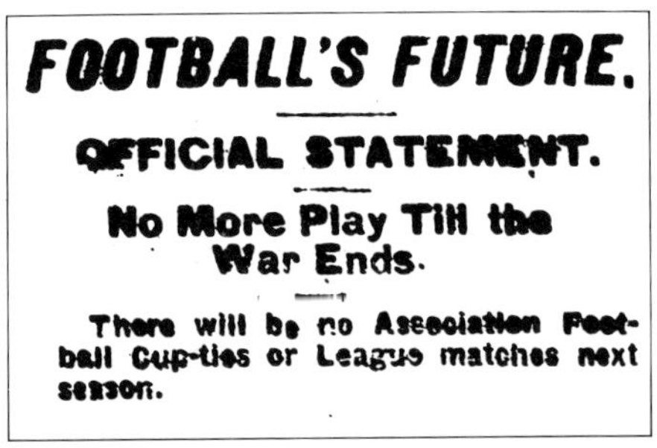
FOOTBALL'S FUTURE.

OFFICIAL STATEMENT.

No More Play Till the War Ends.

There will be no Association Football Cup-ties or League matches next season.

ON GOOD FRIDAY 1915 Manchester United and Liverpool met at Old Trafford, in a first division league fixture that was of little consequence to middle-of-the-table Liverpool but of vital importance to lowly-placed United. By all accounts the game was a dour affair and nobody attached much importance to United's 2–0 victory until a couple of weeks later when there was an accusation in a leading newspaper that the match had been rigged.

The game was played in front of 15,000 supporters in pouring rain with George Anderson shooting United into a first half lead. Late in the match, Anderson added a second goal as a lethargic-looking Liverpool seemed content to drop a couple of points. When Fred Pagnam, the Liverpool centre-forward hit the cross-bar, his team-mates were visibly angered and words were exchanged. It was later alleged that Pagnam had not been a party to the arrangement. There was no immediate speculation about the result although a number of newspapers remarked on Liverpool's miserable showing, with the *Sporting Chronicle* reckoning them to be 'too poor to describe'.

A few weeks later a handbill began to circulate in the Manchester area, signed by a firm of bookmakers known as the 'Football Kings'. On Saturday April 24th, the *Sporting Chronicle* carried a story which reproduced the handbill and alerted the football world to a possible scandal. The handbill alleged that the game had been squared for the home club to win by a certain score, and that a number of players had then laid bets on this score. Investigations were now being carried out, reported the *Chronicle*, and a substantial reward was on offer for any further information.

Although betting on football matches was common in 1915, it was unusual for anyone to bet on the score rather than the result. It was odd then that considerable sums of money had been laid, at odds of seven to one, on United to win by 2–0.

An inquiry was immediately launched by the Football League which began its investigations in Manchester on May 10th and continued late into the autumn, but it was not until Christmas that the final verdict was delivered. It found that 'a considerable amount of money changed hands by betting on the match and ... some of the players profited thereby.' The report was damning and caused a sensation. As a result four Liverpool players were found guilty along with four United players and all eight were suspended from the game for life. United finished the season second from bottom, just two points above Tottenham who were relegated.

It transpired that Jackie Sheldon of Liverpool, a former United player himself, had acted as the go-between, meeting a number of United players in a Manchester pub where the deal had been fixed. Along with Sheldon, the Liverpool players involved were Bob Purcell who had been poached from Queen's Park in 1911 in an illegal deal; Tommy Miller, the former Motherwell, Hamilton and Third Lanark player; and Tom Fairfoul, another Scot. The United culprits were Sandy Turnbull, Enoch 'Knocker' West, Arthur Whalley and Laurence Cook, although West was the only United man to have played in the match. As a gesture of goodwill the FA lifted the bans following the war, except for Enoch West whose ban continued until 1945 even though he always maintained his innocence. For Turnbull, killed in action, the pardon came too late.

Allegations Against Players.

A Commission consisting of Messrs. J. Lewis, H. Keys, and C. E. Sutcliffe, who had investigated certain complaints, reported as follows:—

We have made very careful inquiries and full investigation into certain rumours that an important League match played recently had been squared, but in view of the facts hereinafter set forth we are withholding any report at present.

A football coupon issued last week has been brought to our notice containing the following announcement:—

£50 Reward.—We have solid grounds for believing that a certain First League match played in Manchester during Easter week-end was "squared," the home club being permitted to win by a certain score. Further, we have information that several of the players of both teams invested substantial sums on naming the correct score of this match with our firm and others. Such being the case, we wish to inform all our clients and footballl public generally that we are upholding payment on these correct score transactions, also that we are causing searching investigations to be made with the object of punishing the instigators of this reprehensible conspiracy.

With this object in view we are anxious to receive reliable information bearing on the subject, and we will willingly pay the substantial reward named above to anyone giving information which will lead to punishment of the offenders.

The coupon referred to is issued by "The Football King."

The allegations referred to are not made in connection with any particular match, and may refer to either of two.

We can readily understand the serious unwillingness of bookmakers to be robbed by a conspiracy on the part of players, and we are just as determined that League football shall not be degraded, disgraced, and ruined by such reprehensible practices as those referred to in the coupon under notice.

If, as is stated therein, direct bets have been made by players such conduct is contrary to the rules of the F.A., and in accordance with declarations by the F.A. and the Football League any such player found guilty would be put out of football for ever. The conspiracy alleged is a criminal offence upon which the aggrieved parties can take action.

If the injured parties are not prepared so to act and will furnish us with any information justifying such allegations, or either of them, we are prepared to pursue our inquiries to the utmost and fearlessly impose adequate punishment, and anyone willing to supply any information should communicate with the Secretary of the Football League, Mr. T. Charnley, Castle Chambers, Market-place, Preston, at once.

There is one further alternative. If the party responsible for the issue of the coupon referred to will publicly state the match referred to, and furnish us with his name and address, thus accepting responsibility for the publication of such coupon, the 22 players concenred will immediately take action for libel, and test the whole question in the Courts before a Judge and jury.

If this challenge is not accepted within 14 days we shall know what construction to place on the anonymous allegations, and shall issue a further report based upon our investigations.—J. Lewis, H. Keys, C. G. Sutcliffe.

It was decided to hold the next meeting of the committee in London, on Monday, **May 31, 1915.**

Sporting Chronicle, 24 April 1915

Jackie Sheldon

Tom Miller

Tom Fairfoul

1915

THE 1915 Cup Final will always be remembered as the 'Khaki Cup Final'. It was played at Old Trafford in typically wet, miserable Manchester weather with the terraces swaying with soldiers huddled inside their buttoned up, damp khaki trench coats. Britain was at war and although the ground swelled to the noise of cheering servicemen, few elsewhere cared much for the game's outcome. Soccer was about to come to a temporary halt and the Final would prove to be virtually the last major competitive fixture in England for four years.

The game was fought between Sheffield United and Chelsea with the Yorkshire club running out comfortable winners by three goals to nil. Simmons had given United the lead with Fazackerly adding a second seven minutes from the end. Kitchen scored a third with only minutes remaining and the Cup was on its way to the Steel City for the fifth time (Sheffield Wednesday having won the Cup twice). It would remain there for the next five years.

The papers cared little for the match. On the Saturday of the game the *Daily Mirror* carried just one sentence merely announcing that the game was taking place. In stark contrast to the previous season, there was no analysis, no photographs, no predictions. News of hostilities was at a premium in papers that had greatly reduced their size to help the war effort. The following morning,

A KHAKI FINAL.

To-day's Great Match at Old Trafford.

Big as is Old Trafford, the home of Manchester United—it will accommodate about 70,000—there are abundant signs its capacity will be fully tested to-day when the final of the English Cup between Chelsea and Sheffield United will be decided.

This year's final can, from many points of view, be called a khaki final, for soldiers will be present in their thousands. Army officers from all over the country have made application for tickets, and in addition to the soldiers quartered in and around the city hundreds of wounded soldiers, representative of the South, Scotland, Ireland, and Wales will be present in large numbers.

While the Army and Navy will be strongly represented at Old Trafford, naval officers and sailors at sea have sent postal orders with requests for the scores to be wired to them. The soldiers in the trenches are also interested in this great national event, and they will be eager to know whether Chelsea or Sheffield United have lifted the Cup.

Sporting Chronicle, 20 April 1915

SHEFFIELD'S THIRD CUP.

Chelsea Beaten by 3 Goals to 0 in Final Tie at Manchester.

A crowd of 50,000 people saw Sheffield United win the English Cup at Manchester on Saturday for the third time in the history of the club. Chelsea never reproduced the form which got them to the final stage and were well beaten by 3 goals to 0.

A wet morning was followed by a very dull afternoon, and towards the end of the game it was difficult to distinguish the players on the far side of the ground. The turf, however, was in fair order, and Chelsea had no excuse on that score for their failure.

Sheffield outplayed their opponents completely, and, on the whole, it was a somewhat disappointing match. There were long periods in the game when the football was of a distinctly mediocre quality, and although a fine pace was maintained the struggle left a feeling of disappointment.

As to the superiority of Sheffield United, however, no two opinions could exist, and, as Mr. Kirby said in seconding Mr. Claggs's vote of thanks to Lord Derby for presenting the Cup and medals, "the better team won."

Quicker on the ball and always looking more dangerous in attack, the United forwards at times played splendid football, and their defence was so superb that only during the closing moments of the first half did they experience any really anxious time. Chelsea's failure was entirely due to their forwards, who played without any conception of combination.

Whatever their shortcomings in attack, however, Chelsea had nothing to reproach themselves with in regard to defence. Logan was superb, and even if Betteridge was rash at times, he did not make many mistakes, and Molyneux in goal, although beaten three times, kept out many other shots in great style.

Utley, the Sheffield captain, will always be able to look back upon the game with the greatest degree of personal satisfaction. Indefatigable in all he did, he smashed up the occasional attacks of the Chelsea right wing in masterly fashion.

Simmons scored the first goal for Sheffield after thirty-six minutes' play, and it was not until seven minutes from the end that Fazackerley obtained the second. This was followed almost immediately by another from Kitchen, who scored after a brilliant individual effort.

After presenting the Cup and medals, Lord Derby, addressing the huge crowd, said that the clubs and their supporters had seen the Cup played for, and it was now the duty of everyone to join with each other and play a sterner game for England. He felt sure he would not appeal in vain; we had a duty before us which every man must face and do his best.

Daily Mirror, 26 April 1915

the Sundays also gave scant coverage to events in Manchester, concentrating instead on the battlefront that was spread across Europe. It was left to the *Sporting Chronicle* to pen the phrase 'Khaki Cup Final' that would last forever. Only the *Athletic News* delivered the kind of coverage football fans would normally have expected, while on the Monday morning the *Daily Mirror* in its brief report devoted more space to Lord Derby's stirring speech. 'After presenting the cup and medals,' reported the *Mirror* somberly, 'Lord Derby, addressing the huge crowd, said that the clubs and their supporters had seen the Cup played for, and it was now the duty of everyone to join with each other and play a sterner game for England.' Doubtless many of those present did so, and doubtless many never returned to see soccer again.

BELOW: *Wounded soldiers were among the 50,000 crowd at the 'Khaki Cup Final' of 1915*

THE FIGHT FOR THE ENGLISH CUP.

IT is difficult to say which section of the community, civilians or soldiers, takes the greater interest in the Final Tie for the Association Cup, to be played on the ground of Manchester United to-day. There was a politician who, years ago, said that we were all Socialists May it not be said with even more truth that to-day we are all soldiers, or sailors, or making munitions for the men who fight, or manufacturing something that the Forces need. The nation is engaged in a huge conflict, and has sons of Empire in action in six or seven different parts of the world. But those who are in our island will rest awhile to-day.

Sporting Chronicle, 24 April 1915

1919

AFTER FOUR years of friendly football and regional competitions, league soccer eventually returned to England on September 1st 1919. World War One had ended too late in 1918 for a new league season to commence, so officials had postponed the opening day until the following year. When the new season kicked off, nobody knew quite how the crowds would react. Would there still be the old enthusiasm for the game, or would the retirement and death of so many pre-war stars have led to a fall in playing standards?

On the first Saturday of the season, with the league tables as they had been before war interrupted, there were few signs that any of the old spirit was missing. More than 50,000 turned up at Highbury to see Newcastle beat Arsenal by a single goal while 35,000 supporters lined the terraces at Roker Park. In the second division, Tottenham, relegated in 1915, began their fight back with a 5–0 trouncing of Coventry while Blackpool beat Leeds City 4–2 in one of the day's most exciting encounters.

When soccer had been disbanded in 1915 Everton had been the champions, but four years later there were a couple of absentees and advancing years had slowed some others. They opened the season against Chelsea at Goodison Park which coincidentally had been their final league match prior to the war. Then they had clinched the first division championship with a 2–2 draw but now they lost 3–2. Only five of the Everton team which had played in that 1915 game lined up at the start of the 1919/20 season. By the end of the campaign Everton were in sixteenth place while West Bromwich Albion surprised everyone by capturing their first title, and Tottenham, not unexpectedly, won promotion back to the first division.

> **A THRILLING OPENING.**
> Chelsea Conquer the Champions at Goodison.
> **FIVE VICTORIOUS VISITING CLUBS.**
> **CHELSEA'S FOX-TROT** | **ROVERS BRILLIANT.**
> How They Extinguished Everton. | Shea and Dawson in Scoring Form.
> Chelsea ....3 *Everton ....2 *Blackburn Rovers .4 Preston North End .0

Athletic News, 1 September 1919

ABOVE: *From* Gamages Football Annual *1919–20. Eddie Latheron was just one of the many fine players – amateur and professional – killed during the Great War*

> **The Real League Football Resumed. 50,000 Spectators at Highbury.**

Athletic News, 1 September 1919

1920

ON SATURDAY August 28th 1920, league football took a giant stride forward with the introduction of a third division. A decision had been made in May 1920 at the League's annual meeting to introduce a third division at the start of the 1920 season and providing it was successful, a northern section the following year. And so, on that sweltering Saturday afternoon in late August a new era of football began. The change also meant that the back pages had to respond by adding a third league to their network of results and reports. More space and more reporters were needed to cover the games and once the Northern League had been added, football was soon spreading onto a second page.

All the teams forming the new division had been members of the Southern League with the exception of Grimsby Town who had failed to gain re-election as full members of the Football League after finishing bottom of the second division. One of the previous season's Southern League clubs, Cardiff City, were elected to the second division in their place. All but one of those teams playing on that first day remain members of the league, with only Merthyr having dropped out while some are currently members of the first division. That the decision to form a new division was popular was quickly shown by the crowds they attracted. Even on that opening Saturday with the cricket championship still undecided, Millwall could draw 25,000 to The Den while both Portsmouth and Queen's Park Rangers attracted 20,000 each. That may have been down on the average second division gate and well down on the 60,000 at St James' Park but it demonstrated that the public was keen for more soccer.

There were plenty of goals in the third division as well, with Swindon Town slamming nine past Luton while unfancied Merthyr Town beat Crystal Palace 2–1. By the end of the season, however, Palace were champions five points ahead of Southampton. But on their first day Southampton could only manage a draw, at Gillingham, who eventually ended the season bottom of the table.

BELOW: *Crystal Palace FC, the first champions of the third division south*

THE LEAGUE.—DIVISION III

				Attendance.
Exeter City (Wright, Vowles, Feebury.)	3	**Brentford**	0	8,000
Gillingham (Gilboy.)	1	**Southampton** (Dorning.)	1	12,000
Grimsby Town (Macauley 2.)	2	**Northampton**	0	12,000
Millwall (Broad 2.)	2	**Bristol Rovers**	0	25,000
Newport County	0	**Reading** (Bailey.)	1	12,000
Plymouth Argyle (Heap.)	1	**Norwich City** (Whitham.)	1	14,000
Portsmouth (James, Springfellow, Reid.)	3	**Swansea Town**	0	29,000
Queen's Park Rangers (Birch.)	1	**Watford** (Ronalds, White.)	2	20,000
Southend United (Fairclough 2.)	2	**Brighton & H.**	0	9,000
Swindon Town (Fleming 4, Batty 2, Davies, Jefferson, and Parker, own goal.)	9	**Luton Town** (Simms.)	1	10,000
Merthyr Town (Walker, Chesser.)	2	**Crystal Palace** (Milligan.)	1	13,000

Daily Herald, 30 August 1920

1921

A YEAR AFTER the third division south had been introduced, it was the turn of the north. This time however there was no league to automatically assume the mantle as there had been with the Southern League. Instead, applications were invited from any northern clubs equipped for the professional game. The result was that a wide variety of teams – primarily from the Lancashire Combination, the Midland League, the Cheshire League, the Central League and the North Eastern League – applied to join the new division. Among the many unusual names kicking off on that first Saturday were Ashington, Durham City, Stalybridge Celtic, Accrington Stanley, Nelson, Wigan Borough, Southport and Barrow, none of whom remain in the Football League today.

The opening fixtures brought a 6–3 win for Rochdale over Accrington, a 4–1 victory for Tranmere against Crewe and a 1–0 defeat for Grimsby at Ashington. The first ever league table, after just two games, showed Durham City and Tranmere Rovers in the top spot, both with three points from two matches. But it was a very different picture by the end of the season with Tranmere third from bottom and Durham hovering in the middle of the league which had been won by Stockport County.

NEW NORTHERN BANTLING.

A Rude Awakening for Some Team Builders.

WALSALL'S WELCOME

Poor Forward Line Loses them Match with Lincoln.

**Lincoln City.......1 Walsall..........0*

AFTER 28 YEARS.

Accrington, Stanley's Return to League Football.

**Rochdale.........6 Accrington Stanley.3*

Athletic News, 29 August 1921

GRIMSBY'S GLUT OF GOALS.

Halifax Town Startle The North-Country.

THE LEAGUE.—Division 3. NORTHERN SECTION.

*Chesterfield ....4 Stalybridge Celt ...0
Butterworth, Williams, Marshall, Ormston.

*Crewe Alexandra...1 Tranmere R............1
Rowlands. Prentice.

*Accringt'n Stan. ...4 Rochdale..................0
Makin, Green (2), Hosker.

Nelson ....4 *Wigan Borough ...1
Halligan, Hargreaves, Jacques, Marsh. Balmforth.

*Durham City ....2 Southport 0
Young, Cousins.

*Grimsby Town ......6 Ashington 1
Miller (3), Deacey, Gillow, Carmichael. Thompson.

*Halifax Town..........5 Darlington 1
Woods 2, Dent 2, Hetherington. Edmunds.

Wrexham ....1 *Hartlepool U. 0
Moorwood.

*Walsall ....3 Lincoln City 0
Reid (2), Barber.

* Home club.

RESULTS TO SATURDAY, SEPT. 3 (Inclusive).

	Pld.	Won	Lost	Drn.	For	Agst.	Pts.
Durham City	2	1	0	1	3	1	3
Tranmere Rovers	2	1	0	1	6	2	3
Stockport County	1	1	0	0	2	0	2
Grimsby Town	2	1	1	0	6	2	2
Walsall	2	1	1	0	3	1	2
Hartlepools United	2	1	1	0	2	1	2
Halifax Town	2	1	1	0	6	3	2
Nelson	2	1	1	0	6	3	2
Stalybridge Celtic	2	1	1	0	6	4	2
Accrington Stanley	2	1	1	0	7	6	2
Rochdale	2	1	1	0	6	7	2
Chesterfield	2	1	1	0	4	6	2
Darlington	2	1	1	0	3	5	2
Wigan Borough	2	1	1	0	3	5	2
Wrexham	2	1	1	0	1	2	2
Ashington	2	1	1	0	2	6	2
Lincoln City	2	1	1	0	1	3	2
Crewe Alexandra	2	0	1	1	2	6	1
Southport	2	0	1	1	1	3	1
Barrow	1	0	1	0	0	2	0

Athletic News, 5 September 1921

GRIMSBY'S ATONE.

Miller's Three Goals in Polished Style.

Athletic News, 5 September 1921

RIGHT: *Stockport County at the end of the 1919/20 season, winners of the third division north*

1922

LIVERPOOL WERE the team of the early 1920s, capturing their third league championship in 1922 before following that up with their fourth triumph the next year. It was much the same team over the two years, with players such as captain Don McKinlay, England internationals Harold Chambers and Tom Bromilow and the dashing inside-forward Dick Forshaw. After winning two championship medals with Liverpool, Forshaw sensationally moved to Goodison Park where he linked up with Dixie Dean to help Everton win the title in 1928. At Anfield he averaged a goal every other game.

Yet if the team owed more to any one player it was goalkeeper Elisha Scott. The Irish goalkeeper followed in a grand tradition of outstanding goalkeepers at Anfield. The first had been Ned Doig, the Scottish international who guarded during the early years of the twentieth century. He was followed by Sam Hardy, the great England international who made 239 appearances for the Reds before departing for Aston Villa. During an international career spanning 13 years he won 21 caps. Kenny Campbell, another Scottish international, followed, only to hand over finally to Scott in 1920. But Scott was possibly the finest of them all. He played 430 league games for Liverpool between 1912 and 1934 and made 31 appearances for Ireland, winning his first cap in 1920 and his last at the age of 42 in 1936. At 5 ft 9½ inches he was on the short side for a goalkeeper. But this, coupled with his lack of weight, seemed to make him more agile than most keepers. During their two championship seasons Liverpool conceded only 67 goals, an unusually low number considering the high scoring times. In the 1922/23 season they conceded a mere 31 goals – a new first division record.

Scott was unmistakable. He lined up wearing two pairs of socks and even in the mild spring weather pulled on three sweaters, while in the winter he would add a pair of darkened long-johns and knee pads to his outfit. He arrived at matches hours before anyone else, quickly changed and then spent an hour hurling the ball against the dressing room wall and catching it. One wonders if this did not irritate his teammates! During the 1930s, derby matches with Everton were always billed as a confrontation between Dixie Dean and Scott. It was even said that when Dean met Scott in the street one day he nodded politely, and the agile Irish goalkeeper reacted by instantly flinging himself to the pavement to save some imaginary header. The story is almost certainly fictional but it was all part of the legend of Elisha Scott.

ABOVE: *Elisha Scott, characteristically clad in gloves and sweater*

EN PASSANT

The Champions of the League.

THE supreme event in the Eastertide football was the decision of The League championship. When Liverpool had the honour of defeating last season's winners, Burnley, and on the same day Oldham Athletic overcame Tottenham Hotspur at Boundary Park, the premiership of the First Division was beyond argument, for the North London club, which alone threatened to wrest the prize from Liverpool, could not do so even if they won all their matches and Liverpool finished their programme in absolute ignominy.

With their visit to Cardiff City merged in the past, the Liverpool eleven have their fixtures with West Bromwich Albion to decide. These will be most interesting, as no doubt the new champions will be eager to prove that their exit from The Association Cup was one of those misfortunes which overtake the best, while the Albion will be keen to keep the champions as far as possible below the record 60 points which the South Staffordshire club established in 1919-20.

This is the third time since this century dawned that Liverpool have been League champions, as they gained this distinction in 1900-01 and in 1905-06, but it is doubtful if they ever had such an evenly-balanced and consistent set of players as at present.

Necessarily the figures are incomplete, but we anticipate that their achievement will bear analysis and comparison with their performances in those years.

Athletic News, 24 April 1922

1923

ABOVE: *crowd on the touchlines;* BELOW: *cartoon from the* London Evening News

THE FIRST EVER Wembley Cup Final could so very easily have resulted in a major disaster and may never have even taken place had it not been for one man, a police officer mounted on a white horse. It was his brave action that saved the day and allowed the game to kick off as he cleared the pitch of thousands of supporters. The *Daily Mirror* had no doubts that he was the hero of the day.

The problem was that nobody had expected that so many would flock to see this inaugural event at Wembley. The newly-completed stadium had clearly caught the public's imagination. Its capacity was put at 127,000, but the *Empire News* estimated that a crowd of around 300,000 had besieged the ground with at least 200,000 of them managing to gain entry. They swarmed over walls, climbed turnstiles and knocked down exit gates, ignoring gatekeepers and police threats. Even then, thousands remained outside, unable to force their way through the multitude and into the stadium. The police were powerless and for a full hour the pitch was a seething mass of spectators before the officer on his famous white horse appeared to bring some semblance of order. The players appeared but there was little they could do; some retreated to the dressing rooms, others stayed to try and persuade the crowd back to the terraces in the hope that the presentation of the teams could go ahead.

Eventually at 14 minutes to four, play began with thousands packed around the goals and touchlines. But they were not ideal conditions for a football match and the north-south clash between Bolton Wanderers and second division West Ham United never lived up to expectations. Bolton won by two goals to nil, with David Jack securing the honour of scoring Wembley's first goal just three minutes into the game while John Smith added a second shortly after half time. At the final whistle the pitch once more was invaded and after a breathless struggle captain Joe Smith and his men finally made their way up the steps to the Royal Box to be presented with the trophy by King George V.

CUP RIOT PREVENTED
BY POLICE RESOURCE.
Officer on a White Charger Hero of the Day.
COAXING A MULTITUDE.

(Continued from page 3, column 1.)

At first they were so utterly outnumbered as to be helpless. The foot police were whirled away like twigs in a Severn spate by that rush of thirty thousand men flinging themselves over and through the barriers.

There were about half a score mounted constables, and they did wonders, but of course were all too few.

When a horseman came prancing upon the intruders they retired a little before him, only to push forward again as soon as he rode to some other part of the line.

One officer on a white charger won the unstinted admiration of the "gallery," and was often and deservedly cheered.

Energetic, undaunted, resourceful, at once decisive and good-tempered, he dominated the crowd by the sheer force of his personality, and wherever he appeared he received willing obedience and made a little oasis of order in the general chaos

But he could not be everywhere at once, and the temporary clearances he and his scanty band of comrades made, with the two football teams assisting, were soon submerged.

A MATCH AFTER ALL!

For an hour it looked as if it would be utterly impossible for the match to be played that day.

Then, at long last, came the reinforcements. A whole squadron of mounted men rode upon the ground, and a strong company of foot police followed. A regiment and a battalion would not have been too many.

Slowly and with great effort the multitude was jostled and herded back just clear of the goal posts and lines, policemen sat down on the turf in front. So the game was played, as best it could be, with a seated policeman or too-prominent spectator having occasionally to be shifted for a corner kick and the ball frequently flying right into the depths of the serried ranks of onlookers.

Daily Mirror, 30 April 1923

THE DAILY MIRROR, Monday, April 30, 1923.

CHAOS AT CUP-TIE FINAL: WHO WAS TO BLAME? SEE P. 7

The Daily Mirror

NET SALE MUCH THE LARGEST OF ANY DAILY PICTURE NEWSPAPER | **24 PAGES**

No. 6,079. Registered at the G.P.O. as a Newspaper. MONDAY, APRIL 30, 1923 One Penny.

POLICE v. CROWD: WEMBLEY'S FIRST CUP FINAL

Daily Mirror, 30 April 1923

ABOVE: *The overflowing crowd surging onto the pitch at Wembley*

Official records will claim that the first contest to be staged at the Empire Stadium, Wembley, was the final for the Football Association Challenge Cup between West Ham United and Bolton Wanderers. The many thousands who journeyed to Wembley on Saturday will, however, long retain the memory of an earlier struggle in which the opposing elements were police and public, the ultimate victory resting with the force, whose efforts eventually produced order from utter chaos.

Daily Mirror, 30 April 1923

1924

GALLACHER'S GREAT FEAT.

Athletic News, 15 September 1924

THE HISTORY of Airdrieonians Football Club is hardly littered with jewels. Formed in 1878 they became members of the Scottish League in 1894. Nine years later they climbed out of the second division as champions to join Scotland's élite in the first division. But there was precious little else to cheer about for another two decades. Then suddenly as the 1920s dawned Airdrie, for a brief time, became a major force in Scottish football, thanks mainly to one man – Hughie Gallacher.

Gallacher was born in Bedshill in Lanarkshire in 1903 and began his illustrious career with Airdrie during the 1921 close season. In his first year with the Waysiders he made just 11 appearances but notched up seven goals to issue a warning of what was to follow. The following season, 1922/23, Gallacher played 18 games and scored 10 goals, helping Airdrie into the runners-up spot behind the mighty Rangers. It was the beginning of a remarkable period in Airdrie's history. The following year they were in second spot again but capped that by beating Hibernian 2–0 at Ibrox to capture the Scottish Cup for the first time in their history. Gallacher scored 33 times in 34 appearances. A year later they were runners-up to Rangers yet again, though this time only three points behind the champions as Gallacher rattled in another 32 goals in as many appearances. In 1926 they completed an astonishing run by being runners-up four years in succession when Celtic beat them to the title. But that was really the end of Airdrie, for Hughie Gallacher had already left to try his luck with Newcastle United.

He signed for Newcastle in December 1925 for £6,500, bringing with him a slice of the luck that had helped Airdrie. Within a little over a year he had skippered Newcastle to the league championship. Gallacher, the doughty centre-forward, netted 23 goals in just 19 appearances during the 1925/26 season. And a year later as Newcastle topped the first division he hit 36 goals in 38 games – a club record which stands even to this day. He remained with Newcastle until May 1930 when Chelsea paid £10,000 for his services, but his goals and luck were now beginning to evaporate and after four years with the London club he signed for Derby County for £3,000. Two years later he was on his way to Notts County, and then Grimsby, before he ended his days as a £500 transfer to lowly Gateshead. His final game was played in the third division north the day before war broke out, bringing to an end a career that had spanned 543 league games in Scotland and England and had produced 387 goals.

ABOVE: *Hughie Gallacher, the finest goalscorer of his day*

He won his first Scottish cap at the age of 21, and lined up for his twentieth and final international honour against England in 1935. He scored a record 21 goals in the home international championships during that period and hit five for the Scottish League against the Irish League in Belfast in November 1925. He was also a member of the illustrious Scottish side that destroyed England 5–1 at Wembley in 1928.

At 5 ft 5 inches Gallacher may have looked more like a shopkeeper than a dashing centre-forward, but he had the courage and tenacity of a man twice his size and was always to be found in the thick of the action. But above all it was his speed on the ball and his natural goalscoring instinct which made him the finest goalscorer of his day.

Off the field his life was as stormy as it was on it. He was divorced, unusual for those times, and in 1957 committed suicide by throwing himself under an approaching train while awaiting a charge of ill-treating his son. It was a sad end for one of the greatest goalscorers in English and Scottish football.

RESULTS TO SATURDAY, SEPT. 13 (Inclusive).

	Pld.	Won	Lost	Drn.	Goals For	Goals Agst.	Pts.
Airdrieonians	6	5	0	1	16	3	11
Rangers	6	5	0	1	15	3	11
Hibernians	5	5	0	0	10	4	10
Celtic	6	3	0	3	14	4	9
Hamilton Acad.	6	4	2	0	8	8	8
Partick Thistle	6	2	1	3	14	7	7
Falkirk	6	3	2	1	8	5	7
Dundee	5	2	1	2	11	4	6
Cowdenbeath	6	1	2	3	13	10	5
Hearts	6	2	3	1	13	16	5
Queen's Park	6	2	3	1	7	10	5
Third Lanark	5	1	1	3	4	6	5
Ayr United	6	1	2	3	7	11	5
Motherwell	5	1	2	2	6	5	4
Kilmarnock	6	1	3	2	8	11	4
Raith Rovers	5	1	2	2	3	5	4
St. Johnstone	7	1	4	2	9	18	4
St Mirren	5	1	4	0	3	11	2
Aberdeen	5	0	4	1	4	12	1
Morton	6	0	5	1	4	24	1

Athletic News, 15 September 1924

1925

THE START of the 1925/26 season heralded a major change in the rules of football. Until then, a player had to make sure there were three opponents between him and the goal. From now on, there need be only two. This change in the offside law was to have a dramatic effect on the game, cutting down the confusion and continual stoppages that had resulted under the old rule.

As the season kicked off on Saturday August 29th nobody knew precisely how the new rule would operate and whether it would indeed be beneficial. But it soon became clear. After careful consideration of the results, Monday's *Daily Mirror* gave its opinion. 'Generally speaking the verdict was that the change is for the better. The game was faster, more goals were scored,' it reported, adding that, 'the referee's whistle was scarcely heard.'

The one result which had swayed everyone was Aston Villa's ten goals against Burnley. The poor old Lancastrians simply could not adapt to the change. But there were other big hitters. Bradford, Plymouth and Rochdale all opened their accounts with six goals and in the weeks that followed there were numerous surprises as favourites took a pasting. Sunderland, for instance, shocked everyone by knocking six goals against the cup holders Sheffield United. As for the crowds, they loved it and flocked in even greater numbers to the games. Charles Buchan who had just been transferred from Sunderland to Arsenal summed it up for the nation in his weekly column in the *Sunday Express*, arguing that 'to player and spectator alike, it has been almost a new game'.

OPENING DAY OF REVOLUTIONISED FOOTBALL

Daily Mirror, 29 August 1925

Revolutionised football starts to-day in **all** parts of the country. The new offside **rule**, by which only two opponents are necessary between the player and the goal when the ball was last played by a member of his own side, comes into the game. Is it for good or ill? Time alone will show.

BELOW: *Centre-forward Walker scores Villa's eighth goal against Burnley*

1926

ABOVE: *Huddersfield Town, top of the first division, 1925*

ON THE EVE of the 1926 General Strike Huddersfield Town wrote their name in the history books when they became the first Football League side to win the championship three years in succession. On Easter Saturday, April 10th, Huddersfield beat West Ham United 2–1 with Alex Jackson hitting both goals in front of a 20,000 crowd at Leeds Road. On the same day Arsenal lost 2–1 at Sunderland and Huddersfield leapt into an unchallengeable eight-point lead. Theoretically it was still possible for the Gunners to catch them but it was a wild dream. Two days later the Yorkshiremen made certain of their third title by beating Bolton Wanderers 3–0. It was an astonishing feat that would be matched in later years by only Arsenal and Liverpool.

Huddersfield's record began when Herbert Chapman arrived at Leeds Road in 1920 after a spell with Leeds City. At that time the town was more noted for its famous rugby league side than for football, although the soccer team had just narrowly lost to Aston Villa in its first Cup Final appearance. Indeed Huddersfield were lucky still to be in football after the League Management Committee had ordered that they amalgamate with the new Leeds United when financial mismanagement had been discovered at the club. But after a public appeal and the sale of a few players, they managed to raise enough cash to satisfy the League that they had put their house in order. And within two seasons Chapman had guided them back along the Wembley trail, this time to a 1–0 victory over Preston in the 1922 Cup Final. The following year he steered them into third place in the first division and the next season they were champions, winning the title on goal average from Cardiff City.

In 1925 they headed the table again, two points clear of West Brom, and although Chapman then surprisingly resigned to join Arsenal he left behind a team still capable of claiming its third championship, this time from his new club Arsenal. The next two seasons saw them as runners-up behind Newcastle and Everton. In 1928 they lost at Wembley to Blackburn Rovers and again in 1930 to Chapman's Gunners in one of the outstanding inter-war Cup Finals.

At Leeds Road, Chapman discovered and imported some fine talent. Players like Clem Stephenson, Alex Jackson, George Brown, Billy Smith, Ted Taylor, Sam Wadsworth and Roy Goodall made the 1920s an astonishing period in Huddersfield's history. Sadly, like the town itself, the football club has had little to shout about since then.

ELECTRIC SHOCK FOR HUDDERSFIELD.

West Ham leading at half time, but a message from Sunderland spurs on Huddersfield.

JACKSON (Huddersfield).

Yorkshiremen in an impregnable position. Worthy winners of the Championship.

By THE SPOTTER.

Huddersfield Town 2, West Ham 1.

Daily Express, 12 April 1926

1927

ONLY ONCE in its long history has the FA Cup been wrenched from the firm grip of English football. In 1927, first division Cardiff City beat Arsenal by a single goal at Wembley to take the Cup to Wales, thanks to a mistake by a Welshman.

It was a result nobody had really bargained for as Arsenal, runners-up in the league the previous season, took on middle-of-the-table Cardiff on a gloomy Saturday afternoon in April. But as so often happens in the Cup, a slice of luck or a mistake can easily determine the outcome. And so it was that with the game 15 minutes away from a goalless draw, Dan Lewis, the Arsenal and Wales goalkeeper, fumbled an awkward shot from the Cardiff centre-forward, Hugh Ferguson. Lewis watched in despair as the ball bounced tantalisingly under his body and trickled towards the goal for Cardiff's Len Davies to race in and help over the line. Ferguson claimed the goal but Lewis would always be haunted by his costly mistake. Well, we assume it was an error, though he was no doubt welcome in the hillsides of Wales for the rest of his life.

CITY BRING THE ENGLISH CUP TO WALES.

WELSH PLAYER'SCOSTLY MISTAKE
GIVES THE BLUEBIRDS VICTORY.

FERGUSON, LEN DAVIES AND THE GOALKEEPER HAVE A HAND IN THE WINNING GOAL.

The F.A. Cup, never before wrested from English football since the competition started in 1871, has come to Wales.

Cardiff City, thwarted in their hopes two years ago, renewed this challenge to-day against the Arsenal with the glorious result—a 1—0 victory for Wales.

South Wales Football Echo, 23 April 1927

It was an amazing goal credited to Ferguson that decided the great issue.

Ferguson shot at Lewis, the Arsenal goalie, who fumbled the ball. and Len Davies is believed to have helped it over the line.

It will ever be a debatable point as to who actually scored the goal, but obviously it came about primarily through Lewis's costly blunder.

It is an irony of fate that Lewis, who is a Mardy boy, should thus unwittingly helped the City to their great triumph.

(By "ARTHURIAN.")

The trek to Wembley has ended and the honour of competing in the final stage of the F.A. Cup competition has been gained by Cardiff City and the Arsenal, worthy competitors, and each with a huge following to cheer their every effort.

A Royal final this, for his Majesty the King was present, and the contest became national in character as the Cardiffians fought for the Principality.

Their appearance on this delightful enclosure, which looked for all the world like a well-kept lawn, recalled a previous visit two years ago when they suffered a narrow defeat. but they gained fame in the football world. They were referred to as the wonder team of post-war football.

Few imagined that in the short space of time Wales would again provide one of the finalists.

All along the line it has been made abundantly clear that the City's strength was practically centred in defence. They were able to beat down determined opponents even though the latter appeared to excel by comparison as a well balanced and clever side. Their methods recall a parallel in sport provided by the "stone walling" batsmen who concentrate upon the task of tiring the expert bowlers as a preliminary to opening out. 'Tis true that defence alone could not have carried the City through, but it has been so fine in character that one is apt to pay less than fair tribute to the occasional flashes in attack, which prove that there is real merit in the City forward line. Yes, there is a fund of talent distributed amongst the raiders, though it has manifested itself at unexpected moments, and on lines that may not be regarded as orthodox.

There is no doubt that Wake's claim for inclusion would have been favoured if he had not met with an unfortunate accident; and so the team is made up with Curtis on the right flank, where he will not fail through lack of effort, for he is a "live wire."

The Arsenal officials have had their share of worry owing to the injured players, and the constitution of their team was not decided upon until the last moment.

EARLY SCENES.

Conditions Ideal for a Great Game.

Welsh and English enthusiasts, wildly excited though they were expected to become when play started, were tame enough during the period of waiting for the kick-off in harmony and community singing.

Colours, favours and mascots took part in this preliminary affair, though there was much evidence of a huge Welsh crowd when, accompanied by band of either the Grenadier or Irish Guards, they joined in singing.

Conditions seemed ideal for a rattling game of football for there was an absence of dazzling sunshine. The enclosure was a perfect picture, with sufficient green turf to provide a grip while firm enough to enable the players to make full use of their speed. There was perhaps a little too much wind to be pleasant for there was just a chance that it would have its effect upon the play.

The announcement that all tickets had been disposed of made a full attendance assured, but the scene on the ground was in marked contrast to that of two seasons ago, and thousands of seats were unoccupied as far advanced as 35 minutes from the start.

The King arrived at 2.30.

Coloured Berets.

It was a splendid sight that was to be obtained from the Press stand. Here and there were umbrellas of the respective colours of the sides, giving a splash of relief to the fierce faces, whilst it was interesting to notice how groups of partisans had banded themselves together wearing berets, so that while at one spot was to be seen a bank of blue and white, at another the red and black patch marked the situation of the Arsenal supporters.

The latter accepted the boy's appearance with a notice board containing intimation of a change in the Arsenal side from that given on the official programme. On top was the name of the Arsenal, with A. Kennedy being shown as playing instead of Cope. This change, however, was really made yesterday. Beneath Cardiff's name was "Nil."

The Arsenal supporters looked on this as an omen of what the Welsh side's score would be. Cardiff's supporters thought differently.

As the clock approached half-past two the bands massed in front of the Royal box, and at once the crowd was on tip-toe. Hitherto the weather had been dull and overcast, but as the first note of the National Anthem was struck the sun burst forth in full glory until the chorus, lustily taken up by the huge throng, had been completed and cheers given.

King's Wish Granted.

His Majesty had announced his intention of being present earlier than he had intended in order to hear the community singing. His wish was immediately acceded to, the crowd at once responding in fine style with "Pack up your troubles in your old kit bag and smile, smile, smile," it being followed by "Tipperary" and other popular [illegible].

So impressed was his Majesty with the singing of the Welsh National Anthem that he asked for an encore. His desire was acceded to, and friend and foe vied with each other in its rendering.

RIGHT: *The rival captains – Buchan (Arsenal) and Keenor (Cardiff) – shake hands before the start of the game*

BELOW: *The winning goal, scored by Ferguson*

1927

THE FIRST football broadcast was heard over the airwaves on Saturday January 22nd 1927 from Highbury, where Arsenal met Sheffield United in a first division fixture. A week earlier the rugby international between England and Wales had been successfully relayed from Twickenham and the BBC hurriedly decided to extend the experiment to soccer. And so for the first time the broadcasting schedules in the Saturday morning newspapers read: '2.5. Community singing and Arsenal v Shef-

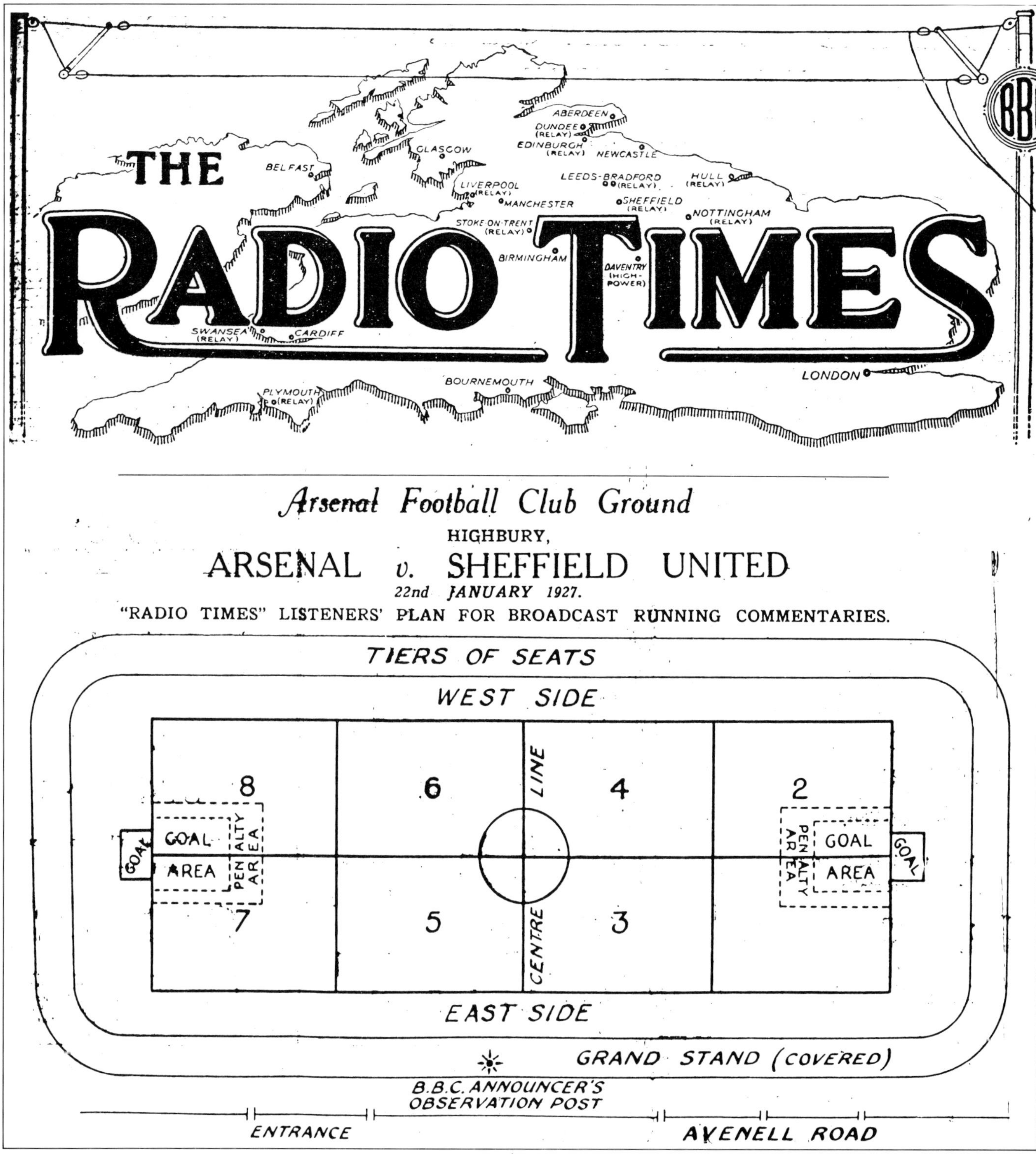

field United Association football Match (relayed from Arsenal ground, Highbury).' The match was to be described by Mr H. B. T. Wakelam with local colour provided by Mr C. A. Lewis. Some newspapers also published a plan of the pitch, divided into eight numbered sectors. The idea was that Mr Lewis would call out the number of the section the ball was in, as his co-commentator described the action.

By all accounts it was another highly successful relay and the *Guardian*'s broadcasting column added its blessing the following Monday, rating it as 'more successful than that from Twickenham the previous week.' In the rugby commentary there had been only one commentator while at Highbury listeners had benefited enormously from the plan of the ground and the second commentator. So successful was that initiative that it remained part of broadcasting for many years.

The *Guardian* gave those who had missed the broadcast a brief taste of the commentary. 'One commentator gave listeners a graphic description of the game while the other called out the section in which the ball was actually being played. Listeners heard: 'Oh! Pretty work, very pretty (section 5) . . . now up the field (7) . . . a pretty (5, 8) pass . . . Come on, Mercer . . . Now then, Mercer; hello! Noble's got it (1, 2).'

> **THE HIGHBURY RELAY.**
>
> The broadcast of running commentaries of the Arsenal v. Sheffield United match at Highbury on Saturday afternoon was more successful than that from Twickenham the previous week. In the Rugby match listeners heard only one commentator, whereas on Saturday there were two, and with the aid of the plan of the ground issued by the B.B.C. and their information, it was possible to follow fairly closely the movements of the ball.
>
> One commentator gave listeners a graphic description of the game, while the other called out the section in which the ball was actually being played. Listeners heard:—
>
> Oh! Pretty work, very pretty (section 5) . . . now up the field (7) . . . a pretty (5, 8) pass. . . . Come on, Mercer. . . . Now then, Mercer; hello! Noble's got it (1, 2).
>
> With the chart before one, it was fairly easy to visualise what was actually happening, and the cheers and groans of the spectators helped considerably the imagination of the listener.
>
> It has been decided to instal a wireless receiver in the convict prison at Horsens (Jutland) to enable selected convicts to hear sermons, concerts, and lectures. The prisoners are making their own apparatus.
>
> *Manchester Guardian, 24 January 1927*

The *Guardian*'s reviewer added that 'with the chart before one, it was fairly easy to visualise what was happening, and the cheers and groans of the spectators helped considerably the imagination of the listener.' *The Times* agreed, reckoning that 'his descriptions of swift passing movements, long clearances up field and shots at goal were totally vivid and impressive.'

Three months later a further landmark was reached when the Arsenal v Cardiff Cup Final was broadcast live from Wembley to homes all over the country. The previous commentators Wakelam and Lewis had by this time been replaced by George Allison, later to become manager of Arsenal, and Derek McCulloch, soon to become better known to millions of children as 'Uncle Mac' of BBC Radio's 'Children's Hour'.

LEFT: *Commentator George Allison*

1928

EVEN THE ENGLISH newspapers had to admit that England had been disgraced. 'Never was a country more humiliated on its own soil and before its own partisans,' wrote the *Sunday Chronicle*. None of the papers had predicted a defeat even though the signs were evident enough. In the home championships England had been beaten 2–0 in Belfast and 2–1 by Wales at Burnley while the team selected to take the field at Wembley against the Auld Enemy hardly set the heart beating with anticipation.

ENGLAND'S FOOTBALL HUMILIATION.

SCOTS PILE ON AGONY.

Sporting Chronicle, 2 April 1928

Our Biggest International Disaster for 46 Years: By T.C.

TO the skirl of the bagpipes Scotland caused the rose of England to wither and die at Wembley in the most sensational international match since the early years of the competition for the triple crown of Soccer.

Not since 1882 had England forfeited five goals to the Scots in this series of games; what a tragedy in view of the universal expectancy that England would have something like a walk-over against the lightest and smallest attack the land of the Thistle has ever had in a match of this sort!

The result completes England's confusion by creating a stampede in the councils of the game. The fact that the "wooden spoon" comes once more into our possession is of small account beside the revelation that the Scots are still our "daddies" at the game.

We thought English representative football plumbed the depths in the Welsh match at Burnley in November, yet we find the Scots putting up the biggest score they have ever registered in an international played in England with the exception of their 6–1 win at the Oval in 1881, the year before they triumphed at Glasgow by a score similar to Saturday's.

Once more we have to start taking kindergarten lessons in the science of the game. The heavy going—rain fell almost throughout the game, which was almost as much a procession as the boat race the same day—was all to the liking of the "wee frees"—the midget inside forwards of the Scottish team—who, aided by Alec Jackson's tearaway speed on the right wing, became juggernauts.

The Huddersfield right winger scored three goals, and James, Preston North End's inside left, the other two, while Kelly, of Huddersfield, obtained England's crumb of comfort—England's second goal in the tournament—from a free kick just before the farce ended.

"NOT SO BAD AS PAINTED."

King Amanullah must think we are a strange race after seeing the Grand National and International fiascos! And we are thinking that, too.

The Scots prefer heavy turf to light ground because it makes all the difference to the harmony of their ball control and jugglery, but we cannot complain of lack of equality of opportunity.

Scotland could not possibly have anticipated victory, to say nothing of one of such proportions, as there was no logical basis for such an expectancy. The ultimate finding in any analysis of cause and effect must therefore be that the Scots' fervour in these games is incomparable with that of any other country, not forgetting Wales, and that the "international spirit" of English players is the poorest of all.

We have all still to learn that the inspiration of an early success is half the battle in any branch of sport, and that no alteration of rules can prevent luck playing a part.

There is bound to be an "inquest" on this match, but we must not lose our sense of proportion and sight of the fact that the luck goes round.

I wonder if the Scots would have "curled up" if England's outside left, Smith, had scored instead of hitting the post in the first half minute of the game. Some have already scouted that idea, and I think they are mistaken.

"THE BEST EVER!"

The basis of the Scots' victory was the perfect passing, mostly on the floor, between their halves and forwards. The ball was made to "find" the man with uncanny precision, with the result that the English halves had no chance after Scotland's opening goal, scored in the third minute.

ABOVE: *Alec Jackson*

LEFT: *The Scottish team take the field, led out by Hughie Gallacher*

ABOVE RIGHT: *A shot from Jackson glides into the net, leaving the English goalie floundering in the Wembley mud*

RIGHT: *Scottish visitors show their delight at their team's victory. Scotland's captain, Jimmy McMullan, runs the gauntlet of his admirers*

1928

Only Dixie Dean, now established as the regular England centre-forward, looked a threat. Scotland, on the other hand, had more than its share of exciting and skilful players including Tom Bradshaw the Bury centre-half; Alex Jackson, one of five Huddersfield players on duty that day, Jimmy Dunn, who was to join Dean at Everton only a week later; Hughie Gallacher of Newcastle; Alex James, the gifted Preston inside-forward and Alan Morton of Rangers. It was a forward line that would strike fear into any defence.

Within three minutes the diminutive Jackson had hit the first of his three goals to set the Scots among the 80,000 crowd delirious. Alex James added another just before half time as Scotland's middle line began to stroke the ball around Wembley, giving the finest demonstration of passing anyone could remember. The second half was barely ten minutes old when Jackson swooped on the ball again to make it 3–0 and before the final whistle had blown he and James had added two further goals with Bob Kelly scoring a consolation for England.

The *Daily Mirror* was unusually generous in its praise of the Scots: 'England were not beaten at Wembley. They were routed and outpaced by Scotland and thrashed by five goals to one. And the wonder is that the score was not bigger.' The *Sporting Chronicle* regarded it as nothing short of a sensation: 'To the skirl of the bagpipe Scotland caused the rose of England to wither and die at Wembley,' it wrote. 'Not since 1882,' it continued, 'had England forfeited five goals to the Scots in this series of games; what a tragedy in view of the universal expectancy that England would have something like a walk-over against the lightest and smallest attack the land of the thistle has ever had in a match of this sort.'

England ended up with the wooden spoon while the Scottish team – which soon found itself written into the history books as the 'Wembley Wizards' – went on to enjoy one of its finest spells in international football, winning seven out of the next eight games, and drawing the other. And the team to finally beat them? Yes, England by five goals to two at Wembley in April 1930.

1928

THE FIRST football competitions in the press, introduced in the 1890s, proved to be immensely popular with readers and quickly led to the introduction of a variety of other games. They were reckoned to have increased newspaper circulations, and soon the old favourite where you had to forecast the results of twelve matches was joined by a variety of others, all aimed at increasing readership. There were competitions to win tickets for major matches such as Cup Finals and a novel one where the reader had to recognise a particular football ground from an aerial photograph. But in 1928 the *Athletic News* introduced a new competition that was to prove so popular it would still be going sixty years later. It was called Spot the Ball.

Spot the Ball was simple, yet tantalising. All you had to do was put a cross where you thought the ball – which had been deliberately obliterated from a photograph – should be. It cost just sixpence to enter with a prize of £500 for the most accurate guess, and soon proved to be just as popular as trying to forecast the results. It looked easy but when the photograph was published a fortnight later with the ball included, few would have guessed the ball could possibly have been in that spot. Most people tried to follow the line of the players' eyes but that was no solution. The ball was nearly always in the most unlikely place.

Being a football expert did not help. In fact the game proved to be most popular with women readers. The competition was adopted by many newspapers including the *News of the World*, where it continued for a number of years as a regular feature.

£500 for "SPOT THE BALL."

Great Opportunity for Readers to Win Weekly Summer Prize.

TO-DAY the *Athletic News* presents to its readers a new and alluring competition in "Spot the Ball," the full details of which, together with entry form, are published below. Here is a fascinating test of football skill, for which £500 MUST BE WON. The entrance fee is sixpence.

Here is a wonderful chance for everyone who has an interest in football. The picture reproduced is of an actual incident in a football match. The football itself has been purposely obliterated. Now, can you, after studying the positions and attitudes of the players, judge where the ball was at the moment of the snapshot?

It is a test of skill. You must indicate the position of the centre of the ball, and to do this you must mark, in pen and ink, a cross. The centre of the cross must coincide with the centre of the football.

The competition calls for careful judgment, and is a splendid opportunity for exercising football knowledge. You can bring into your own home the thrills of the game itself—a summer competition for all.

.... CUT HERE. ....

"SPOT THE BALL" PUZZLE, No. 26.

The sealed solution is lodged with the Westminster Bank.

WHERE WAS THE BALL AT THE INSTANT THIS PHOTOGRAPH WAS TAKEN?

The right of reproduction in "Spot the Ball" Football Skill Competition is protected under the Patents Acts, and copyright **is** strictly reserved.

In entering this competition I agree to abide by the Editor's decision, and enclose Postal Order.

No. .... Value ....

SIGNED ....

ADDRESS ....

A.N. 26 .... (Write in Block Letters.)

.... CUT HERE. ....

CONDITIONS.

1.—This competition is complete in itself; no factor other than competitive skill will be taken into consideration in adjudicating the prizes.

2.—The sealed solution will not be opened until after all the competitors' entries are received.

3.—A prize of £500 will be awarded to the competitor who sends in a correct solution to the puzzle. If there is more than one correct solution the £500 will be equally divided.

4.—In the event of there being no correct solution, the prize of £500 will be awarded to the competitor who "spots" the ball in a position nearest to the spot marked on the sealed solution. If there is a tie, the £500 will be equally divided between the successful competitors.

5.—Competitors must mark on the picture the position of the football the instant the photograph was taken. According to your judgment and knowledge of the rules of the game, mark on the photograph with pen and ink a cross indicating the position occupied by the football.

6.—The photograph used in this competition is an actual photograph of a football match.

7.—Coupons must be filled in in ink and all names and addresses clearly written in block capitals. The coupon must be accompanied by a postal order value 6d., which must be made payable to Allied Newspapers Ltd.

8.—Postal Orders must be crossed & Co., and the date of sending the order, complete with the name and address of competitor, must be written on the back. The number of the postal order must be written in the space provided in the coupon.

9.—Entries must be posted (envelopes must bear 1½d. stamp) so as to arrive here not later than Saturday, May 5, and addressed to:—

"SPOT THE BALL," No. 26,
"ATHLETIC NEWS,"
PUMP YARD, MANCHESTER (Comp.)

No coupon from any other competition run by Allied Newspapers Ltd. must be enclosed in the same envelope as "Spot the Ball."

10.—The Editor cannot hold himself responsible for any coupon or coupons lost, mislaid, delayed in the post, or otherwise, and proof of posting cannot be accepted as proof of delivery or receipt.

11.—In all cases the proper form and coupon must be used, upon which only one indication of the position of the ball must be shown.

12.—The result of this competition will be published in the *World's Pictorial News*, on sale May 11, and in *Empire News* of May 13, and in our issue of May 14. Any competitor who claims to have sent in a solution which is the same as one of those published as winning a prize may have a scrutiny by demanding same before Saturday, May 19. After this date no claims will be considered.

13.—If such a claim is found to be correct the prize in question will be divided equally between the competitors sending in the same solution.

14.—Every request for a scrutiny must be accompanied by a remittance for £5, which will be returned to the competitor if his claim proves to be valid. With the exception of a demand for a scrutiny no correspondence can be entered into concerning this competition.

15.—The Competition Editor's decision on all matters relating to this competition must be accepted as final and legally binding in all respects and acceptance of these rules is an express condition of entry.

16.—Employes of Allied Newspapers Ltd. are not allowed to compete. The contest is run in conjunction with the *World's Pictorial News* and the *Empire News*, and coupons from those papers may be enclosed, but not those for any other competitions in those papers.

Competitors who are unable to obtain copies of the "Athletic News" from their usual newsagent can be supplied by making an application to the Subscription Department, "Athletic News," Withy Grove, Manchester, or 200, Gray's Inn-road, London, W.C.1. Price 3d. per copy, post free.

Athletic News, 30 April 1928

1928

LEFT: *William Ralph Dean, the finest goalscorer of all time*

DEAN BREAKS RECORD.

"Hat-trick" Against The Arsenal at Goodison.

RAPID FIRING.

Fifty-nine Goals In a Season.

By THE SERGEANT.
Everton 3, Arsenal 3.

Sunday Express, 6 May 1928

WILLIAM RALPH DEAN, the greatest goalscorer in the history of English football, broke George Camsell's league scoring record of 59 goals on Saturday May 5th 1928 in front of a full house at Goodison Park. What a pity that the *Sunday Express* the following day could not get their statistics right. They reckoned Camsell had scored 58 goals and as Dean had bettered that by one, he must have hit 59. But they were wrong. Fortunately the rest of Fleet Street could add up. Dean had scored an astonishing 60 goals.

Everton were already league champions when they met Arsenal at Goodison in the final fixture that spring Saturday afternoon. Dean had scored 57 goals but to expect him to hit a hat-trick against the Gunners was perhaps asking too muuch even from such a goalscoring ace. Arsenal, whose illustrious servant, Charles Buchan was retiring after that game, were equally determined to give their man a victorious send off and before Everton had even settled Arsenal had shot into a one goal lead. But almost from the restart Dean had equalised with his team's one hundredth goal of the season. A minute later Everton were awarded a penalty and the ball was tossed casually to Dean. The 21-year-old confidently stepped up, placed the ball and, before a hushed Goodison, slammed it into the back of the net. He had equalled Camsell's record and there was now every prospect that he could go on to beat it. Half time came and went with Arsenal levelling the score but Everton and Dean could not find a third. Then, with just minutes remaining, Everton's tiny Scottish winger, Alec Troup, took a corner and lofted the ball delicately into the penalty area where Dean climbed high above the entire Arsenal defence to head it home. He had done it and within seconds was buried beneath a crowd of blue and red shirted players as they raced to congratulate him. Only Charlie Buchan stood at a distance, his farewell overshadowed by the young man's outstanding feat.

Besides his 60 league goals which included seven hat-tricks, Dean had scored a further three in the FA Cup while in other internationals, representative and charity games he had scored 37 bringing his season's total to 100 goals in 56 matches. When he finally left Everton to join Notts County in 1938 he had scored a career total of 377 goals in 431 league and Cup games for the Goodison Park club.

BELOW: *This is believed to be the only surviving picture of Dean's historic 60th goal of the 1927/28 season*

1928

IT WAS INEVITABLE that the £10,000 transfer would arrive and, as ever when a magic transfer barrier is broken, there was the usual hue and cry. Only days before the deal was signed, Sir Charles Clegg, President of the FA, was warning that no player in the world was worth £10,000. 'If a club is sufficiently foolish to give £10,000 for a player, it deserves to be let in and I would not be sorry if they were,' he was reported as saying in the *Daily Mirror*. But the deal did take place and late on the Saturday evening of October 13th 1928, David Jack of Bolton Wanderers became an Arsenal player for the princely sum of £10,000.

RECORD SUM FOR A FOOTBALLER.

DAVID JACK.

Arsenal Pays Out Over £10,000.

HIS OWN STORY OF THE DEAL.

By ADJUTANT.

DAVID JACK, the Bolton Wanderers and International inside right, has been transferred to Arsenal at a fee which easily exceeds any fee hitherto paid for a footballer.

The Bolton Wanderers' directors will not divulge the sum received, but I can state definitely that it exceeds £10,000. The previous record was about £6,500 so far as is known. That amount is about the sum paid by Burnley for Hill, by Newcastle for Gallacher, and by Aston Villa for Gibson.

The transfer was completed late on Saturday evening, and, actually, I was

DAVID JACK (Bolton Wanderers).

the first person to acquaint the Wanderers with the fact that the transaction had been completed.

So far as the clubs were concerned, the matter was settled on Thursday evening; it remained for the Arsenal to complete arrangements with Jack himself.

Daily Dispatch, 15 October 1928

Jack was always the likely candidate to beat the barrier. Capped four times by England, the nippy inside right was among the half-dozen outstanding players in the country. Born in Bolton, the son of the former Wolves left-winger and Plymouth Argyle manager, he had joined the Lancashire club in 1920 and had gone on to claim two FA Cup winner's medals and had the distinction of scoring the first goal at Wembley. But even greater honours awaited him at Highbury. Initially both clubs were reluctant to disclose the fee but Fleet Street had no doubts that the £10,000 barrier had finally been breached. The fee had in fact been £11,500.

LEFT: *Record transfer David Jack proved an astute purchase by helping Arsenal to three league titles*

Jack had been bought by the Arsenal manager, Herbert Chapman, to replace Charles Buchan who had retired at the end of the previous season, Chapman, perhaps the game's greatest innovator, was searching for a star and had no qualms about paying the enormous asking price. Some, like Sir Charles Clegg, considered it unsporting to buy your way to honours but Chapman wanted the best and if that meant paying for it, then pay for it he would. Jack turned out to be an outstanding purchase, appearing in two more Cup Finals and helping the Gunners to three league championships as well as winning a further five England caps. When he retired in 1934 after just over 200 games in the red and white of Arsenal, he could be reckoned to have been a bargain buy, even at £10,000.

ENGLAND'S FIRST FALL.

HOT WEATHER A BIG FACTOR IN DEFEAT IN SPAIN.

The first defeat abroad of an English F.A. team embracing professional players has just been suffered at the hands of Spain, at Madrid, and in the first International played between the two countries. The result was 4–3.

BY A MEMBER OF THE PARTY

THE Spaniards are fast—very fast—and not lacking in skill and finesse. They make ground by speedy dribbling, which is cruder than the Corinthian style, but is never carried to excess. This happy mixture of individual and combined movements is a feature of their play.

We were beaten, and one never likes to make excuses for defeat. But in all fairness to the team it must be placed on record that the English players did wonderfully well considering the tremendous handicap of playing after our heavy season at home and of renewing their activities in intense heat.

"DRENCHED."

Indeed, no words of mine could describe the torrid conditions which prevailed for this match at Madrid. I sat in the stand drenched with perspiration. Beads of perspiration were dropping off the chins of our players as they ran about.

It was not football weather, and this explains how our goals were scored early in the first half and early in the second. The men were more or less fresh then and more able to make the pace, which the heat gradually reduced. That is why we lost our half-time lead.

Athletic News, 20 May 1929

1929

ABOVE: *The legendary Zamora, pictured here saving from Dixie Dean, as England take their revenge two years later at Highbury with a 7–1 victory over Spain*

ENGLAND'S FIRST defeat abroad, at the hands of Spain, caused barely a ripple in the English press. It had to happen sooner or later, suggested the *Athletic News*, and anyhow there were genuine excuses considering the sweltering conditions.

England had arrived in Spain after a short continental tour that had seen them defeat France 4–1 and go one better in Belgium by beating the home nation 5–1. George Camsell, the prolific Middlesbrough centre-forward had already notched up six goals in those two games but was forced to cry off in Madrid through injury. Nevertheless, England began their first-ever game against Spain as hot favourites and by half time led comfortably by two goals to nil, thanks primarily to the opportunist Sunderland forward, Raich Carter. But then in the second half Spain struck back and although England led at one stage by three goals to one, their weary legs were visibly wilting in the torrid heat of Madrid's mid-May afternoon. England had sought a later kick-off time but the Spanish football authorities had turned down their request and England's fears were now coming to haunt them.

The Spanish, with the legendary Zamora, the world's finest goalkeeper, keeping the English forwards at bay, soon began to take control of the game and when they levelled the score at 3–3 they initiated a pitch invasion that had the England players looking on in disbelief. 'Drawn Swords At Football' screamed the headline in the *Daily Mirror* as their football correspondent described how the Civil Guard had been forced to draw swords in order to disperse the excited crowd. Spain finally wound up 4–3 winners as England steadily grew more tired and disinterested in the outcome. Without Dean or Camsell to score goals England looked a mediocre side and, even with Dean, had gone down by one goal to nil earlier in the year at Hampden. It was not by any count an outstanding English side but although they had lost their one hundred per cent record against foreign competition, at least the game had benefited with the emergence of Spain as a major footballing nation and its football interest well fuelled.

1930

THE 1930 Cup Final brought together the two finest teams of the inter-war period but it was not the respective stars of Arsenal and Huddersfield Town – Alex James and Alec Jackson – who stole the headlines the following morning but the German airship *Graf Zeppelin* which hovered menacingly over Wembley. 'Graf Zeppelin gatecrashes the Cup Final' ran the front page lead in the *Sunday Dispatch* while the *Sunday Chronicle* and the *News of the World* also carried page one stories about the airship's dramatic appearance. Arsenal's momentous victory was forced to take second place.

The *Sunday Chronicle* reported that the vast Wembley crowd had booed the airship and reminded its readers that 'not since the Zeppelin had come on a mission of destruction had one flown over London.' But memories of World War One were far from the mind of the *Sunday Dispatch* which reported cheering and waving from the spectators and their guest of honour, the King. The *Sunday Express* on the other hand opted out of this particular dispute and simply reckoned the 92,000 crowd had ignored it. Whether or not they did, all were agreed that the droning noise had been deafening. The airship's appearance had been preceded by a dozen or so small aircraft flying low over the stadium before giving way to the enormous silver craft which suddenly and dramatically jutted above Wembley's twin towers, hovering at a height of no more than 350 feet. Its tow ropes dangled tantalisingly just beyond the reach of those spectators at the highest point on the terraces before it swept majestically across the arena and made towards central London.

Only a few were aware that the Zeppelin was to make this guest appearance and although there was a strong protest from Clem Stephenson, the Huddersfield manager, beforehand, its formidable journey across the North Sea had gone ahead. But Stephenson could hardly claim that the Zeppelin's presence had disturbed his team who were already a goal down and staring defeat in the eye when the airship loomed.

Arsenal's victory was well deserved, thanks to goals from James and Lambert, but Huddersfield Town had shown all the grit and fight that had helped make them the finest team in post-war Britain. Herbert Chapman, who had previously managed the Yorkshire club and been the man primarily responsible for their rise to fame, was now in charge at Highbury where he was bringing his flair and genius to bear, welding together players like Alex James, Cliff Bastin, David Jack and Eddie Hapgood. Their 2–0 victory that day brought Arsenal their first trophy under Chapman and heralded a flood of honours that would soon find their way into the Highbury boardroom. Huddersfield Town's reign as the kings of soccer was over. Arsenal's victory and the appearance of the Zeppelin turned out to be an uncanny portent of what the 1930s would hold.

THE DAILY MIRROR Monday, April 28, 1930

Wilfred at the Zoo: See page 14

Daily Mirror

THE F.A. CUP COMES BACK TO LONDON—GRAF ZEPPELIN OVER WEMBLEY

Daily Mirror, 28 April 1930

LEFT: *The Graf Zeppelin airship hovers menacingly as Arsenal and Huddersfield contest the 1930 Cup Final*

The giant German airship, Graf Zeppelin, passing low over the Wembley Stadium during the Cup Final in which Arsenal beat Huddersfield Town by two goals to nil and thus brought the Cup to London for the third time since 1882. The airship was booed by some of the crowd who regarded its presence as likely to distract the players. Arsenal won the match on their merits, but Huddersfield played hard throughout and did not lose their form. The King presented the trophy and medals.

Daily Mirror, 28 April 1930

1930

ALTHOUGH ENGLAND had suffered their first international defeat by a foreign side only the year before, there remained a supremacist assumption within the country that we still boasted the world's finest football team. But it was a view which had more to do with our Empire than with any reality.

On July 30th 1930 an event took place 12,000 miles across the Atlantic, that was almost totally ignored by the British press but which forty years later would be regarded as the biggest soccer occasion of all, the World Cup Final. The first final was played that day in Montevideo, Uruguay, between the host nation and Argentina, yet there was barely a mention in the British press. Only the *Guardian* noted the event and then with just a short paragraph buried down the sports page which referred haughtily to the game as 'the so-called World's association football championship'. Meanwhile the lead story that morning was that rain had wiped out the entire previous day's cricket.

The *Athletic News* made two references to the finals. As they got underway in mid-July the weekly arrogantly reported that 'by way of a send-off Argentine beat Mexico 6–3 on Saturday. This doesn't sound much like a world championship? No, but it is – in title.' Reporting on the final itself a week later, it commented that 'the first world soccer championship has come and gone. As expected it ended in a victory for the home country, Uruguay beat Argentine 4–2 in the final and a little revolution.' The 'little revolution' was not the birth of a great new competition but the demonstrations that had followed in the streets of Montevideo. The paper's commentator condescendingly added that 'I don't see how soccer can continue in these countries. Surely they will kill off all the referees.' He rounded off his short piece by putting the entire nation's mind at rest: 'Finally I am able to deny the rumour that the FA proposes to enter a team for the next world championship.' Indeed, it would be another twenty years before England entered.

Association

WORLD'S CHAMPIONSHIP.

Uruguay Again Beats the Argentine.

(Press Association Foreign Special.)

MONTE VIDEO, WEDNESDAY.

Scenes exceeding in enthusiasm even those of an English Cup final were witnessed here to-day, when 100,000 people assembled to watch Uruguay and the Argentine meet in the final of the so-called world's Association football championship. Twenty special trains unloaded thousands of people from up country, and fleets of aeroplanes brought spectators from remote towns. All the shops and offices in the city were closed, and business was at a standstill. Among the early arrivals were fifty members of Parliament. It will be recalled that Uruguay and Argentine fought out the Olympic final at Amsterdam in 1928, when, after a draw, Uruguay won by two to one.

Uruguay won to-day by four goals to three.

Manchester Guardian, 31 July 1930

Making that long trip to Uruguay for the first competition were France, Mexico, Argentina, Chile, Yugoslavia, Brazil, Bolivia, Rumania, Peru, Belgium, Paraguay and the United States. England were ineligible, having recently left FIFA but judging from the insularity of the British press, sporting events on the other side of the world were of little consequence.

ABOVE: *Argentina's goalkeeper Botazza dives in a vain attempt to stop Uruguay scoring their third goal in the World Cup Final*

1931

A DAY OF CASUALTIES

SCOTTISH FOOTBALL MARRED BY ACCIDENTS

THE CROWDS AND THE REFEREES

SURPRISE DEFEATS OF HEARTS AND HIBERNIANS

Every incident in Scottish football on Saturday was overshadowed by the tragic happening at Ibrox Park, Glasgow, where John Thomson, the young Celtic and Scotland goalkeeper, received injuries that proved fatal.

The Scotsman, 7 September 1931

AS IF Glasgow football were not explosive enough, the tragic death of Celtic goalkeeper John Thomson, in the annual old firm clash, gave sectarianism another excuse on which to thrive. Thomson, capped four times by Scotland, died in Glasgow's Victoria Hospital at 9.25 on the evening of Saturday September 5th 1931, just five hours after he had been stretchered unconscious from Ibrox Park. Thomson's death was accidental, although there are still those who wish to perpetuate the myth that his fate was somehow deliberate. But all the newspapers agreed that there was no blame attached to the Rangers' forward, Sam English, with whom he had collided.

Thomson was killed as he sprinted out of his goal and dived daringly at the feet of English, who was chasing a loose ball. The Rangers' player had every reason to believe that he could reach it and Thomson, always a brave goalkeeper, likewise felt that he could get there first. In the rush, English's knee caught Thomson on the left temple and the young Scottish keeper was thrown motionless to the ground. Within minutes the 22-year-old Thomson had been gently laid onto a stretcher and rushed to hospital.

BELOW: *John Thomson in collision with Sam English – the daring save that cost him his life*

Sam English was shattered by the news of Thomson's death, but recovered sufficiently to set a Rangers record of 44 goals that season. But the incident continued to haunt him and wherever he played crowds savagely barracked and reminded him of it. A year later he moved to England, joining Liverpool in the hope that he could forget and that crowds would treat him more fairly. But it took a long time for the barracking to ease off, and he eventually returned to his native Ireland.

Thomson immediately became a legend. Those who saw him play rated him the finest goalkeeper to have ever donned Scottish colours, and shortly after his death the ballads that recounted his exploits were being sung in bars across Scotland. More than 30,000 attended his funeral and even to this day his grave at Bowhill Cemetery in Cardenden is a shrine for the many Celtic supporters, young and old, who regularly make the pilgrimage. Even though Thomson was himself a Protestant, his death did little to bridge the religious gulf between the two clubs. A small group of Rangers supporters did write to the *Daily Record* to apologise for the thoughtless chants from the terraces that day, but instead of healing the division Thomson's death only became an excuse to further the hatred.

1932

HITLER MAY well have swept to power in Prussia and riots may have been tearing Delhi apart but the Fleet Street editors knew precisely what sold newspapers. And so, the controversy over Newcastle United's first goal in the 1932 Cup Final held a prominent place, even on the front page of the Labour newspaper, the *Daily Herald*.

By 1932 football was big news and Arsenal were the biggest news of all. Whatever they did, wherever they went, they were followed by a sortie of reporters in search of a few quotes. They were the glamour team of the time with stars such as Alex James, Eddie Hapgood, David Jack and Cliff Bastin and no amount of world news was going to keep them off the front page. It was also a case of Fleet Street convincing itself that Arsenal were invincible. Newcastle may have won the Cup by two goals to one but the papers were determined to prove that United's first goal should have been disallowed, as the ball had passed over the dead ball line before Richardson crossed for Allen to slam home their equaliser. The Arsenal defence had waited, expecting the referee to point for a goal-kick, but instead he awarded a goal.

Advances in technology meant that a print could be taken from the film of the match which had been shot by British Movietone News. And the photograph, although it was some distance from the action, appeared to support Arsenal's claim that the goal should have been disallowed. But no amount of disputing the referee's decision was going to change the result. 'It was a goal,' said the referee. 'As God is my judge, the man was in play. I was eight yards away. I do not mind what other people say.' But what about the ball?

ABOVE: *Jimmy Nelson with the Cup*

CUP FINAL GOAL WAS NOT A GOAL!

FILM PROVES IT—YET IT MUST STAND

NO, IT WAS NOT A GOAL!

Newcastle United defeated the Arsenal by two goals to one in the F.A. Cup Final at Wembley on Saturday—but the camera proves beyond doubt that their first goal was not a legitimate one.

The referee's word is law, however, and there the matter must end.

"Whatever the film may appear to show will not make me alter my decision," the referee, Mr. W. Harper, said yesterday.

To Hannen Swaffer on Saturday, Mr. Harper said:

"It was a goal. As God is my judge the man was in play. I was eight yards away. I do not mind what other people say."

Daily Herald, 25 April 1932

A FILM RECORD made by British Movietone News of the incident that led up to Newcastle's first goal. Richardson's right foot and the ball are clearly over the dead ball line. It was at first thought that it was Boyd who centred the ball.

1932

ABOVE: *The Austrian team arrive at Victoria Station*

WHEN AUSTRIA'S national football side arrived in London in early December 1932, they came with the reputation of being a 'Wunderteam'. Behind them was a string of impressive victories. After drawing 0–0 with England in Vienna two years previously, they had then thrashed Scotland 5–0, outclassed Germany 6–0 in Berlin, beaten Switzerland 8–1 and 3–1, narrowly beaten Italy 2–1 and trounced Hungary 8–2. In all, they had gone 13 games without defeat, winning ten of those while drawing the others. They were the unofficial champions of the Continent, and the game against England at Stamford Bridge was widely regarded as the championship of Europe.

England fielded six of the players who had appeared in the Vienna match and although 1932 was hardly a prime year for English football, the team still boasted players of the calibre of David Jack, Harry Hibbs, Ernie Blenkinsop and Billy Walker. There was considerable excitement about the fixture with the press concentrating on Austria's trainer, the former Burnley and Bolton player Jimmy Hogan. Along with manager Hugo Meisl, he had put together the most skilful side Europe had ever seen, a blend of English strength and continental skills. Goalkeeper Rudolf Hiden already had a keen fan in Herbert Chapman, who in 1930 had brought the young man to Arsenal only to be thwarted by the Ministry of Labour and immigration officials who refused him the necessary visa to play in league football. Up front they boasted Mathias Sindelar, a centre-forward whose only rival during the 1930s was England's own Dixie Dean and who was renowned for his delicate ball control and fierce shot.

In spite of the speculation that had accompanied the pre-match preparations, only 40,000 turned up at Stamford Bridge but they were to be treated to one of the finest exhibitions of football ever seen in Britain. England stormed into the lead after only five minutes when Jimmy Hampson drove home from a corner. Twenty minutes later, the Blackpool man hit his second and although England were now being outplayed, they clung on to their two goal advantage until half time. But the second half was a far different matter as the Austrians emerged with even more vigour. Early in the

RIGHT: *'Wunderteam' tactics being rehearsed*

ENGLAND LUCKY TO BEAT BRILLIANT AUSTRIAN SIDE

OUR VISITORS SHOW US HOW TO PLAY!

Perfect Team Work : Jack and Keen Only Englishmen to Shine

By CORINTHIAN

England 4, Austria 3

A MOST disturbing victory—the kind that leaves one wondering how it happened and a sort of creepy feeling that we were successful by the kindness of some spirit of chance which will never be so good again.

Definitely and beyond all shadow of doubt, Austria played football better than England did at Stamford Bridge yesterday.

Though they were once 2—0 down, and later 3-1 down, our visitors kept on with their good game and made the score 3-2, eventually losing 4-3.

What astounded us all was the fact that, compared with the Austrians, the English forward line was third rate. In general combination the losers were better than the winners.

In style of play, such as making passes along the ground so that the receiver should be able to make good use of the ball quickly; in getting to open spaces to make a pass possible, and even in control of the ball, in every sense the Austrian forwards and half-backs were better than ours

Just two individuals, David Jack and Keen, the accidental selection for left-half, have to be excepted. Those two were at least up to the standard of the losers.

Anxious Defence

Never before has any continental team succeeded in making England's best defence look so anxious, compelled them to take hasty kicks which meant slicing the ball to all sorts of useless positions.

It was the brilliance of these Austrian forwards that occasioned this shakiness among our defenders. The visitors did not possess a forward who was weak, but England did.

The fact that England's backs and half-backs

Individually — I must insist upon dealing with the better team first—the Austrians were also superior. Sindelar is the best centre-forward the Continent has ever sent to England. I cannot remember a move, a touch, a feint, or a pass which was made by him unless it was to the advantage of his side.

Schall the inside-left, was a schemer of the highest class

Daily Herald, 8 December 1932

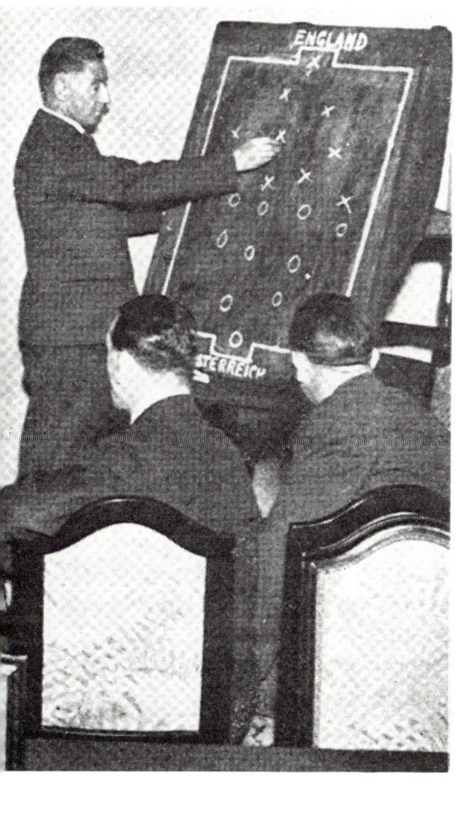

RIGHT: *Austrian goalkeeper Rudolf Hiden in action*

half Ziscek made it 2–1 and just as the Austrians began to look as if they might draw level an unfortunate deflection put them even further behind. Sindelar, playing as well as he had ever played, hit Austria's second goal while David Jack struck England's fourth to make it 4–2. With little time remaining Austria battled back and Ziscek netted his second but there was not enough time and at the end of the day England, although they had been outclassed, had emerged as 4–3 winners.

For once the English press was generous in its praise of continental football. 'Never before has any continental team succeeded in making England's best defence look so anxious,' admitted the *Daily Herald*'s correspondent. 'The losers were responsible for some of the finest team work I have ever seen from any club.' All the papers agreed that the better team had lost.

The Austrians were probably at their peak in 1932. Two years later they lost to Italy in the semi-finals of the World Cup and with the Nazification of their country by the Germans, the 'Wunderteam' was broken up. The German occupation also led to the tragic suicide of the great Sindelar whose Jewish parentage was betrayed by a team-mate.

1933

IF IT WAS not the biggest Cup upset of all time, it is certainly the most celebrated. A BBC newsreader was said to have hesitated disbelievingly as he read the result out, convinced that there must be some mistake on his script. And the newspapers the next morning were equally shocked. The score: Walsall 2 Arsenal 0.

The game was the third round of the FA Cup played on Saturday, January 14th, 1933 at Fellows Park, an apology of a football stadium in the Black Country. Walsall, a third division north outfit, were 54 places below the aristocrats from Highbury, having collected only 24 points from 24 games that season.

Walsall fielded a typical third division side – lots of heart and muscle but little subtlety or style – while the Gunners, at the height of their fame, boasted Alex James, Cliff Bastin, David Jack and Frank Moss among their esteemed ranks with others such as Eddie Hapgood, Bob John, Jack Lambert and Tim Coleman sidelined supposedly through illness or injury. Cup Finalists in 1932, Arsenal had won the championship in 1931, been runners-up the previous season and would go on to win their second title in 1933. Walsall had never been higher than the second division and had spent most of their days languishing in the lower division. There was simply no comparison between the two sides. Even Arsenal's boots were said to have cost more than the entire Walsall team.

The Midlanders won the toss and kicked off, showing little respect for their betters by doling out some rough treatment that led to a dozen free kicks to Arsenal in as many minutes. But the visitors remained calm and might well have gone into the lead had their young replacement centre-forward Charlie Walsh not squandered so many opportunities. For an hour Arsenal looked to be the better side and, although they were making heavy weather of their ordeal, surely it was just a matter of time before Walsall's rugged defence, backed by the inspired Joe Cunningham in goal, cracked. But instead it was Walsall who leapt sensationally into the lead. On the hour they were awarded a corner and Fred Lee's cross was met by Gilbert Alsop, whose glancing header soared past England goalkeeper Frank Moss. One goal up and the Midlanders suddenly began to believe in themselves. Minutes later, as Alsop once more powered into the Arsenal penalty area, Tommy Black the Arsenal left-back deliberately up-ended the bustling centre-forward. A bitter confrontation ensued in the area as Walsall players tore in to the rescue of their prostrate colleague, while the referee pointed decisively to the penalty spot. When order had been restored Bill Sheppard stepped up to take the kick, and as cool as a seasoned international drove his penalty firmly into the net. Arsenal were on their way out of the Cup.

The Arsenal manager Herbert Chapman was furious. Within a week Tommy Black had been transferred to Plymouth and within the month Charlie Walsh was on his way to Brentford. Yet it was always whispered that Chapman himself should have shared the blame as some of his missing stars had been deliberately rested. As for Walsall their dream of Wembley was short-lived. In the fourth round they travelled to Manchester and in front of 52,000 at Maine Road went down 2–0 to Manchester City.

ABOVE: *Walsall (in stripes) on their way to pushing Arsenal out of the Cup*

WALSALL STAGE CUP SENSATION OF THE CENTURY

AMAZING SCENE FOLLOWS PENALTY AGAINST ARSENAL

BLACK.

TEMPERS FRAYED AND BLOWS AIMED

A "TERRIFIC K.O." TO HIGHBURY PRIDE

BASTIN.

Sunday Dispatch, 15 January 1933

1934

DEATH ON ALTAR OF DUTY

FORTUNE MADE FOR HIS CLUB

BUT DIED A POOR MAN

MR. HERBERT CHAPMAN, manager of the Arsenal Football Club, and the outstanding personality in the game, died suddenly from pneumonia yesterday at his home in Haslemere-avenue, Hendon, N.W.

In the adjoining columns is the last article he wrote for the "Sunday Express." Mr. Peter Batten, who knew him intimately, tells the story of "Chapman, the man," and reveals the fact that in all probability the manager who talked in tens of thousands when buying players, and made a fortune for his club, has died a poor man.

Sunday Express, 7 January 1934

HERBERT CHAPMAN was unquestionably the most outstanding manager in the history of British football and his untimely death in January 1934 at the age of 59 almost certainly robbed him and Arsenal of even greater achievements. Chapman died on the morning Arsenal were scheduled to play Sheffield Wednesday in a league fixture at Highbury. He had caught a chill in mid-week watching Bury and by Friday it had tragically turned to pneumonia. News of his death came in the lunchtime papers and quickly spread among the thousands of fans making their way to the game through the busy streets of north London. Shortly before kick-off 50,000 of them stood bareheaded in tribute as four trumpeters sounded the last post while his usual bench at the touchline stood poignantly empty.

The following morning all the Sunday newspapers carried the news and even *The Times* a day later marked his death in its obituary columns. But perhaps the most unique coverage came in the *Sunday Express* which carried not only an obituary but Chapman's final article. A regular columnist with the paper, Chapman had written about the forthcoming third round of the Cup and his fancies for Wembley.

RIGHT: *Herbert Chapman, builder of winning football teams, a manager who was years ahead of his time*

Born near Sheffield in 1875, Chapman had an undistinguished playing career with Sheppey United, Grimsby Town, Swindon Town, Sheffield United, Tottenham and Northampton, becoming player-manager of the latter and taking them to the Southern League championship in 1909. From there he took over the reins at Leeds City but when the Yorkshire club was disbanded in 1919, he travelled just a few miles down the road to crisis-ridden Huddersfield Town. Two years later Huddersfield had won the Cup and over the next three seasons became the first club to capture the league championship three times in succession. In 1925 he moved to Arsenal and immediately took them to a Cup Final though they lost. A year later they were back at Wembley to win the Cup and crowned that with the league title in 1931. The following year they narrowly missed the double but then matched Huddersfield's magnificent feat by winning three championships in a row, the final one just months after Chapman's death. In all, the great man could claim to have had a hand in lifting nine trophies. Years later Bob Paisley would more than match that total but with only two trophies to play for in the 1930s, Chapman's achievement was far more significant. Yet Chapman was also a pioneer, urging the installation of floodlights, the numbering of players' shirts, and building fine stands and facilities for spectators while spending more than £20,000 on David Jack and Alex James alone. He was the first genuine football manager whose legacy has enriched and enlivened the game.

1934

EVEN THE amateurs of the United States, along with Argentina and Brazil, were prepared to make the long sea voyage across the Atlantic to Italy for the 1934 World Cup Finals. But not England, who yet again missed out as the FA failed to patch up its differences with FIFA and turned down the chance to participate in the second World Cup Finals. The British press, as insular as ever, predictably ignored the event except for the final, where the only honourable mention came from the *Guardian*.

Uruguay, the world champions, also declined their invitation, but South America was represented by the Argentinians and Brazilians who along with Egypt and the USA were the only non-European competitors in the tournament. In all, sixteen teams were involved in the final competition, compared with thirteen in Montevideo for the 1930 finals. The favourites were Austria, whose Wunderteam had captured the imagination of fans across the continent, and Italy, the host nation, now basking under Mussolini's dictatorship. In the first round, the Italians easily disposed of the USA by seven goals to one while Argentina, Brazil and Egypt were all eliminated, giving them scant reward for their arduous travels. The Austrians meanwhile overcame a methodical French side by three goals to two, leaving eight European teams to battle out the quarter-finals.

Czechoslovakia, who had beaten Romania in the first round, scraped a place into the semi-finals with a 3–2 win against Switzerland, where they were joined by Germany. Italy now faced Spain, who had recently handed England their first defeat. The initial encounter petered out into a 1–1 draw, but in the replay the only goal of the game gave the Italians a semi-final draw against the Austrians, 2–1 winners over Hungary. This was the game everyone had hoped would be the final, and a match that pitted two of football's finest technicians against each other. And both owed much to the British game.

BELOW: *The Italian team, left to right: (back row) coach Vittorio Pozzo; Combi; Mozeglio; Allemandi; Ferraris IV; Monti; (front row) Bertonili; Guiata; Meazza; Borel; de Maria and Orsi*

Vittorio Pozzo, the Italian coach, had built his team around the basic style of the English game. After helping to found the Italian club Torino, he had travelled to England and while working in Bradford and the Midlands had become much influenced by the Manchester United side of Charlie Roberts. Back in Italy he had coached the 1912 Italian Olympic team, and after the war took over the reigns of the national side, where he

Association Football

ITALY WINS WORLD "CHAMPIONSHIP"

The Urge of the Duce

ROME, JUNE 10.

Forty thousand spectators, including Signor Mussolini, saw Italy win the world football "championship" this afternoon by defeating Czecho-Slovakia 2—1 in the final at the Fascist Stadium. The game was a contrast between the cool, well-co-ordinated play of the Czecho-Slovakians and the more dashing and individualistic performance of the Italians. The Italians won because they were faster than their opponents.

There was no score in the first half, but the Czechs missed several opportunities owing to bad shooting. Puc, the outside-left, was especially wild in his kicking. The Czech goal also had many narrow escapes, Planicka making several wonderful saves. It was half-way through the second half that the first goal was scored, but to the astonishment and dismay of the Italians it was Puc who found the net. The loss of a goal under the eyes of Mussolini stirred the Italians to frenzy, and in ten minutes they had equalised, and at full time the score was still 1—1.

An extra half-hour was played, and so great was the excitement that it was feared at one time that one of the stands would collapse under the stamping of the feet. At one corner of the field, too, a cordon of police was formed to keep back the spectators. The Italians scored their second goal early in the extra half-hour, Schiavio kicking the ball with such force that the goalkeeper seemed to be knocked over by it.

At the finish of the game the two teams paraded with their flags and were joined by the German team, which was third in the championship. Signor Mussolini received the captains and presented the cups. The Italians received the gold championship cup, which is so big that it took four men to carry it and its pedestal on to the field. The Duce's cup was presented to the Czecho-Slovakian team, and the Germans received the Italian Federation's cup.—Press Association Foreign Special.

Manchester Guardian, 11 June 1934

drilled home the disciplines of English league soccer learnt from Roberts and the attacking flair he had seen demonstrated by Steve Bloomer.

Pozzo's opposite number in the Austrian camp was Hugo Meisl, a wealthy Viennese Jew, who had adopted the former Bolton player Jimmy Hogan as his chief aide. Hogan and Meisl successfully grafted the neat passing of Scottish football, that had so impressed Hogan, onto the delicate skills of Austrian league soccer which Meisl cultivated. Between them, they moulded a side that stormed across Europe with a succession of stunning victories. They had even taken their so-called Wunderteam to Stamford Bridge where England undeservedly beat them 4–3.

Italy and Austria finally met under heavy Milanese skies, for their private battle to decide the real world champions. The wet, muddy conditions hardly suited the Austrians who were already showing signs of tiredness while the Italians, urged on by waving fascist flags, found enough energy to run out 1–0 winners. Austria's Wunderteam was past its peak and its crown was duly handed to Vittorio Pozzo.

In the final – played in Rome's Fascist Stadium before an excited Mussolini – Italy faced Czechoslovakia, and to the astonishment of everybody went a goal down in the 70th minute. But eight minutes from time Orsi scored a fluke equaliser, and the match moved into extra time. The Italians' superior fitness, hammered into them by Pozzo, now began to show results and with just seven minutes gone Schiavio danced around the Czech defence, and the World Cup belonged to Italy. Forty thousand spectators looked on as the gold championship cup was brought onto the field. Mussolini beamed from on high and, making his presentation to the Italian captain Combi, called the Italian victory a triumph for Fascism.

ABOVE: *Vittorio Pozzo being carried aloft by the triumphant Italian team*

1934

THE PROSPECT of Italy, the World Cup holders, facing England in London excited football fans everywhere. The first ever World Cup finals in 1930 had been virtually ignored by the press and even the 1934 finals – when England were absent yet again – had received only scant coverage. But everyone knew that Italy had recently won the tournament and they could rightly call themselves the world champions. Such a claim was of course too much for the jingoistic English who had long laid stake to that title. And so just a few months after beating Czechoslovakia to win the Jules Rimet trophy, Italy arrived at Victoria station to a fanfare of publicity and noisy support from London's Italian community.

England v Italy was billed in the papers as a showdown but over the years the match was to be remembered not as a Titan clash of skills but for the seven Arsenal players which England fielded and the bruises that were inflicted. When the England team was announced a week before the game, only five Highbury men had been chosen. They were captain Eddie Hapgood, Wilf Copping, Ray Bowden, Cliff Bastin and goalkeeper Frank Moss. It was a line-up that had Fleet Street nicknaming England 'Nearly All The Arsenal'. But as match day approached, injuries took their toll and when the two teams lined up the five Arsenal men had been joined by two more Gunners, George Male and centre forward Ted Drake, making seven in all. In addition the game was not only played at Highbury, but the England trainer was the Arsenal coach Tom Whittaker and radio commentary came from George Allison, the secretary-manager of the Gunners. The Italians, not to be outdone, fielded five Juventus players.

It was an extraordinary line-up which did not go amiss with the press. 'Drake to Lead This Arsenal Armada' ran the headline in the *Daily Mirror* on the morning of the

UP! THE 7 + 4 :: HUNT OUT—AND IN COMES DRAKE AS CENTRE

World-Wide Interest In This Arsenal Occasion

ENGLAND OR ITALY —WHO WINS?

Our Players Must Go All Out— The Telling Through Pass

By
ARTHUR SIMMONS
Sports Editor

The gates for the England v. Italy match at Highbury today will be open at twelve o'clock. The game begins at 2.30.

ENGLAND or Italy? If you like, Arsenal or Italy?

When the England side was picked last week caps were awarded to five Arsenal players—Moss, Hapgood, Copping, Bowden, and Bastin. That got the goat of my provincial friends. They bombarded me with complaints. Oh! the sarcasm. I was even accused of having worked Bastin and Copping in the eleven.

Daily Express, 14 November 1934

THE RIVAL TEAMS

ENGLAND		*ITALY*
MOSS (Arsenal)	*goal*	**CERESOLI** (Ambrosiana Inter)
MALE (Arsenal)	*right back*	**MONZEGLIO** (Bologna)
HAPGOOD (Arsenal)	*left back & capt.*	**ALLEMANDI** (Ambrosiana Inter)
BRITTON (Everton)	*right half*	**FERRARIS** (Lazio)
BARKER (Derby County)	*centre half*	**MONTI** (Juventus)
COPPING (Arsenal)	*left half*	**BERTOLINI** (Juventus)
MATTHEWS (Stoke City)	*outside right*	**GUAITA** (Roma)
BOWDEN (Arsenal)	*inside right*	**SERRANTONI** (Juventus)
DRAKE (Arsenal)	*centre forward*	**MEAZZA** (Ambrosiana Inter)
BASTIN (Arsenal)	*inside left*	**FERRARI** (Juventus)
BROOK (Manchester City)	*outside left*	**ORSI** (Juventus)

Referee.—O. OLSSEN (Sweden).

Snapshots Of The Players

ABOVE: *Heads to the ball before Eric Brook scored England's first goal*

DRAKE TO LEAD THIS ARSENAL "ARMADA"!

All Italy will be there.—Business in more places than one is likely to be held up this afternoon for the great match at Highbury.

7 'GUNNERS' AMONG ENGLAND
MEN-OF-WAR TO-DAY

Patriotic Frenzy That Would Beat Italy—Ten-Goal Victory Must Be Our Aim

Daily Mirror, 14 November 1934

BELOW: *Carlo Ceresoli, the Italian goalkeeper, makes a spectacular attempt to save a shot from Eric Brook of Manchester City*

match demanding that 'Ten Goal Victory Must be Our Aim'. There was of course no hope of that but with Mussolini in power and xenophobia at its height, the *Mirror* reckoned that 'if we could beat the Italians by ten goals and on the day deserve such a margin, the stock of England, not merely of English football, would jump as it had not jumped for years.' The *Mirror* wanted Stanley Matthews and Arsenal to put Mussolini firmly in his place. Of course it never turned out like that. England won by three goals to two but only after a struggle against ten men.

The game began sensationally as Drake swept through the Italian defence in the first minute, only to be pulled down in the penalty area. Eric Brook of Manchester City calmly stepped up to take the kick and blasted the ball into the crowd. Two minutes later he made up for his error by heading England into the lead. With five more minutes gone, Drake was again tripped, this time just outside the area and Brook was nervously handed the ball. He did not make the same mistake twice, driving his shot neatly into the net for England's second goal. The Italians were later said to be playing like schoolboys, floundering in a grey November mist, though the truth was that they were disorganised after centre-half Monti had limped off injured. Drake added a third goal after 15 minutes and England looked to be well set for the ten goals which the *Daily Mirror* had demanded. But they had not reckoned with some new Italian tactics.

After half time the Italians reorganised their ten men and began to freely dish out some rough treatment to the English forwards. Twelve minutes into the second half they scored and a minute later hit a second goal to send England reeling. As the rain grew worse, so England's performance deteriorated. Once calm and skilful, they were now ruffled and desperate. Italy attacked relentlessly but the equaliser would not come. 'I shudder to think what would have happened if Monti had been there to help Italy,' commented the former Austrian coach, Jimmy Hogan, in the *Daily Mirror*.

The following morning the papers had no praise for the Italians' fighting performance. Instead they were scornful of their rugged tactics. The *Mirror* listed the injuries: 'Hapgood – broken nose; Brook – arm x-rayed; Bowden – injured ankle; Drake – leg cut; Barker – hand bandaged; Copping – bandaged from thigh to knee.' It read like a bulletin from the war front, while on the back page it suggested that the FA might ban further internationals'. English pride had been hurt and although Mussolini's men had been defeated, the Italian dictator who had been receiving regular bulletins on the game's progress had not been made to squirm. Another chapter on English superiority was closed.

1935

JUST TWO weeks after Arsenal's Ted Drake had equalled the league scoring record by hitting seven goals in one game, Tranmere's Robert 'Bunny' Bell went two better and struck nine as the Rovers rattled in 13 goals.

Bell's feat was set on Boxing Day 1935 with Oldham Athletic the visitors at Prenton Park for a third division north fixture. Perhaps Oldham were suffering from a surfeit of turkey and Christmas pudding as they were four goals down within a quarter of an hour. By half time the score was an astonishing 8–1 and although Oldham pulled the game back to a respectable 11–3 with just two minutes remaining, Tranmere still managed to hit a further two goals in the final minutes to make it 13–4. Their thirteen goals equalled Stockport County's record win over Halifax the previous season but it set a new record aggregate score for an English league game which still stands today.

Bell's goals began slowly, his first coming in the seventh minute and his second after 16 minutes when Tranmere were already four up. By half time he had struck five and added the other four in the second half with two in the 88th and 89th minute. And to top it all he managed to miss a penalty. At the end of the game the 24-year-old Bob Bell was carried shoulder high off the field and presented with the ball which today rests in the Tranmere boardroom.

Bell was a prolific scorer in the lower divisions and followed in the distinguished path of another great Tranmere centre-forward, Dixie Dean. With Dean now beginning to age, Everton decided to tempt Bell across the Mersey to Goodison as they had his great predecessor. They obviously hoped for the same result but it was not to be and Bell after only 14 league games (though he did manage a creditable nine goals) gave way to another young centre-forward, called Tommy Lawton.

Bell's record did not last long. Less than four months later, in April 1936, Joe Payne of Luton Town hit ten goals as Luton thrashed Bristol Rovers 12–0.

BELOW: *Bob Bell, scorer of nine goals in Tranmere's 13–4 win over Oldham Athletic. His performance at Everton, however, was not so spectacular*

HIS 9 GOALS IN ONE GAME

Football Record at Twenty-Four

DRAKE, of the Arsenal F.C., who made history by scoring seven goals recently, has a rival in twenty-four-year-old Bell, centre forward of Tranmere.

He broke the League record by scoring nine goals against Oldham. The result was: Tranmere 13, Oldham 4.

Daily Mirror, 27 December 1935

1936

THE PUBLIC loves a sporting hero, especially a no-hoper. And Joe Payne of Luton Town fitted that bill perfectly. Up to Easter Monday 1936, Payne had played in just three first-class football matches and had enjoyed only a handful of appearances in the reserves without ever establishing himself in any regular position. But that holiday Monday, Luton drafted him into their first team at centre-forward to help stop a slide which threatened their position at the top of the third division south. It was an inspired decision and one that wrote Payne's name into the history books.

'Are Luton losing grip?' ran the headline in the *Daily Herald* on the morning of Easter Monday as it reported Luton's goalless draw at home to lowly Millwall. By five o'clock that afternoon Luton had given their answer thrashing Bristol Rovers 12–0 at Kenilworth Road. And the star of the day was young Joe Payne who helped himself to a record ten goals. Three came in the first half with the remaining seven after the interval, although as Payne left the field he was convinced that he had only scored nine to equal Bunny Bell's tally for Tranmere the year before. But the referee generously informed him that one of his efforts had in fact crossed the line before a team-mate had made sure.

Payne's achievement thrust him on to the front pages, unusual for a footballer in those days, but his ten goals were still not enough for Luton to win promotion. They finished as runners-up, but the following season, with Payne confidently playing in the centre-forward spot, they topped the table. Payne managed 55 goals and won an England cap but with the war two seasons away, it was sadly the highlight of his career.

Reserve Scores 10 Goals Out Of 12

ALL LEAGUE RECORDS BROKEN

JOE PAYNE, unknown footballer, sometime of Bolsover Colliery, Derbyshire, smashed all records for League matches yesterday by scoring ten goals for Luton Town against Bristol Rovers at Luton.

He was a last-minute selection. This Third Division game was vital to Luton, fighting to retain their position at the top.

Ball and Boyd, Luton's regular centre forwards, were injured. Whom could the directors choose?

Joe Payne had played half-back, full-back and inside forward for Luton, but never centre. Indeed, he had recently been in the reserves.

Dare they trust the leadership of the attack to him? They did.

Ten times he scored. Originally he was credited with nine goals, but after the match the referee indicated that the seventh goal—already given to Martin—belonged to Payne, who had headed in.

The ball was over the line when Martin charged the goalkeeper.

Daily Express, 14 April 1936

BELOW and BELOW LEFT: *Joe Payne, who became an overnight celebrity when he scored a record ten goals for Luton Town as they thrashed Bristol Rovers 12–0. It was the highlight of his career*

1937

ABOVE: *So near and yet so far. FA Cup semi-final, April 10th 1937; Mangnall scores for Millwall but Sunderland went on to win 2–1*

MILLWALL, LYING seventh in the third division south, almost brought off the biggest sensation in Cup football, when in 1937 they came within a whisker of a trip to Wembley. The first third division side ever to reach the semi-finals of the FA Cup, brave Millwall finally went down by two goals to one at Leeds Road to the eventual Cup winners, Sunderland.

Millwall's daring Cup run began at Aldershot with a 6–1 trouncing of the low-lying third division south side and continued in the next round with a 7–0 victory over Gateshead at the Den. In the third round they drew Fulham, then lying half way up division two for another tie at the Den. A bumper crowd of 35,000 turned up to see one of the surprises of the round as Millwall romped home by two goals to nil.

That victory brought the Lions a plum draw for the fourth round when Chelsea – lying twelfth in the first division – came out of the bag and, as luck would have it, the tie was to be played at the Den. Just over 42,000 packed their tiny ground for the London derby which was played on a bitterly cold January Saturday. The two clubs may have been forty places apart in the league but Millwall made easy measure of their more distinguished opponents, thrashing them by three goals to nil. It was the upset of the round.

In the fifth round Millwall faced another first division side, Derby County, again at the Den. The previous season Derby had been runners up in the league championship and nobody gave little Millwall much hope. But then, the pundits knew nothing of the goalstriking prowess of McCartney and Mangnall. A record cowd, which still stands today, of 48,672 turned up for the David and Goliath clash and witnessed an astonishing battle by the underdogs as McCartney hit Millwall's winner with just four minutes remaining. Derby had been beaten 2–1 and the Den went wild.

A fortnight later in the quarter-finals, Millwall faced their biggest task yet when they drew Manchester City, the eventual league champions. City arrived at the Den with a team of glittering stars, including goalkeeper Frank Swift, England full-back Sam Barkas, international outside left Eric Brook and the gifted Irish forward, Peter Doherty. But Millwall were not to be overawed by such an array of talent. By half time they were a goal ahead, thanks to Mangnall converting a quickly taken corner, and after just 12 minutes of the second half Millwall took an unassailable lead when the legendary England keeper, Frank Swift, misjudged a McCartney centre to allow Mangnall a free header at goal. The 42,000 south-east London crowd were ecstatic and as the final whistle blew, thousands of overjoyed Millwall supporters flooded onto the pitch. McCartney and Mangnall were carried shoulder high from the field while City's stars slunk shamefully away. The press loved it, and

MILLWALL MAKE CUP HISTORY

MILLWALL, a Third Division club, made the big hit of yesterday's F.A. Cup ties by defeating Manchester City, crack First Division club, by 2—0.

This is the first time a Third Division club has reached the semi-final.

At the finish crowds of Millwall supporters swarmed on the pitch, and Mangnall, who scored both goals, was carried shoulder high to the stands.

Sunday Express, 7 March 1937

1937

dubbed Mangnall 'David the Giant Killer', and for a brief weekend the two Millwall forwards enjoyed the notoriety of the back pages.

The Lions were in the semi-finals of the Cup, the first time a third division side had ever reached that stage of the competition, though it was not Millwall's first taste of the semi-finals. In 1900 and 1903 as a Southern League side they had reached this stage of the tournament, but with so few teams entering in those days it hardly compared with the 1937 feat. It was hard to choose between the three remaining teams in the competition, Preston, Sunderland and West Bromwich. All were first division sides with fine Cup-fighting pedigrees and all capable of lifting the trophy. But it being the semi-finals, Millwall were forced to leave the Den where they had experienced such good luck and make the journey north to neutral Leeds Road, to face Sunderland.

It was a mammoth task with just over 62,000 making the trip to Yorkshire from London and Wearside. After just eleven minutes it seemed that Millwall's luck might still hold when Burditt slipped a neat ball through the Sunderland defence for Mangnall to put them a goal ahead. Leeds Road had seen nothing quite like it and for 19 more minutes the dream of Wembley hovered before Millwall's eyes. But Sunderland were not eighth in the first division for no reason. Led by Raich Carter with Gallacher the Scottish international and Gurney of England, they were rated favourites to lift the Cup. Inevitably they equalised and then 23 minutes into the second half Gallacher headed home a free kick to send Sunderland to Wembley. It was a glorious end to Millwall's brave battle.

DAVID THE GIANT KILLER

Sunday Express, 7 March 1937

ABOVE: *Millwall fans invade the field after their team's sixth-round Cup Tie victory over first division Manchester City*

1937

IT WAS the greatest crowd ever to watch a soccer match in Britain when 149,407 poured through the turnstiles of Hampden Park in April 1937 to watch Scotland beat England by three goals to one.

Hampden that season had just opened its new north stand at the back of the terracing opposite the main stand, adding a further 4,500 seats to its capacity, with the Scotland/England game the first test of the ground's increased size. The game however attracted even more spectators than had been anticipated, with a further 10,000 reckoned to have gained free entry after smashing down the gates.

Over the next decade, Hampden ruled supreme as the world's largest soccer stadium – regularly attracting crowds of over 120,000 – until the 200,000 Maracana stadium in Rio opened its gates in 1950. Just a week after the Scotland/England fixture, 144,303 turned out for the Aberdeen/Celtic Cup Final, the highest gate ever to watch two club sides. In 1949 the ground's capacity was cut to 135,000 for safety reasons but it still pulled in a record 136,505 for the Celtic/Leeds United European Cup semi-final in April 1970 and also attracted a record for a friendly when 104,000 watched Rangers play Eintracht Frankfurt in 1961.

The record attendance at the Scotland/England match went largely unnoticed by the press with only the *Sunday Dispatch* making any reference to it. They were more concerned with happenings on the field than on the terraces. With few fixtures played against foreign competition, the home international championships took pride of honour in the international calendar and regularly attracted large crowds.

By all accounts, Scotland deserved their victory although the English press reckoned the scoreline flattered the Scots. England had led at half time by a single goal scored by Freddie Steele, the young Stoke centre-forward. Scotland replied early in the second half when outside-left Delaney cut past the England and Manchester City defender, Barkas, to send in a low cross for O'Donnell of Preston to hammer home. With just ten minutes remaining, McPhail struck to put Scotland into the lead and then with only a minute left the Rangers man hit a second to give Scotland a comfortable-looking win. It had been a disastrous season for England who wound up in third place in the home international table, well behind the winners, Wales, and who could still only count two victories at Hampden since 1900. No wonder nearly 150,000 Scots turned up.

TOMMY WALKER INSPIRED SCOTS

England Played Classy Football, But Failed To Hold Slender Lead

RECORD GLASGOW CROWD GET EARLY SHOCK

SCOTLAND ... ... 3 ENGLAND 1

By JOHN MACADAM

THE greatest crowd in the history of sport watched Scotland beat England by three goals to one at Hampden Park yesterday after a display of glorious football that has not been equalled since the famous Wembley wizards' match in 1928.

Yet Scotland crossed over at the interval a subdued, exploded team in arrears 0—1. It was Tommy Walker, idol of Edinburgh, who turned the tide in their favour. Walker, in the second half, played the part of half a dozen forwards.

He was all over the place on his own, and he did what nobody had done all through the first half—he brought Delaney into the game. He inspired the first two of Scotland's goals, and if there are any medals to be handed out, about 11 of them should be given to Walker.

Strangely, it was England who played the football, apart from an inspired Scottish 20 minutes. The Stoke three—Matthews, Johnson, and Steele—had a great day. The wingers had the measure of the Scottish backs right from the start, and Steele had no trouble in keeping out of Simpson's way.

Grand Stopper

Young was a grand stopper, and, although Bray and Britton did not look like setting the Clyde afire, they made a line that had the Scottish one licked.

Nothing but praise for Barkas—he was unlucky to be what I regard as the unwitting cause of the last goal. Woodley did some great things, but he also made mistakes.

O'Donnell did well for Scotland, but McPhail looked past it. Beattie justified himself in the second half, but here is the game just as I saw it.

SCOTLAND WIN 'NATIONAL

Scotland ...(0) 3 England ....(1) 1
F. O'Donnell, Steele.
McPhail 2.

At Hampden Park, before 149,407—the biggest crowd ever at a football match.

FINAL POSITIONS

	P.	W.	D.	L.	Goals F.	Goals A.	P'ts.
Wales	3	3	0	0	8	3	6
Scotland	3	2	0	1	7	4	4
England	3	1	0	2	5	6	2
Ireland	3	0	0	3	3	10	0

Sunday Dispatch, 18 April 1937

BELOW: *149, 407 may have been Britain's largest-ever soccer crowd, but Hampden was certainly accustomed to record attendances. In April 1933, 134,170 turned out to see Scotland v England*

1937

TELEVISION CAMERAS first appeared on a football league ground as early as September 1937 when the BBC transmitted extracts from a practice match between Arsenal and Arsenal reserves to what must have been a tiny audience watching at home. With Alexandra Palace so conveniently close to Highbury and Wembley, it was inevitable that these two grounds should feature prominently in the early coverage of live soccer.

The first transmission took place on Thursday September 16th 1937 at 3.40 pm, when it was listed in *The Times* as 'Football at The Arsenal. A demonstration by members of the Arsenal team at the Arsenal stadium, Highbury, introduced by George F. Allison.' But that very morning the *Daily Herald* was able to give its readers a sneak preview of the first ever football match on television. Reporter Douglas Walters had managed to get inside the studios and witnessed the secret experiment carried out from Highbury the afternoon before to check that all the equipment was operating correctly. Few at the time recognised the significance. Even after the live transmission no newspapers commented on the event, but Walters was in no doubt about the success of what he had seen and predicted that it would not be long before we were all watching football while sitting by our firesides.

The first live game to be shown in its entirety was the Preston v Huddersfield Cup Final, played on April 30th 1938. There were few television sets in those days and probably less than 10,000 saw the match on TV, compared with the 90,000 in the stadium itself. The coverage of that game aroused no interest in the press and it was not until 1953 when the nation rushed to buy television sets for the Coronation that a mass audience began to watch sport on TV. And only then did Fleet Street wake up to the growing power – and threat – of television.

BELOW: *Arsenal players examine the latest technology – the mobile television unit which had just transmitted the first live football broadcast to TV owners across the country*

GOALS MAY GO ON THE AIR SOON

BY DOUGLAS WALTERS

THE DAY IS NOT FAR OFF WHEN YOU MAY BE ABLE TO WATCH YOUR FAVOURITE FOOTBALL TEAM FROM YOUR FIRESIDE. THE B.B.C. COULD TELEVISE A GAME TO-DAY IF IT WERE TO OBTAIN PERMISSION.

A secret television broadcast outside normal programme hours yesterday proved conclusively that it is possible.

Seated in the G.E.C. television theatre, in the heart of London yesterday evening, I watched members of the Arsenal football team practising at Highbury, N.

Even at 6 p.m., when the light was failing, one could see clearly the farthest touchline and spectators in the far corner. Not once did I lose sight of the ball. The players were distinct.

Yesterday's tests were preliminary to this afternoon's advertised outside television broadcast from the Arsenal ground, when Mr. George F. Allison, manager of the club, will introduce before the camera many Arsenal players. They will be accompanied by their trainer.

Three cameras connected to the mobile television unit will be used and viewers will see field tactics, dribbling, passing, shooting and goalkeeping.

Daily Herald, 16 September 1937

1938

IT MIGHT SEEM incredible that England, just 15 months before the outbreak of war, should travel to Germany and before 110,000 spectators in an Olympic stadium swathed in swastikas give the Nazi salute. Yet that was precisely what happened on Saturday May 14th 1938 when England met Germany in Berlin and even more astonishingly, their gesture passed almost without comment in the British press.

Everyone knew that it was going to happen. On the day of the fixture the *Daily Mail* reported that 'before the start of the match the English players will give the German national salute, in accordance with the practice they have always followed when playing in foreign countries.' Yet still nobody seemed concerned, including the left-wing *Daily Herald*. The only bone of contention about the game was whether Germany, which had recently annexed Austria, should be allowed to field Austrian players. In the end a compromise was reached. There would be no Austrians in the German side but the following day Aston Villa would play a friendly in the same stadium against a German XI which would be almost wholly made up of Austrians.

The international was played late on a sweltering May afternoon in front of most of the Nazi hierarchy, including Goebbels, Hess and Von Ribbentrop. England came out and as planned, standing alongside their German opponents, gave the Nazi salute. *The Times*' football correspondent seemed remarkably proud as he reported that 'the English team immediately made a good impression by raising their arms in the German salute.' The players were said not to be too happy with captain Eddie Hapgood arguing beforehand that standing to attention was sufficient. Some might reckon that England then gave their best response by hammering the Germans by six goals to three. The following day the *Sunday Express* alone referred to the incident, with a photograph of the England team saluting, but suggested that they may have not given, a proper salute, since their arms were a shade too low. The photograph was repeated in the *Guardian* and the *Daily Express* on the Monday morning but it was left to Henry Rose of the *Express* to raise the only objections.

But there was a footnote to the incident which was carried on most of the front pages that same Monday morning. Aston Villa, after a bruising 3–2 victory over the German XI, left the stadium to the derision of 110,000 German spectators without giving the Nazi salute. Whether Villa deliberately refused the salute is a matter of some controversy, but it remains a fact that Fleet Street saw little to concern them in an England team saluting the swastika.

England should have won by 6-0

From HENRY ROSE

BERLIN, Sunday.

A SMALL bunch of Englishmen are walking about with their chests out today. And two Union Jacks are fluttering bravely, surrounded by hundreds of the Nazi flags draped around the magnificent Olympic Stadium here.

Great Britain may win the Walker Cup for the first time in history this year. We may win the Davis Cup. But 1938's snappiest blow for our prestige was struck by the England eleven who trounced Germany by 6—3 here yesterday.

It has been rocketed sky-high. You should be here properly to appreciate the magnificence of the achievement.

Few of us expected it. We were nearly all pessimistic. A draw was the best we hoped for.

A broiling sun beat down on our fellows, who had spent two days in sightseeing, with just one hour of training.

Weighing it all up, I couldn't see an English victory. Could you? But this victory before 110,000 people all rooting for the Germans has put back the calendar a few years for sporting Germany—put them back to the time when we were the masters and they the pupils.

My lasting impression is not of the play of either side, not of the crowd in this majestic concrete arena that makes you catch your breath when you first see it, not of the orderliness and perfection of organisation that sees this huge army of 110,000 marshalled in and out like clockwork.

WHEN THE BAND STRUCK UP

No, my lasting impression is of eleven English professional footballers lined up in the centre of the field giving the Nazi salute as the band strikes up Deutschland uber Alles and the Horst Wessel.

They were not happy about it. And they are not happy about it now

Hapgood, the captain, looks along the line. There is a shuffle, and orders being orders, hands are raised. They are lowered as one anthem finishes (I detect relief) and raised again with some diffidence.

There was a good deal of talk about it among the players before the game, and there has been a good deal since. There was no unanimity about the decision of the committee in charge that the salute should be given.

Hapgood, the captain, thought standing to attention, as all British teams do on the Continent, should have been sufficient.

Another member of the team told me: "I know that when my father sees a picture of me giving the salute, he won't be too pleased."

ENGLISH ARE WORLD CHAMPIONS

German writers are full of praise for the England team. Here are typical comments quoted by Reuter:—

FUSSBALL WOCHE (official organ of the Football Board): They are world champions of football after all, these English. They buried the fairy tale of English mechanised football. It was perfect football.

DEUTSCHE ALLGEMEINE ZEITUNG: They were superior to our players, especially in physical fitness, speed and form.

MORGENPOST: The English are still the perfect artists.

BERLINER TAGEBLATT: England played as if they were at home, despite the unaccustomed climate. That is the simple explanation of their great victory.

Daily Express, 16 May 1938

RIGHT: *England give the Nazi salute*

ALL SPORT BROUGHT TO A HALT

Restart When Safe for Crowds

FOR the moment all sport has been brought to a halt. The concentration of Britain's whole effort on winning the war makes its continuance undesired and inappropriate.

The Government have let it be known that the assembly of crowds in the open or indoors is at the present time to be avoided, and all events which would attract the public in any numbers have been prohibited.

Future Will Show

It may be possible in due course to minimise or remove the restrictions which have been imposed. Meanwhile, all sportsmen and sportswomen will realise the need for the Government's action.

In view of the fact that since Saturday this country has declared war, the results of League football, racing, and other sports events during the week-end have no significance.

Although the conditions may now be different, the war of 1914-1918 did not prevent the resumption of racing and other sport after a short stoppage. It will be the hope of all that the present interference will be as brief. *Daily Mail, 4 September 1939*

1939

WHEN WORLD War One broke out, football continued almost as if nothing had happened. It took more than a year before the footballing authorities finally stepped in and brought a halt to the game, and then it was only declining attendances that persuaded them. But there was no such danger that anything similar would happen in 1939.

The day before war was declared, Saturday September 2nd, turned out to be the final day of league football. Blackpool were top of the table with maximum points from their three games while league champions Everton were held to a 2–2 draw at Blackburn with Tommy Lawton scoring both their goals. At 11am the following morning with Hitler ignoring the British demand that he withdraw German troops from Poland, World War Two was officially declared. The following day's newspapers were a grave and sombre collection with sport relegated to the briefest of mentions. Page ten of the *Daily Mail* carried the all too obvious message: 'All Sport Brought to a Halt,' though there remained some hope that it was only temporary and that if matters improved, sport would be back again. Two days later the Football League Management Committee met at Crewe and acknowledged that the season, though only three games old, was over. With no sports news, the back pages disappeared overnight. But it would not be too long before soccer returned on a friendly basis with regional leagues, though it would never be the same until the Football League returned.

RIGHT: *With official sport ended, it's do your own thing – tin hats and all!*

1944

LEAGUE FOOTBALL may have vanished with the outbreak of war, but soccer did not disappear altogether. People still needed some respite from the weekly slog of the war effort and as long as football did not interfere with nor drain resources, there was general agreement that it should continue, albeit in a different form. So, instead of the old league structure, a system of regional leagues was introduced. This minimised travel as well as costs and to assist those clubs which had lost players to the forces, a guesting system was permitted. It meant that clubs could invite any locally-based servicemen to play for them, and inadvertently helped many third division clubs gain some extra kudos as they eagerly went in search of any footballing servicemen in their area. It led to an unusual mixture of talent with some

INTERNATIONAL

England ...... 2 Wales 2
Carter, Lawton. Dearson, Lucas.
H.T. 2—2. Att 38.483. £6,285.
(At Anfield, Liverpool.)

FOOTBALL LEAGUE—NORTH

Accrington S.. 2 Bradford City. 3
Conroy, Malcolm. Barclay, Newman. Shepherd.
H.T. 1—0. Att. 4,000

Aston Villa ... 3 Wolves 1
Parkes, Iverson. Haycock. Acquroff.
H.T. 2—1. Att. 20.000

Barnsley ...... 2 Derby County. 0
Robledo Smith
H.T 1—0 Att. 7.000

Bolton Wan... 1 Blackpool ... 0
Hamlett
H.T 0—0. Att. 10,000

Bradford ...... 1 Newcastle Utd 0
Horsman.
H.T 1—0. Att. 8,309.

Burnley .... 3 Southport 1
Kinghorn (2), Brocklebank. Coates.
H.T. 1—0. Att. 4.000.

Bury .... 1 Everton 4
Drury. Wyles (2), Stevenson. Rawlings.
H.T. 1—3 Att 4.000

Coventry City 0 Birmingham .. 1
H.T 0—1 Att 9.927 Faulkner.

Crewe Alex ... 0 Tranmere Rov. 1
H.T. 0—1. Att 3.500 Alder.

Darlington ... 2 Hartlepools ... 1
Brown, Ward. Horton
H.T. 0—1 Att. 6.736.

Gateshead .... 5 Middlesbrough 5
Johnson (2), McCormack, Bohills. Dudgeon. Stobbart (4), Warburton.
H.T 2—2. Att. 2.000.

Grimsby Town 2 Doncaster Rov. 1
Kurz (2). Tindill.
H.T. 1—0. Att .000

Hull City .... 2 Halifax Town 0
Talbot, Sergent
H.T. 1—0. Att. 8.000.

Lincoln City... 0 Chesterfield ... 1
H.T. 0—1. Att. 3.000. Pringle.

Manchester C.. 2 Liverpool 2
Smith, Sproston Dix (2).
H.T. 1—1. Att. 10.000.

Northampton.. 1 Stoke City ... 1
Perry. Bowyer.
H.T. 1—1 Att 2,500.

Nottm. Forest 2 Sheffield U. .. 2
Inskip, Baxter. Brook (2).
H.T. 1—2. Att. 8,000

Port Vale ..... 0 West Brom A 0
Attendance 6.000

Preston N.E. 4 Oldham Ath.. 1
Livesey, McIntosh. Iddon, Bond. Chapman.
H.T. 2—1. Att. 4,000

Rochdale ...... 2 Blackburn Rov 0
Ainsworth, Acton.
H.T. 1—0. Att. 2.500.

Rotherham U. 0 Mansfield T... 0
Attendance 7.000.

Sheffield Wed 6 Notts County 1
Catlin, Massarella (2). Froggatt. Thompson (2). Morrad.
H.T. 3—0. Att. 10.000.

Stockport C. .. 4 Manchester U. 4
Barkas (2), Worsley. Catterick. Smith, Mycock (2) Bryant.
H.T. 2—2. Att. 6,000.

Sunderland ... 5 Leeds United .. 1
Whitelum (2) Laidman (2), Walshaw. Mahon.
H.T. 0—1. Att. 8.000.

Walsall ...... 0 Leicester City. 1
H.T. 0—0 Att 5,000 Mercer.

Wrexham ... 1 Chester 1
Roberts. Neary.
H.T. 0—0. Att. 9,000.

York City ... 1 Huddersfield... 3
Dawson. Price (2), Glazzard
H.T 1—0. Att. 5.000.

FOOTBALL LEAGUE—SOUTH

Aldershot ... 1 Clapton Orient 0
Halton.
H.T.: 0—0 Att. 4,000

Brighton & H. 1 Fulham 7
Offord. Rooke (4), Leyfield. Potts (2)
H.T.: 1—4 Att. 4,500.

Chelsea ...... 8 Crystal Palace. 2
Payne(3), Foss, Mitten (3), Walker. Dawes (A.), Robson.
H.T.: 6—0 Attd 20.000

Luton Town... 1 Brentford ... 3
Daniel. Manley, Boulter, Thomas.
Half-time: 1—1. Attendance 3,500

Millwall ...... 1 Charlton Ath. 3
Jinks. Turner (3).
Half-time: 1—2. Attendance 6,600.

Queen's P. R. 0 West Ham U.. 1
H.T: 0—1 Att. 8.000. Goulden

Southampton . 0 Arsenal 2
H.T.: 0—1 Attd 18,000. Drake, Farquhar.

Tottenham H. 1 Portsmouth ... 1
Walters. Guthrie.
Half-time: 1—1. Attendance 14,167.

Watford ...... 2 Reading 2
Brain, Jackson McPhee, Layton.
Half-time: 1—2. Attendance 3.695.

	HOME W.	L.	D.	F.	A.	AWAY W.	L.	D.	F.	A.	Pts.
S'thampton	1	1	0	9	2...	2	0	0	9	5...	6
Reading ...	1	0	1	5	4...	1	0	1	10	4...	6
Brentford	1	1	0	6	7...	2	0	0	7	3...	6
Crystal P.	2	0	0	12	6...	1	1	0	6	10...	6
Tottenham.	1	0	2	7	3...	0	0	1	0	0...	5
Portsmouth	2	1	0	12	8...	0	0	1	1	1...	5
Chelsea ...	1	0	1	9	3...	1	1	0	9	7...	5
Fulham ...	1	0	1	9	6...	1	1	0	11	6...	5
Aldershot .	2	0	0	7	3...	0	1	1	1	2...	5
Arsenal ...	1	0	0	1	0...	1	1	1	4	6...	5
West Ham	0	0	0	0	0...	1	1	2	8	8...	4
Charlton....	1	1	0	5	10...	1	1	0	4	6...	4
Luton T....	0	1	2	3	5...	0	0	1	3	3...	3
Brighton...	1	1	0	4	8...	0	2	0	4	11...	2
Watford ...	0	1	2	7	9...	0	1	0	0	9...	2
Q'n's P.R..	0	2	0	4	6...	0	1	1	6	9...	1
Clapton O.	0	0	1	3	3...	0	3	0	2	9...	1
Millwall...	0	2	0	2	7...	0	1	1	3	6...	1

FOOTBALL LEAGUE—WEST

Aberaman A. . 0 Bristol City ... 4
H.T 0—2. Att. 400. Owen (2), Thomas. Collins.

Bath City ... 2 Cardiff City .. 2
Barron, Sloan. Rees, Wood
H.T 2—1 Att. 5.000.

Lovell's Ath.. 5 Swansea Town 0
Guest, Clarke (2). Edwards (2).
H T 2—0. Att. 2 000.

	HOME W	L.	D.	F.	A	AWAY W	L.	D.	F	A.	Pts.
Bristol C...	3	0	0	8	2...	1	1	0	5	4...	6
Bath City.	1	0	1	5	3...	1	1	0	3	3...	5
Cardiff C...	2	0	0	6	2...	0	1	1	2	5...	5
Lovell's A.	1	1	0	6	2...	1	1	0	5	5...	4
Swansea T.	1	1	0	5	4...	1	1	0	6	9...	4
Aberaman	0	2	0	4	10...	0	2	0	3	8...	0

OTHER MATCH

Norwich City. 9 R.A.F. XI... 1

SCOTTISH SOUTHERN LEAGUE

Albion Rovers 2 Motherwell ... 0
Moodie (2) H.T. 2—0.

Clyde .... 5 Falkirk 1
Galletly (2), Gordon, Wallace, Johnstone. Fitzsimmons.
H.T. 2—0.

Dumbarton .. 0 Celtic 3
H.T. 0—2 Gallacher (2), Delaney

Hamilton Ac.. 5 St. Mirren ... 2
Herd (2), Jones McShane, Burns. Linwood, Murdoch.
H.T. 1—1.

Hearts ...... 4 Third Lanark 1
Donaldson, Johnson, Philip, Bolt (o.g.). McIntosh
H.T. 3—0

Morton ...... 2 Partick Thistle 0
Kelly, White H.T 0—0.

Queen's Park . 0 Hibernian 2
H.T 0—1 Devlin (2)

Rangers ...... 2 Airdrieonians .. 0
Smith, Gillick. H.T. 1—0.

SCOTTISH N.-E. LEAGUE

Arbroath...... 1 Dundee 4
Brand. Turnbull (3), Auld.
H.T. 1—1.

Dundee United 3 Rangers (N.E.) 0
Juliussen (2), McGillivray. H.T. 1—0.

East Fife ...... 5 Aberdeen 4
Jarvis (2), Duncan. Wilson (2). Waldron, Buchan (2). Munro.
H.T. 1—1.

Falkirk (N.E.). 0 Dunfermline... 3
H.T. 0—0 Harrower, Houliston. Logie.

Raith Rovers . 3 Hearts (N E.). 0
Junior (2), Conner. H.T. 0—0

	HOME W.	L.	D.	F.	A.	AWAY W.	L.	D.	F.	A.	Pts.
Dundee.....	2	0	0	7	4...	4	0	0	13	5...	12
Aberdeen...	3	0	0	12	3...	1	2	0	10	7...	8
Dunfrmline	1	0	1	5	4...	2	1	1	10	7...	8
Rangers.....	2	0	1	10	1...	1	2	0	8	9...	7
Raith R....	3	1	0	11	5...	0	1	1	4	5...	7
Dundee U.	2	2	0	7	5...	0	1	1	3	4...	5
East Fife...	1	1	1	8	11...	0	2	1	4	11...	4
Arbroath...	2	1	0	8	7...	0	3	0	0	9...	4
Hearts N.E	0	2	1	6	9...	1	2	0	7	9...	3
Falkirk N E	0	3	0	1	13...	1	2	0	3	9...	2

Empire News, 17 September 1944

Scotland Again Well Beaten by England

SCOTS will remember yesterday's International match at Wembley if only for the fact that their almost unknown team, brilliantly led by Matt Busby, held England—in the first half—before a Royal assembly.

I thought Scotland were decidedly unlucky not to get the upper hand quite early in the game when Ditchburn, the young 'Spurs goalkeeper, for the first and only time, showed signs of "Wembley nerves."

Ditchburn fumbled a ball—in fact, dropped it—with Dodds in close attendance. Nine times out of ten that would have meant a goal.

England were class from start to finish, but it was not until the second half that they were given an opportunity to display the form which gave them the title of the best England team ever.

Cullis Kept Busy

SCOTLAND'S team is well worth persevering with. Flavell and Caskie did their jobs well, but I thought Dodds was too frequently left to plough a lonely furrow, although it must be many seasons since Cullis had to face a more determined rival.

Busby was the man who kept the Scots together in the first half, but nothing could have stopped Matthews in his inspired spell after the interval.

The way he took the ball right up under Stephen's nose, showed it to him, and then was gone was audacious to say the least.

Empire News, 20 February 1944

LEFT: *England v Scotland, 4 March 1944. Grozier saves from Lawton*

of the lower clubs fielding international stars while many of the first division clubs found themselves scratching around to field a side.

At the end of the first wartime season, the ten-league regional structure was scrapped and the nation simply split into two with northern and southern leagues that operated until 1945, with the exception of 1941/42 when a number of London and southern clubs broke away for the one season and formed the London League. Wages were strictly regulated with a flat fee of 30 shillings for each match, later increased to £2, although this did not stop one or two players auctioning their talents to the highest bidder. International fixtures continued, although they were restricted to the four home nations. England and Scotland met regularly, with England usually getting the better of the encounters and often by high scores. A cup competition was also introduced, again played on a north/south basis, and with a two-leg final.

Yet although the game continued, it hardly flourished. Attendances were low and only local derbies and internationals attracted crowds above 25,000. Genuine competition was always absent, even in cup matches, and the press took little interest in proceedings. Paper was in short supply and the number of pages had to be slashed to a minimum, with coverage from the war front always taking priority over any frivolous activities on the sports field. The war also tragically cut many careers short with some like Tom Cooper, the England and Liverpool full-back, killed while serving in the forces. In all, more than 70 professional league players gave their lives. For others, the war had broken out just as their careers were reaching a peak and by the end of hostilities their playing days were all but ended without their talents having been fully recognised. A number of grounds, including Old Trafford, Ashton Gate and The Den were also severely damaged by aerial bombing, bringing an end to any hope of football in some cities until peacetime. When the game finally returned to normal in 1946, it was hardly surprising that it should be greeted with a resurgence of interest.

LEFT: *Internationals between Scotland and England were regular crowd-pullers, by wartime standards. Here Carter tries a shot for England, 19 February 1944*

1945

WHEN MOSCOW Dynamo arrived in England in November 1945, the nation was in the grip of pro-Soviet fever. Along with the United States, the Soviet Union had been Britain's closest ally throughout the dark days of the war and cultural relations were at a new high as the team stepped off the plane at Croydon Airport after their eleven-hour flight from Moscow. Coupled with this was a football-thirsty audience, eagerly awaiting the return of league soccer and desperate to see any competitive match. With visiting foreign clubs still a rarity and no Soviet team ever having played in Britain, it was hardly surprising that the Dynamo should attract huge interest.

A 'monster crowd', as *The Times* put it in one of its rare football reports, turned out for the first game against Chelsea at Stamford Bridge on a bitterly cold Tuesday afternoon. Almost 75,000 paid to see the match, with the gates closed long before kick-off and an estimated further ten thousand clambering over the fences to secure any vantage point available. With the vast crowd spilling onto the pitch the two teams appeared side by side, the Dynamo players each clutching a bouquet of red and white flowers which they proudly presented to their much embarrassed opponents. It was the kind of gesture the press relishes and led to the *Daily*

'Thanks'–In 11 Bouquets

THE biggest-ever crowd at Stamford Bridge yesterday saw the Moscow Dynamos trot on to the field carrying red and white bouquets. Each Dynamo presented one to his Chelsea counterpart.

Daily Herald, 14 November 1945

This pleased but puzzled the crowd.

Last night, at a Café Royal reception, the Dynamos explained.

The bouquets were a sign of gratitude for the warm welcome they had received.

Well might they have been pleased. They drew a crowd of 85,000—a record for Stamford Bridge—to their first match in England.

Five minutes before the kick-off Fulham-road from Walham Green station to the turnstiles was one solid mass, and as the gates closed there was a roar.

BELOW: *A packed Stamford Bridge looks on with puzzled amusement as the Russian Interflora team take the field*

Herald reporting on its front page that it had 'pleased but puzzled the crowd'. Chelsea, with new signing Tommy Lawton up front, quickly went two goals ahead and that was how it remained at half time with the Russians having missed a bagful of opportunities including a penalty. But once the second half was underway, the Dynamo were transformed and gave the Londoners a memorable lesson in skills with the final score level at three apiece.

A few days later they travelled to Cardiff and in front of another huge crowd gave the Welshmen a 10–1 hammering. At half time they were a mere three goals ahead but within 20 minutes of the second half had added a further five. They 'flashed and weaved', wrote *The Times*, which by now was as caught up as everyone else in its enthusiasm for Soviet soccer. The *Daily Herald* described the Dynamo as 'thawing out in front of the warmth of British sportsmanship', but within days of their return to London the warmth turned to chill as they were caught in an unfortunate and unnecessary diplomatic incident. Their next opponents, Arsenal, with many of their regular players serving overseas, wanted to field a number of guest players including Stanley Matthews and Stan Mortensen. The Russians protested angrily arguing that Arsenal, fearing they might be beaten, were trying to field a representative England side. But the Russians had little need to worry as even with Matthews and Mortensen, the Arsenal went down 4–3 in front of 55,000 amid a typical London fog at White Hart Lane. A week later they travelled North to Glasgow where more than 90,000 at Ibrox watched them force a 2–2 draw with Rangers.

The Communist Party newspaper the *Daily Worker* revelled in this sudden friendship with the Soviets and carried daily reports, mostly on the front page, of Dynamo's activities. There was even an editorial which seized on the interest shown by the public and the huge crowds which the team was attracting. 'The more some politicians and diplomats seek to spread suspicion as to the objectives of the Soviet Union, the more the common people of Britain are intent on showing that they want a strengthening of relations between the two countries,' they wrote, adding that 'such visits should also kill any lingering idea that socialism means dull, spoilsport austerity.' And so at the end of the month, despite attempts to arrange extra fixtures, the Soviets returned home undefeated, leaving behind an army of fans that would remember their famous visit for many years to come.

BELOW: *Tommy Lawton scores for Chelsea*

AS I SEE SPORT BY CLIFFORD WEBB

MOSCOW THUNDERBOLTS SPLIT SIX WITH CHELSEA

Speed That Staggered The Fans

FOR "Dynamo" read "Dynamite." Drawing 3-3 with Chelsea before a crowd which overflowed to the Stamford Bridge touchlines yesterday, the Moscow footballers blew skyhigh any suggestions that they were not up to top-class British standards.

The match, which began with presentations of bouquets from each Russian player to his Chelsea opposite, ended with a weary London side walking slowly off the field wondering what had hit them.

Daily Herald, 14 November 1945

1946

ABOVE: *The Associated Press explanation of the tragic scene at Burnden Park*

SADLY, IT TOOK another disaster to thrust football back onto the front pages again. The huge crowds that had flocked to see Moscow Dynamo the previous year continued to pour into the football grounds throughout the immediate post-war years. Even third division clubs could boast regular gates of over 15,000 as Britain relaxed and enjoyed its football after years of austerity and war. But on March 9th 1946, for the crowd that poured into Burnden Park, Bolton, it was to have dire consequences.

On that day Bolton Wanderers were entertaining Stoke City in the second leg of the sixth round of the FA Cup. Bolton had won the first leg 2–0 and 65,000 spectators turned up to watch some of the country's finest players. It promised to be a stirring Cup-tie with Lofthouse, Matthews, Mortensen and Steele on display but instead it was to be remembered for the tragedy that struck on kick-off.

The gates had been locked by 2.30 pm as the 65,000 spectators swayed and sweated in the spring weather. Even before tragedy struck a wall caved in injuring a handful of fans, but then shortly before the teams kicked off a gate was forced open at the Railway End and thousands flooded into the ground. A further gate was tragically picked open by a father wanting to escape the inside crush with his young son. The result was catastrophic as more swarmed in, the crowd pressed forward and a barrier collapsed.

Veteran *Sunday Chronicle* reporter Ivan Sharpe sitting in the safety of the press box watched horrified as 'screams rent the air as the helpless crowd began to stumble and fall.' Suddenly Sharpe found himself covering a major front page story instead of his usual back page report. Within minutes 33 lay dead and more than 500 were injured. It was soccer's worst tragedy. The footballing authorities met days later and an official inquiry was set up by the Home Office but although the blame was laid at the gatecrashers and weak crowd barriers, the truth was that many of Britain's soccer stadiums were too old and could not safely hold large crowds. Unfortunately it would take many more deaths and thirty more years before the authorities would legislate to restrict the capacity of soccer grounds.

After a brief stoppage the game continued but petered out into a goalless draw that gave Bolton a place in the semi-finals. Professional to the end, Ivan Sharpe amid the carnage also wrote his back page report of the game for the *Sunday Chronicle*. It was a brief sketch which ended, 'I have no heart or pleasure in writing about the match.'

BRITAIN'S WORST FOOTBALL TRAGEDY OCCURRED AT THE BOLTON-STOKE F.A. CUP-TIE YESTERDAY.

Thirty - three people, including one woman, were trampled to death or suffocated when two barriers suddenly collapsed under the weight of the crowd, 15 minutes after the start. At least 500 people were injured, four seriously.

Sunday Graphic, 10 March 1946

33 KILLED : 503 INJURED

when seventy thousand Cup-tie crowd bursts the barriers at Bolton

Crushed spectators trampled to death on the touchline

Sunday Express, 10 March 1946

1947

THE FIRST post-war winter was the worst on record. The freeze, beginning in January, stretched on until mid-March with even the quarter-finals of the FA Cup played on snowy frozen surfaces. It seemed that it would never end as one cold snap followed another, bringing soccer and horse racing to a halt. For much of the period temperatures were well below freezing, forcing the postponement of dozens of games each Saturday. And this was at a time when match officials were reluctant to cancel games unless conditions were impossible. On the first Saturday in February only three first division matches were played; two weeks later 23 games were off and on March 8th there was no soccer in the Midlands at all as 20 league games were postponed. Well over 120 games were called off altogether. For ten weeks, players slithered and slid their way through the fixtures, narrowly avoiding serious injury and almost freezing to death in the bitterly cold westerly winds.

The problem was compounded by an industrial crisis which further forced the postponement of mid-week games. With coal stocks frozen solid and railway lines iced up, it became difficult to move the nation's vital sources of energy. Industry ground to a halt and post-war reconstruction plans had to be hastily redrawn. When coal stocks did move and production began to improve again, the Government asked the Football League to postpone its mid-week fixtures in order to maintain the nation's production at as high a level as possible. And so the season wore on with League officials finally forced to extend fixtures into June. Most clubs wound up their season on the final day of May but tabletopping Liverpool had to wait another two agonising weeks for Stoke and Sheffield United to play each other before they knew they were the League's first post-war champions. Even the newspapers had their problems. Producing and delivering them was a tricky task and with no racing pages and little football, the number of pages shrank dramatically.

MID-WEEK GAMES OFF: SATURDAY 'NATIONAL'

Daily Express, 12 March 1947

Sport sheds the load (except ice hockey)

Express Staff Reporter

FIRST effects last night of the Government's request to officials that mid-week sport be stopped for the emergency were: (1) the cancellation of 13 Football League matches next week; and (2) the postponement of the Grand National from Friday, March 28, to the following day.

ABOVE: *Blackpool's goal slides in quite literally – v Chelsea at Stamford Bridge, March 8th 1947*

1947

TWENTY YEARS after the first Cup Final broadcast in 1927, radio coverage of the great game had become a serious challenger to newspapers. Most football fans either owned their own wireless or at least had access to one so that those who could not witness the occasion at Wembley usually spent Cup Final afternoon huddled around a set, listening to the commentary of Raymond Glendenning.

ABOVE: *The inimitable Raymond Glendenning*

" IT'S CHARLTON'S turn now . . . they're swarming in . . . Brown is back with Strong blocking the goal.

Glendenning was without doubt the first outstanding sports broadcaster. Wherever British sportsmen and women competed, he would be there to give his inimitable coverage, his staccato voice crackling over the airwaves. He was also contracted to the *Sunday Graphic* and provided a regular weekly round up column. So what could be more natural than for the *Sunday Graphic* to devote its coverage of Charlton's cup win over Burnley to the man himself? Extracts from Glendenning's radio commentary served as perfect captions for a series of photographs that showed the best of the Cup Final action.

" . . . AND HERE is Bartram going up . . . fingers stretching out . . . every muscle straining . . . but he doesn't get near it . . . it rises over his head . . . and over the bar. The crowd—particularly the Lancashire lads, cheer, but it's just another hope that failed.

" CHARLTON ARE MOVING down . . . Hurst has the ball on the right wing . . . he passes to Robinson . . . The centre-forward is going through . . . He's right down at the Burnley goal . . . He centres . . . a beauty . . . just over Don Welsh . . . Duffy is on it . . . he half-volleys it into the net . . . It's a goal . . . Charlton have scored . . . Duffy (No. 11) throws his hands up . . . jumps for joy . . . This is it . . . Charlton players are crowding around . . . shaking his hand . . . and the hands of Johnson and Phipps, those magnificent defenders."

Sunday Graphic, 27 April 1947

1947

IN MAY 1947 a special challenge match between Great Britain and the Rest of Europe was held at Hampden Park, Glasgow. It was arranged to mark the re-entry of the four home nations into FIFA, as well as a gesture of friendship to help heal the wounds left by six years of war.

Just over 134,000 crammed into Hampden for the encounter, and most left convinced that British soccer was the finest in the world. It was a talented British side with Frank Swift, the big Manchester City and England goalkeeper, George Hardwick of Middlesbrough and England, Billy Hughes of Birmingham City and Wales, Archie Macaulay of Brentford and Scotland, Jack Vernon of West Brom and Ireland, Ron Burgess of Spurs and Wales, Stanley Matthews of Stoke and England, Wilf Mannion of Middlesbrough and England, Tommy Lawton of Chelsea and England, Willie Steel of Morton and Scotland and the flying Scottish winger Billy Liddell from Liverpool.

The Rest of Europe were captained by Johnny Carey, the elegant Manchester United and Eire full-back, and brought together a mixture of Scandinavians with the odd French and Italian. Football in Germany was still disrupted and consequently there were no Germans or Austrians in the line-up. And considering the quality of pre-war Spanish soccer, it was also surprising that Spain was not represented.

England quickly shot into the lead, thanks to Wilf Mannion. Nordhal, the Swede, equalised but in a five-minute burst shortly before half time England swept into a 4–1 lead. In the second half they added two more to wind up comfortable winners by six goals to one. The flawless Mannion, rated the man of the match, had bagged two as had Tommy Lawton. Parola, the Italian centre-half, had been the most impressive European but the much-anticipated fixture had unarguably been a case of masters versus pupils.

The back pages gleefully reported British superiority, but also tucked away in their columns were two transfer stories. Both emerged from Hampden where the expected transfer of Stanley Matthews from Stoke to Blackpool for £12,000 was confirmed. Elsewhere it was reported that league champions Liverpool had made a world record bid of £15,000 for Morton's inside-left Willie Steel, but the lure of Anfield was not as irresistible as it is these days and the Scottish international went instead to Derby County. With record transfer fees and big crowds, British football was clearly at a peak but already its days were numbered.

Britain gives Rest of Europe six-goal lesson in football

Sunday Express, 11 May 1947

MANNION—MAN OF MATCH

GREAT BRITAIN .... 6 **REST OF EUROPE** 1
(Mannion 2, Steel, Lawton 2, Parola, own goal) (Nordahl)
H.T.: 4—1. Attendance 134,000. Receipts £31,000.

BELOW: *Mannion scores the fourth goal for Britain. In the picture are (left to right) Mannion, da Rui of France, Parola of Italy and Tommy Lawton*

1948

THE *News of the World* had no doubts that this was the finest Final seen at Wembley and few other newspapers disagreed with their conclusion. Manchester United, runners-up in the league that season and the season before, were considered the most consistent and skilful outfit in the first division. They would be runners-up twice more before finally clinching the title in 1952. Blackpool, on the other hand, with Stanley Matthews, Harry Johnston and Stan Mortensen, boasted some of the most exciting players in the land. It came as no surprise then that both teams, dedicated to attacking football, should serve up a six goal feast to be remembered.

It was Blackpool who stole the lead after 12 minutes when Mortensen was brought down in the area by United's Chilton, with Shimwell converting the spot kick. Fifteen minutes later United were back on level terms as Rowley beat goalkeeper Robinson in a desperate dash for the ball. Within five minutes however Blackpool were ahead again, when Mortensen slammed home one of his specials from Hugh Kelly's free kick. And that was how the score remained for the next forty-five minutes.

Matthews was making dazzling runs down the right but the United defence, inspired by Irishman John Carey, held firm. It took another free kick to bring the fourth goal, this time to United when Jack Rowley headed home Johnny Morris's free kick to level the scores. Ten minutes later and United were in the lead for the first time as Pearson latched on to Anderson's delightful through ball. Wembley erupted but there was more to come when with just seven minutes remaining John Anderson's snap shot from 25 yards soared into the net. United had won the Cup for only the second time in their history. And as skipper Carey received the trophy from King George VI, the *News of the World* elsewhere reported him as saying, 'Thank ye sir, and God bless ye!' A case of journalistic licence, surely!

THIS WAS WEMBLEY'S FINEST FINAL

Six-Goal Thriller

By HARRY J. DITTON

MANCHESTER UNITED 4, BLACKPOOL 2

What a magnificent Cup Final! It really was terrific. It had everything—intense drama, including six thrilling goals and some of the most delightful ball play Wembley has ever seen.

Above all, it was contested in a grand sporting spirit in spite of the fact that fouls preceded both of Blackpool's goals.

Yes, this was a game that will leave an imperishable memory with all who saw it—a classic exhibition which reflected nothing but the highest credit on every one of the 22 players.

There could be no possible doubt about the merit of Manchester United's triumph. After a slow start, in which they found themselves twice in arrears, they hit back bravely and finally developed form which was so irresistible that no side in England could have held them.

In the moment of Blackpool's defeat it is pleasant to be able to record that there need be no recriminations about Manager Joe Smith's decision in omitting centre-forward McIntosh and playing Mortenson at centre-forward with Munro at inside-right. Indeed, Munro was one of the heroes of this match.

He was a veritable will-o'-the-wisp, always to be found where the fight was thickest. He took many bold tilts at the United defence and in addition put in some magnificent defensive work. No one in this game gave more in sheer industry than this veteran Scot.

What made this game such a fascinating spectacle was the way both sides went all out from the first kick to scheme and score goals.

There was none of the negative safety-first tactics which have characterised so many Wembley finals. Here we saw craft matched with craft and more true Soccer science than we normally see in half-a-dozen games.

Manchester were always the greater artists, for whereas Blackpool depended largely on the skill and initiative of Matthews, plus the industry of Munro, United's attack was definitely five-pronged and decidedly pointed.

Some of the attacking moves of Delaney, Morris, Rowley, Pearson and Mitten were brilliant in the extreme, and, as the score suggests, carried tremendous goal-scoring possibilities.

Blackpool have no reason to be critical of themselves, particularly their defence. Young Crosland, suddenly finding himself pitchforked into such a momentous struggle, stood up to his task with great courage and no small degree of efficiency.

The only goal that Blackpool might have saved was the equaliser obtained by Rowley after half an hour.

The ball could easily have been cleared by Hayward, but Robinson rushed out of his goal, called for the ball, and then failed to "make it," with the result Rowley was left with a sitter, which he accepted with avidity.

The goal scoring began 15 minutes earlier when Blackpool were awarded a penalty. They had set a cracking pace with Matthews dazzling at outside-right and Mortensen thrusting up boldly through the centre.

Chilton, United's centre-half, was clearly unnerved by Mortensen, and in a despairing effort to stop him lunged out his foot and brought the Blackpool flier down.

There was only one punishment to fit this crime, and Shimwell, taking the kick with the coolness he might show at shooting in practice on a Tuesday morning, scored easily.

News of the World, 25 April 1948

ABOVE: *Blackpool in the lead as Shimwell scores from a twelfth-minute penalty . . .*

ABOVE: *. . . but the victory goes to United. The triumphant team is greeted by thousands in Manchester's Albert Square*

1949

Eggs and Sherry Team Still in Cup

Yeovil's Victory is the Toast of the West

YEOVIL, part-time professional footballers who trained on glucose, eggs and sherry, are to-day the toast of the West Country. After beating Sunderland, First League team, by two goals to one, they are included in the 16 teams going into to-morrow's draw for the fifth round of the F.A. Cup.

Seventeen thousand saw Yeovil make Cup history —compared with the season's record of 82,771 who watched Manchester United, the Cup-holders, draw with Bradford. The 16 ties drew a total attendance of 640,000.

Arsenal were knocked out by Derby County, Aston Villa by Cardiff City, and Everton by Chelsea. Both Sheffield clubs were defeated and Huddersfield could only draw with Newport County.

News of the World, 30 January 1949

YEOVIL will always be remembered as the greatest giant-killers of all. Proud in victory, magnanimous in defeat, the lowly Southern League side captured the hearts of post-war Britain, and drew 81,500 to Maine Road to watch their fifth round clash with Manchester United.

Their exploits began in the qualifying competition with a 3–2 win at Lovell's Athletic (fellow Southern Leaguers), followed in the first round proper by a comfortable 4–0 home win over the Isthmian League side, Romford. In the second round they were drawn away to the Western League side, Weymouth, where they struck another four goals to win 4–0. The third round brought the big clubs of the first and second division into the tournament and Yeovil found themselves at home pitted against second division Bury. But in a thrilling 3–1 win on their notorious sloping pitch, Yeovil gave notice that something sensational was happening. Yeovil's victory was rewarded with a plum tie – first division giants Sunderland at home. The Wearsiders were enjoying a good season with England international Len Shackleton leading their ranks and Willie Watson, a future England cap, behind him.They were the biggest spenders in soccer with a team that had cost £60,000 and many football writers reckoned they might be a good bet for the Cup that season. But it was not to be.

On the slope at the Huish the, might of Sunderland came a cropper against the 5,000-to-one part-timers. Just before kick-off, Sunderland's hopes were boosted even further when the regular Yeovil goalkeeper cried off through injury and 23-year-old Dicky Dyke, a solicitor's clerk, donned the jersey for his first big match. A record 17,000 were jammed into every corner of the Huish which had it been twice the size would still not have satisfied the thousands who wanted to see this game.

The match was barely 26 minutes old when Yeovil, showing no respect for their betters, sensationally swept into the lead through their player-manager, Alec Stock. The score remained like that until the 62nd minute when Dyke made his one and only mistake and it was 1–1. But Yeovil were not dispirited and continued to play their own brand of aggressive, push and run football. At 90 minutes the score remained level and under the government's austerity scheme designed to avoid too many journeys and loss of working hours, extra time was played and the two teams kicked off again. Then with just one minute of the first period remaining, Yeovil's Bryant put the Somerset side into the lead. Now all they had to do was hang on. The ball was belted upfield, into the stands, back to the keeper, anywhere as long as Sunderland did not get hold of it. In the end their tactics paid off and as the final whistle blew, the crowd invaded the pitch.

'Eggs And Sherry Team Still In Cup,' ran the headline on the front page of the *News of the World* as it revealed Yeovil's secret training diet and joined in the national hysteria for the victorious under-dogs. But the draw for the fifth round was not

1949

"I told you it was a mistake fixing it for Cup-tie day!"

News of the World, 30 January 1949

ABOVE LEFT: *Alec Stock (standing, centre) discusses tactics*

LEFT: *Yeovil wives do their duty*

kind. This time there was no home tie, but an away game with glamorous Manchester United, the Cup holders. The two teams met a fortnight later at Maine Road where United were playing while Old Trafford was repaired following war damage. More than 81,000 crammed into the ground with the gates shut 20 minutes before kick-off leaving thousands more outside. But within five minutes Yeovil's dream was shattered when Jack Rowley scored the first of his five goals. By full time United had rattled up eight goals without reply and although Stan Hall in goal had been injured after 20 minutes, Yeovil could muster no excuses. Their daring Cup run had come to a sad but courageous end.

1950

IT WAS not unknown for English league footballers at the end of their days to make the long trek to South America to take up coaching positions. Many clubs, such as Southampton, Nottingham Forest, Everton and Spurs, had visited the far-off continent, Southampton as early as 1904, and British football had contributed much to the development of the South American game. But in May 1950 Neil Franklin, the Stoke City and England centre-half, became the first British star to play for a South American club while still in the prime of his career.

The 1949/50 season had just ended with first division Stoke finishing dangerously close to the relegation zone when Franklin secretly packed his bags, and along with team-mate George Mountford, boarded a plane for New York before catching a further flight to Bogotá. Stoke knew nothing of Franklin's intentions until the FA discovered his disappearance as they attempted to draft him as a late replacement for the England squad about to visit Portugal. It was then that they discovered that he was on his way to Colombia, supposedly to take up a three month coaching job.

When the two, along with their wives, arrived in New York they told waiting pressmen that they 'just wanted to take a look at the situation'. But by the time the small party arrived in Colombia it was announced that Franklin and Mountford had both signed lucrative contracts to play for Santa Fe of Bogata. Stoke City were furious, to say the least, having lost out on a possibly large transfer fee, and with Colombia not even members of FIFA there was little hope of any recompense.

The 28-year-old Franklin had already faced problems with the FA that year after refusing to go to Brazil with the England team for the World Cup because the FA would not allow him to take his wife. He was also known to be unhappy at the pitiful wages paid to English footballers and was able to boast upon his arrival that he was to be paid £3,500 a year plus a £1,000 signing-on fee, compared with £12 per week in England. 'We came for the money,' he was reported as saying. 'They are paying for a maid for our children and everything we want. Next week they are finding us a big house with a separate wing for each family. We'll be paid enough for our own servants.'

The Franklin story hit the headlines for days but it was the *Daily Express* which quickly had a reporter on the scene who scooped everyone by turning not to Franklin and Mountford for their story, but to Vera and Phyllis, the players' wives. 'My semi-detached at Stoke beats these,' joked the *Express*'s front page headline. 'It's nothing like we dreamed it would be,' the two wives admitted to the *Express*'s seemingly sympathetic reporter over their fifth plate of steak and chips that week. 'The kitchens are primitive – great dirty looking iron cookers with a tank on top, old-fashioned sinks, even a stone to scrub the washing on.' Franklin and Mountford with their bulging bank balances may have been the envy of every football league player but their wives were clearly unhappy. Within days of the Franklin and Mountford disappearance, another league player, Billy Higgins, the Everton centre-forward, was signing for the Colombian club, the Millionaires. Meanwhile, it was reported that the great Stanley Matthews and the Liverpool winger Billy Liddell had also been approached and certainly Liddell was made a tempting offer but neither joined the exodus. Nor did

BELOW: *Stoke City's flying centre-half Neil Franklin*

My semi-detached at Stoke beats these—Mrs Franklin

Neil Franklin and George Mountford played their first game for the Santa Fé club last night and helped to beat Medelli 3—2. Mountford, former Stoke winger, scored the winning goal.

From EVELYN WEBBER

BOGOTA (Colombia), Sunday. — Mrs. Vera Franklin and Mrs. Phyllis Mountford, young and pretty wives of the former Stoke footballers, were dispirited tonight.

Their husbands are believed to be getting £3,500 a year here, against £600 in England, and the wives sat down to steak and chips for the fifth time this week.

But they have been house-hunting—rents are about £20 a week —and their conclusion is: "It's nothing like we dreamed it would be."

The kitchens—oh!

Said Mrs. Franklin: "We thought we would walk into a streamlined American home.

"But the kitchens are primitive—great dirty-looking iron coal cookers with a tank on top, old-fashioned sinks, even a stone to scrub the washing on.

"Our little semi-detached back in Stoke was better. [*Stoke City bought it for them. Cost: £3,000.*] I have not seen a washing machine.

Daily Express, 15 May 1950

ABOVE: *Capped 27 times, Franklin was the pillar of the England defence*

anyone else for that matter. Perhaps Vera and Phyllis had dropped the word where it really mattered – on the front page of a national newspaper. By the end of 1950 Franklin had returned home, disillusioned with football in Colombia. After suspension he joined Hull City and later Crewe Alexandra and Stockport County. He eventually tried his hand at coaching in non-league football and in February 1963 was tempted abroad again, this time to Cyprus to become coach of Apoel Nicosia.

1950

BRITISH SPORT MEETS ITS WORST DAY

Daily Express, 30 June 1950

THURSDAY JUNE 29th 1950 was the grimmest day in English sporting history. In the second test at Lord's, Clyde Walcott's touring West Indies won an historic first-ever Test victory on English soil while 12,000 miles away in the simmering heat of Belo Horizonte in Brazil, the England football team lost 1–0 to an amateur USA side and were all but eliminated from their first World Cup. It was humiliating.

England who had been beaten on only a handful of occasions outside Britain were hot favourites to capture the Jules Rimet trophy but had begun their campaign with an unimpressive 2–0 victory over Chile. Against the USA they did everything but score and a few days later, following another defeat, this time by Spain, they were on their way home.

Fleet Street's bastion of patriotism, the *Daily Express*, was horrified and ran the tale of two defeats on the front page under the headline 'British Sport Meets Its Worst Day'. It searched desperately for excuses: Matthews should have played but had been mysteriously left out of the line-up by manager Walter Winterbottom. But the truth of the matter was that world sport was changing with the developing nations now equipped to tackle the strongest. In cricket the West Indies would continue to swashbuckle their way to international success while Brazil were already emerging as an exciting and skilful force in world football.

The papers of course failed to realise all this and the press corps which had accompanied the England team returned home on the same plane. As far as they were concerned a final without England hardly counted, and so Uruguay's 2–1 victory over Brazil a week later barely rated even a paragraph in most papers.

BELOW: *A grim day for England: Bert Williams makes a save but cannot prevent England's ignominious 1–0 defeat by the Americans at Belo Horizonte. It was one of the biggest shocks in World Cup history*

Now U.S. beats us at Soccer

Express Staff Reporter

BELO HORIZONTE (Brazil), Thursday. — U.S. footballers—who ever heard of them? — beat England 1—0 in the World Cup series today. It marks the lowest-ever for British sport.

For the Americans were 500—1 outsiders. Soccer being America's least-practised and least-expert game.

Yet the England team was unchanged from the side which beat Chile 2—0, and the U.S. team—again, whoever heard of it?—had only one change from the side which lost to Spain.

Right after today's match it was learned that Eddie McIlveny, Glasgow-born captain of the American team, is to be signed by Manchester United.

Twenty thousand people saw England's ignominy under heavy cloud, with glaring sun breaking through intermittently.

They also saw the England players leave the field—under an equally heavy cloud. No sun broke through this. Their heads were downcast.

Daily Express, 30 June 1950

1951

EVERYONE WAS agreed: floodlit football was dramatic and was here to stay. Although two Sheffield representative teams had met under lights in front of 20,000 excited spectators as far back as October 1878, the experiment had quickly fallen into disrepute as power failures brought a sudden halt to most games. The first major game to be held under lights in Britain was on the evening of Wednesday September 19th at Highbury with the unusual kick-off time of 7.30 pm. During the 1930s it had been the dream of the then Arsenal manager, Herbert Chapman, that football would one day be played beneath lights but it took another 20 years and another Arsenal manager, Tom Whittaker, to fulfil that dream after he had visited Rio and witnessed for himself the delights of floodlit Brazilian football.

Arsenal's opponents that evening were Hapoel of Tel Aviv and although the Gunners ran out comfortable 6–1 winners, it was not the manner of their victory which was on everyone's lips the next day but the switching on of Highbury's illuminations. Whittaker had a fine sense of theatrical timing and had designed his production with all the skill of an impresario. Roy Peskett, writing in the *Daily Mail*, was like all those alongside him seeing floodlit football for the first time. Yet he captured the mood precisely, showing that football reporters can also on occasion write as well as those who hog the feature pages. 'Perhaps floodlit league football is not so very far off,' commented Peskett. In fact, it would be another five years before the Football League relented and allowed league fixtures to be played under lights. But at least Fleet Street had the foresight to recognise that floodlit soccer had arrived.

FLOODLIGHTS PULL FANS

Daily Mail, 20 September 1951

The Arsenal Show Made 44,000 'Ooh'

By ROY PESKETT

Arsenal ....6 Hapoel-Tel-Aviv 1

THE darker it became, the more you could see last night. at Highbury, where Arsenal staged the complete Soccer show in colour, featuring the League side against Hapoel-Tel-Aviv from Israel.

Under the massed banks of 84 1,500-watt lamps, stage manager Tom Whittaker turned producer.

A few minutes before kick-off time he ordered the electricians to put on the lights at half power. The switch-on was greeted with the "ooh's" you get at a firework display.

But, with perfect timing, he waited until the two teams were entering the field before switching on full power.

I am certain that this moment and the spectacle which then unfolded before the 44,000 crowd will attract many new customers to Highbury, while it also opened up visions of night football played in the perfect setting.

It was all there. The bright emerald pitch, the table-tennis white of the ball, Arsenal in their red and white and the Israel side in the light blue, the flashlights from the cameras, and the cigarette smoke vanishing into the sky above the many lights which, although bright enough to give a daylight glow, never dazzled

I am glad there were many high officials of the Football Association and Football League to see this extraordinarily attractive spectacle. Perhaps floodlit League football is not so very far off.

ABOVE: *Hapoel goalkeeper Hodorov makes a save during the floodlit match*

1952

ANYONE WHO supported football during the 1950s will fondly remember Charlie Buchan's *Football Monthly*. In attics and cupboards all over the land, collections no doubt lie to this day, neatly strung and stored. They are waiting for the moment when they can be brought down, carefully dusted and given to grandchildren to devour. It was a time when football was its peak; a time when crowds flocked to matches, and a time when heroes were really heroes. Charlie Buchan's *Football Monthly* had them all: Nat Lofthouse, Tom Finney, Billy Liddell, Stan Matthews, Trevor Ford, Raich Carter, Wilf Mannion, Jackie Milburn, and the elegant Johnny Haynes. Wolves, Manchester United, Portsmouth, Newcastle and Tottenham. These were the big names and outstanding teams featured every month in colour and black and white photographs that would live forever.

Every month the magazine was packed with 50 or more pages of cartoons, crosswords, match reports, Scottish news, editorials, programme swaps, history features and the players themselves talking about the game or passing on their skills. Among the contributors during the early years were players like Tommy Lawton, Peter Doherty, Eddie Baily, Jimmy Logie, Laurie Hughes and Stan Seymour, as well as commentators such as Ken Wolstenholme, Eamon Andrews and Brian Glanville. And every month there was a prized colour front cover – just right for cutting out and pasting in a scrapbook. Charlie Buchan's *Football Monthly* is football nostalgia at its best, re-living an age when soccer was at its peak.

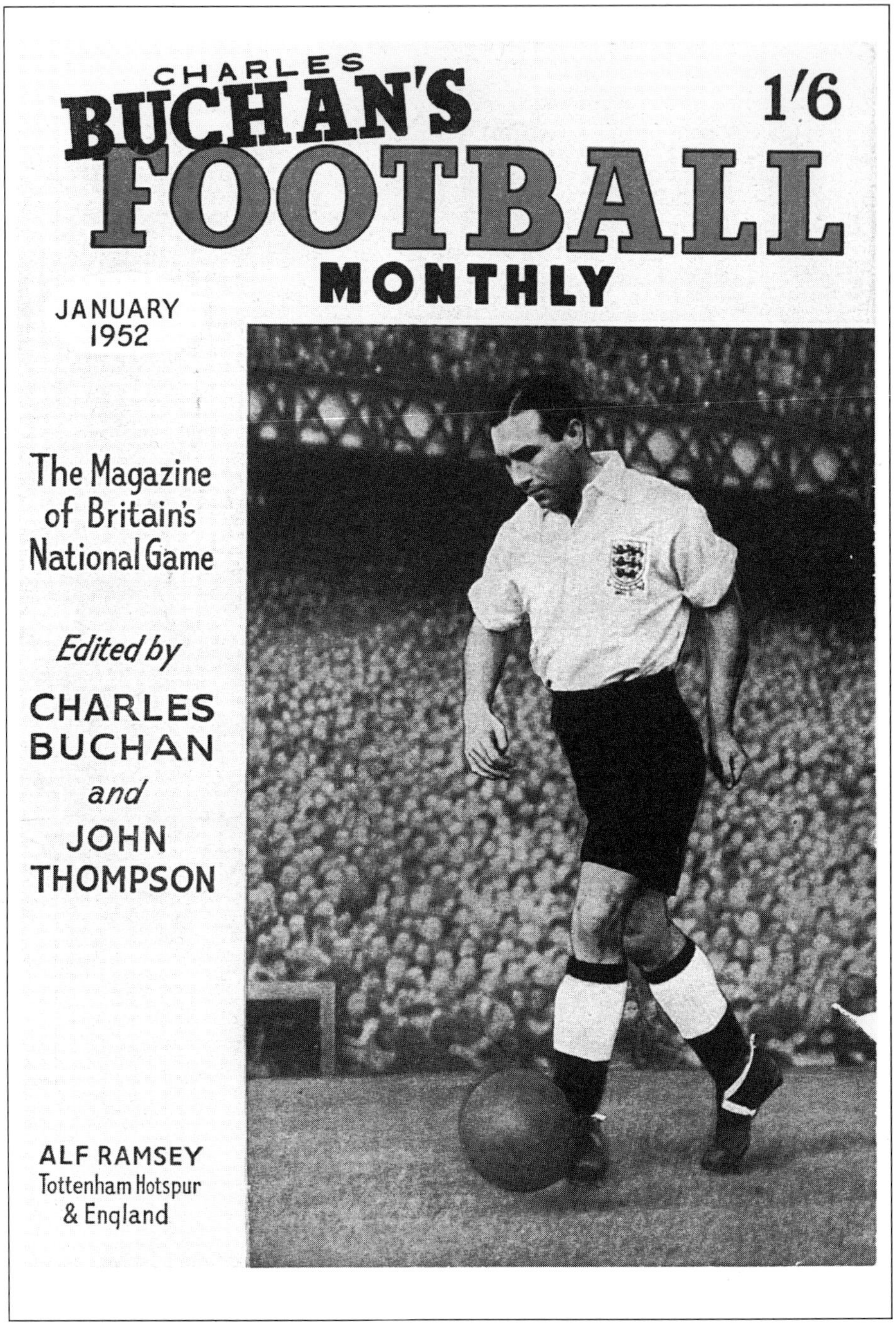

It was founded by the great man himself in September 1951 after a career in football had been followed by a second successful career in journalism. The nippy inside-right was always reckoned to be years ahead of his time. Born in Plumstead, home of Woolwich Arsenal, he had watched Arsenal as a boy, played four games for the reserves and then walked out on the club in 1909 after a row over expenses. He subsequently joined Northfleet and then Leyton but in 1911, at the age of nineteen, was transferred to Sunderland for what was then an enormous transfer fee of £1,200. At Roker Park he helped Sunderland to the league title and the Cup Final in 1913. Surprisingly, he was capped only six times by England, spanning the years between 1913 and 1924, although he did captain his country on a number of occasions.

In 1925 Arsenal's new manager

1952

CHARLES BUCHAN'S FOOTBALL MONTHLY

Edited by . . . . CHARLES BUCHAN and JOHN THOMPSON

Associate Editor . . J. MAXWELL SARL

JANUARY, 1952 No. 5

Contents:

Published by Charles Buchan's Publications Ltd., 408 Strand, London, W.C.2.
Printed in Great Britain by Bournemouth Times Ltd., Branksome, Bournemouth.
Distributed by Thorpe and Porter Ltd., Oadby, Leicester.

The Editors write . . .

WHILE the majority of you have asked for "the mixture as before" in your comments on our editorial policy, we would like to say how much we appreciate the ideas given us by those of you who have put forward constructive suggestions for improving "Football Monthly."

For this has been and always will be YOUR magazine, and we doubt if there has ever been a publication with a more co-operative circle of readers. We have certainly learnt much from you and promise that the lessons will be put to good account.

J. FROGGATT

Some of your ideas, you will notice, have already been adopted. We will get round to the others as soon as we can.

The spirit in which we are happy to work was summed up by the reader who wrote: "I like above all the *friendliness* of your book." And that, sincerely, is the impression we hoped to give.

Now for a word or two about the next issue. The cover picture will be of Jack Froggatt, the Portsmouth and England star, and there will be controversial opinions from such distinguished players as Roy Bentley, of Chelsea, Joe Mallett, of Southampton, and Jackie Sewell, of Sheffield Wednesday.

Arthur Rowe, who guided Tottenham Hotspur to the championship, will tell us what football has taught him, and Clifford Webb, the celebrated sports columnist, will be our leading guest writer.

On our principle that the "outsider" often sees more of the game than those of us close to it, we will also publish a fine feature by Bernard Darwin, one of the greatest writers of our day.

In addition to several other grand articles there will be the usual drawings, photographs and cartoons.

In all, it is what you have asked for. We hope you continue to like it.

5

Football Monthly, January 1952

Herbert Chapman rectified the club's earlier mistake by signing the 33-year-old for £2,000 and £100 for every goal scored in his first season with them. It was money well invested as Buchan scored a total of 20 League and Cup goals in his initial season at Highbury and helped Chapman lay the foundations for Arsenal's future success before retiring in 1928. His final league match was at Goodison Park on the day Dixie Dean scored his sixtieth goal.

At the age of 36, Buchan joined the *Daily News* (later the *News Chronicle*), as a football reporter before starting up his own football magazine. Although *Football Monthly* continued into the 1970s the magazine was never the same after Buchan's death in 1960, and will always be best remembered for the warm picture it painted of soccer in its heyday.

ABOVE: *Following a career with Sunderland and Arsenal, Charles Buchan enjoyed a second equally successful career as the editor of* Football Monthly

1953

EVERYONE REMEMBERS the 1953 Cup Final. Not only was it the first major televised sports event – reaching millions of new sets just purchased for the Coronation – but it was also to be immortalised as the Stanley Matthews Final. The Blackpool and England winger had played in two Cup Finals in 1948 and 1951 but on both occasions had finished up with only a loser's medal. So would it be third time lucky for football's favourite son, as Blackpool took on fellow Lancastrians Bolton Wanderers before a crowd of 100,000 that included the new young Queen, just a month away from her Coronation? With just three minutes remaining, it looked highly unlikely as Blackpool trailed 3–2. But then Matthews took charge and in the most dramatic turnabount in Cup Final history, the 38-year-old twisted and tortured a tired Bolton defence to set up two last-minute goals that won the Cup for the seaside club. If Matthews was not already a national hero, he certainly was the following day as he found his picture beaming from the front pages of all the Sundays.

Bolton had stormed into the lead as early as the second minute when Blackpool's Scottish international keeper George Farm fumbled Nat Lofthouse's 25-yard drive. It took Blackpool half an hour to equalise but by the 55th minute Bolton had swept into a 3–1 lead and all seemed lost until Matthews took over. Thirteen minutes later after the old man

ABOVE RIGHT: *Blackpool's 'Wizard of Dribble' in action*

RIGHT: *All seems lost for Blackpool as Bell slams home Bolton's third goal in the 55th minute*

I 'WON' MATTHEWS THAT JINX MEDAL FROM THE LINE!

by ALLAN BROWN

Sunday Chronicle, 3 May 1953

ROYAL 'FINAL' HERO

BELOW: *Blackpool raise the Cup after their 4–3 extra-time victory*

had dazzled his way down the broad acres of Wembley, he sent in a low cross for Mortensen to make it 2–3. And that was how it remained with just three minutes ticking away on the stop watch. With Matthews again leading the charge, Blackpool won a free kick and Mortensen drove the opportunity through the gap and into the net. That was 3–3 and with extra time looking inevitable, Matthews brought off the miracle when he glided down the wing towards the line before sending in the perfect cross for Bill Perry to slam home. Matthews had his winner's medal at last. It was football romance at its best. The *Sunday Chronicle* told the story through the eyes of Alan Brown, unable to play because of injury.

The Final 12 million saw...

Sunday Graphic, 3 May 1953

1953

IN THE endless debates about who was the finest player of all, the name of Alex James will always loom large. If Herbert Chapman masterminded Arsenal's surge to glory during the 1930s, then James was his commander in the field. And when the famous Scot died on the eve of the Coronation in 1953, even *The Times* felt obliged to acknowledge his death in its obituary columns – rare indeed for a footballer to be so fêted by the establishment newspaper.

Born at Mossend, near Glasgow, in 1901, James began his footballing days in 1922 with Raith Rovers but was soon spotted by Preston North End who brought the young man south in 1925 for £3,275. Four years later he was transferred to Arsenal for the then astronomical sum of £9,000, in a deal that followed hard on the heels of the £10,000 which Arsenal manager Herbert Chapman had paid for Bolton's David Jack. The nation gasped at such extravagance but Chapman had no hesitation and by the time James retired eight years later, he had helped Arsenal to four league championships, and three Cup Finals.

The Times' obituary described James as 'compact in build, [with] a smiling chubby face which added to the picture of a player who looked quite unconcerned about the fortunes of a match.' He may well have looked unconcerned but he was continually inspiring and organising his troops. He had begun his career as a goalscorer, netting 53 goals in four seasons at Deepdale but at Highbury he was transformed, albeit reluctantly, into a scheming provider of goals. His dazzling dribbles and daring runs set Highbury alight, as they had set Wembley alight in 1928 when he had torn the English defence apart in Scotland's 5–1 trouncing of the 'auld enemy'.

As Arsenal's fame grew, so did James's. He appeared on front pages, in gossip columns, on radio and was acknowledged to be the most influential inside forward of his generation. Yet despite his fame, he surprisingly won only eight Scottish caps, four each with Preston and Arsenal before retiring in 1937. During the war he served with the Maritime AA Regiment and afterwards rejoined the Highbury staff as a coach. His death at the age of 51 robbed football of a rare genius.

OBITUARY

MR. ALEX JAMES

Mr. Alex James, the Scottish international, Preston North End, and Arsenal footballer who made his name in the late 1920s and early 1930s, died in hospital in London yesterday at the age of 51. He had been ill for a long time.

Although capped eight times for Scotland, James will be remembered principally for his association with Arsenal, whom he joined in 1929 and, before retiring in 1937, had helped to win the F.A. Cup twice and the Football League championship four times. James was one of the cleverest inside-forwards of his time. Compact in build, he had a smiling, chubby face which added to the picture of a player who looked quite unconcerned about the fortunes of a match, but the appearance of James belied his ability. He was always on the watch for an opening, he could get off the mark in a flash, he had a powerful shot, could beat much taller men in the air, and, above all, possessed an extraordinary knack of tricking opponents merely by feinting and swerving. The Arsenal forward line of Hulme, Jack, Lambert, James, and Bastin was, perhaps, the best which has represented the club.

James was born at Mossend, near Glasgow, and played at school with another boy destined to become a great Scottish footballer—Hughie Gallacher. Raith Rovers was the first big club James played for, and he stayed three seasons with them before going to Preston. After James retired from the Arsenal team he took up a position with a football pools firm. Later he went in for sports reporting and also did pig-farming. He never lost his interest in soccer and in recent years coached Arsenal youngsters in the finer points of the game. James leaves a widow, two sons, and a daughter.

The Times, 2 June 1953

ABOVE: *Although only 5ft 6ins, James was unmistakable on the field, defeating many a taller opponent with his combination of skill and cunning*

NOW IT'S BACK TO SCHOOL FOR ENGLAND—WITH HUNGARY THE SOCCER MASTERS

THE NEW WEMBLEY WIZARDS

THE VISIT of Hungary, the 1952 Olympic and World Youth Football champions was eagerly anticipated by the press. Whilst none of the football writers underestimated them, they all reckoned England would still overcome the East Europeans. After all, England's only home defeat by a foreign side had been the 2–0 victory by Eire at Goodison Park in 1949. Somehow that did not count, nor did the disastrous showing in the 1950 World Cup. But the writing was clearly on the wall, even if the football writers could not read it. And so, on a cold and slightly misty Wednesday afternoon in late November, England lined up to face the Hungarians. Ninety minutes later the Mighty Magyars, as they had suddenly become christened, had changed the map of international football. England 3 Hungary 6: that was the scoreline that stunned the nation and the world. England were 'outplayed, outpaced and outshot'.

One hundred thousand watched in disbelief and growing admiration as the Hungarians tore England apart, going ahead within the first minute. By half time they were four goals to two in the lead and shortly before full time led 6–2 until Alf Ramsey converted a late penalty to make the score slightly more respectable. An England team with names such as Wright, Dickinson, Matthews, Mortensen and Ramsey had been thrashed.

To their credit, the football writers made no excuses and instead heaped their praises on the skills of Puskas, Czibor, Kocsis and three-goal Hidegkuti. The writing on the wall had finally been deciphered. Six months later the Hungarians proved that their Wembley victory was no fluke when they ran up a 7–1 victory in Budapest.

ABOVE: *The magnificent Grosics leaps into the air to thwart another England attack*

Make 'em run? —We couldn't

By CHARLES BUCHAN

England .... 3 Hungary 6

IT had to come. England have been beaten by a Continental side on their own soil. There can be no complaints. We were outplayed, outgeneralled, outpaced and outshot by a great Hungarian side.

Hungary are Olympic champions. They may be world champions after the World Cup series in Switzerland next summer. I rate them superior to Uruguay and Argentina, the best teams I saw during the tour of the Americas last summer.

They taught us two lessons which we must take to heart before the Switzerland trip. 1. The value of positioning. 2. Accurate distribution of the ball.

News Chronicle, 26 November 1953

BELOW: *Hungary, with Ferenc Puskas on the left, line up before their epic victory over England*

1954

FLOODLIT FRIENDLIES against the best of foreign competition were the fashion of the early 1950s. It reached its peak in 1954 when Moscow Spartak, Honved, Red Banner and Inter Milan were among the many famous visitors to these shores. They were all formidable competitors, with Inter Milan slamming West Ham by six goals to nil while Spartak comfortably beat Arsenal 2–1 at Highbury after knocking five goals past them in Moscow. But when they came face to face with the Mighty Wolves it was a very different tale.

Wolves were the current league champions and the team everyone wanted to test their skills against. In Billy Wright, Bert Williams, Ron Flowers, Denis Wilshaw, Peter Broadbent, Jimmy Mullen and Bill Slater they boasted the finest exponents of English League football. First into the lions den of Molineux in early March were Racing Club of Buenos Aires, beaten 3–1. In October First Vienna scraped a lucky draw but two weeks later Maccabi of Tel Aviv paid for that lapse with a 10–0 drubbing. Then followed what many commentators reckoned were two of the finest games ever seen anywhere, let alone at Molineux.

Moscow Spartak arrived fresh from their victory at Highbury to meet a Wolves team sitting comfortably on top of division one. Spartak were determined to maintain the outstanding record which Russian clubs had against British opponents. But it was not to be. In front of a capacity crowd of 55,000, the men in black and old gold played their hearts out. With three minutes remaining they were one goal up. Then in a pulsating final 180 seconds they scored three times to leave Spartak dazed and reeling. Fleet Street was equally stunned.

'Goal Storm Shatters Spartak,' was the headline on the front page of the *Daily Mirror*. 'Our greatest post-war soccer victory' wrote their football correspondent as he waxed lyrical about the good old-fashioned skills of English soccer. But better was about to follow.

GOAL STORM SHATTERS SPARTAK

By PETER WILSON

IT was a great and glorious victory at Molineux, Wolverhampton, last night—Wolves 4, Spartak 0.

And the Russians' display was the most complete collapse I have ever seen from a club in first-class football.

For more than fifty minutes there was no score. Then Wilshaw cracked in a goal for Wolves at firing squad range from a goalmouth melee following a free kick.

As the fog deepened, nerves twanged like snapping violin strings. Paramonov went off injured and Issaev took his place.

But Welsh referee Mervyn Griffiths made the substitute go off again until he received official permission to come on.

Then came Wolverhampton's most fortunate escape. **Right back Stuart saved what had seemed a certain Spartak goal by being in the right place at the right time by the right luck.**

But Stuart had hurt himself making the vital save.

He was treated on the field and the Russian captain Simonian appeared to protest to referee Griffiths that he should be **OFF** the field.

Simonian had been involved in a similar incident when Slater was hurt, and Griffiths pushed him away.

In the meantime Pritchard had peeled off his sweater and had run on to the field as a substitute.

HE was ordered off.

Then—the match was over and the slaughter began. Hancocks put one in. Wolves 2, Spartak 0.

Before the roaring of the crowd had died away, Swinbourne, moving like a knight on a chess board, zig-zagged through to score goal number three. Wolves 3, Spartak 0.

Even more rapidly Hancocks got another in the net—but this was rightly disallowed for off-side.

But the Wolves had not finished yet—although Spartak had and were.

A minute later Hancocks scored again. Wolves 4, Spartak 0.

The Russian side had no hope now. Had this been a fight the referee would have stopped it.

But time spared Spartak—it expired and everything was over.

It was a vindication of a great English club and—I repeat—the most astonishing collapse of a first-class side that I have ever seen.

Russians say Wolves played well

By BOB FERRIER

IN the Spartak dressing room after the match Mr. Antipenok, chief of the Russian party, told the Press in front of the Spartak players: "Wolves deserved the victory. They played well."

Told that Spartak's sporting play was liked by the Wolverhampton crowd, he said: "It is not enough to be sporting. Matches are not won by standing still."

Stan Cullis, Wolves manager, said: "From a prestige point of view we have struck a great blow for English football.

"I did not allow a substitute for Stuart when he was injured because I was determined to play the game the good old British way.

"This is the proudest day of my life, more so than when Wolves won the Cup."

"Wonderful Wolves!"—Page 15.

Daily Mirror, 17 November 1954

A month later Honved, the Hungarian champions, lined up at Molineux with some of the greatest names in European football among their ranks. Kovacs, Bozsik, Kocsis, Czibor and the great Ferenc Puskas who almost alone had destroyed England a year earlier at Wembley, stood ready for action. Within fourteen minutes Honved had all but destroyed Wolves as they swept into a two-goal lead. A full house watched in amazement. But Wolves were not to be pushed aside so easily. At half time they came out a different team, spurred on by manager Stan Cullis. Within minutes they had been awarded a penalty which Hancocks neatly converted. For almost thirty minutes Wolves battled against Honved's solid defence until Roy Swinbourne hit the equaliser in the 76th minute. Wolves were now rampant and two minutes later Swinbourne appeared again to hit the winner. It had been an astonishing performance and one which would be remembered by all those watching.

'Wolves the Great' ran the headline in the *Daily Mirror*. 'After the greatest first half I have ever seen, in which the Hungarians played brilliantly and proved themselves master footballers, Wolves summoned up apparently superhuman reserves of strength and courage to grind Honved into the Molineux mud,' wrote Bob Ferrier. 'One of the greatest matches ever played anywhere,' he called it, adding that 'Wolves ... can rightly claim themselves club champions of the world.'

1954

Drama by floodlight

WOLVES THE GREAT!

WOLVES 3, HONVED 2

HANCOCKS (pen.) 49 mins.
SWINBOURNE 76 mins.
SWINBOURNE 78 mins.
Attendance: 60,000.

KOCSIS ...... 10 mins.
MATHOS ..... 14 mins.
Referee: Mr. R. Leafe (Nottingham).

THEY HAD THE NELSON SPIRIT

By BOB FERRIER

THEY DID IT AGAIN! AFTER SPARTAK, HONVED. WOLVES BEAT HONVED LAST NIGHT.

Just savour that for a moment. Wolves beat Honved, champions of Hungary and the greatest club side in the world, in one of the most glorious games I have ever seen.

It had everything—furious speed, blinding skill, pounding power, superlative goalkeeping, and something more.

Daily Mirror, 14 December 1954

FAR LEFT: *Captain Billy Wright leads out the Wolves team for their confrontation with Spartak*

BELOW: *Honved line up before their floodlit encounter with Wolves*

1955

IT WAS the French sporting daily *L'Equipe* which had the novel idea of a European Cup competition between the champions of the various European leagues. But sadly, there was little interest in England. League champions Chelsea were invited to participate and were keen to accept the invitation but the Football League intervened and refused permission. 'The management Committee felt that additional fixtures might prove difficult to fulfill,' the *Daily Mirror* reported on July 27th 1955. But it was clear from the amount of space which the *Mirror* devoted to the story and its failure to launch a campaign that it, too, had little enthusiasm for European competition.

The *Daily Herald* felt much the same way though at least it pointed the finger directly at the Football League noting that 'the Football League do not want to be represented in the European Cup. That's the obvious explanation behind yesterday's news that Chelsea have withdrawn from the competition.'

The Scottish FA, however, had no such qualms and champions Hibernian became the first British club to participate in European competition when they defeated Rot Weiss Essen 4–0 in Germany. Virtually every English newspaper failed to even give the result, let alone carry a report of the match. And so yet again, the press failed miserably to foresee a major development in the sport.

Chelsea drop out of the European Cup

CHELSEA, Football League champions, have withdrawn from the European Cup. Their notification to the Football League that they were entering the competition came before the League's Management Committee recently and after careful consideration the committee decided to ask Chelsea to consider the matter. The Management Committee felt that the additional fixtures might prove difficult to fulfil.

Daily Mirror, 27 July 1955

BELOW: *Chelsea, thwarted in their attempt to be the first English club in the European Cup*

1956

THE 1956 Cup Final belonged to two men – Don Revie and Bert Trautmann. Devising the role of the 'deep lying centre-forward', Don Revie, the Manchester City striker, displayed all the tactical expertise that would come to fruition in later years as manager with Leeds United.

Revie, however, was one of a number of City players not expected to play at Wembley that day. At odds with the club for most of the season, he had played in only one Cup game and was hardly in favour at Maine Road. There were also doubts about centre-forward Bobby Johnstone, injured with a damaged knee, and right-back Bill Leivers with ankle problems. In the event, both Johnstone and Leivers passed fitness tests, while outside-right Bill Spurdle fell ill at the last moment, leaving City manager Les McDowall with a selection problem. After consulting his directors, McDowall switched the injured Johnstone to the right wing and surprisingly handed the number nine shirt to Revie. Nobody gave City much chance except for the gipsy who claimed to have seen Revie's face in the Cup.

Manchester City's opponents, Birmingham, looked a far better prospect with the acrobatic England keeper Gil Merrick in goal and the elegant Jeff Hall at right-back. But within three minutes Manchester City, losing finalists the previous season, had struck as Don Revie set up and then back-heeled a pass for Joe Hayes to slam home. Birmingham equalised 12 minutes later through Noel Kinsey, but Scottish international Bobby Johnstone, his left knee heavily strapped, was ready to answer those who had doubted the wisdom of his selection. Twenty minutes into the second half he set up Jack Dyson's goal, and then five minutes later struck City's winner. But if Revie and Johnstone were City's stars, the unsung hero was German goalkeeper, Bert Trautmann.

Captured during the war, the former paratrooper had taken up goalkeeping with St Helens Town. Impressed by his agility, Manchester City snapped him up in 1949 when a number of other interested clubs hesitated about the reaction to signing a German in these post-war years. They should never have feared for Trautmann's bravery soon made him a favourite not only at Maine Road but won him the honour of Footballer of the Year in 1956.

GIPSY SEES DON IN CUP

• Johnny Hart may play after all—and Revie

• Johnstone's knee gone now: Spurdle doubt

Daily Herald, 5 May 1956

BELOW: *Don Revie, mastermind of Manchester City's triumph, hands the trophy to the injured Bert Trautmann*

Trautmann knew no fear and in the Wembley final showed remarkable courage after diving bravely at the feet of Birmingham's Peter Murphy. For a minute the blond keeper lay stunned. Five minutes later he was in another collision and again collapsed. Dazed, he once more lifted his giant frame and, rubbing his painful neck, carried on as if nothing had happened.

It was not until three days after the final when Trautmann had been persuaded to have an X-ray that the full extent of his injuries became known. He had a broken neck, and yet had continued regardless. It was a moment when the former soldiers on the terraces forgot about those years of fighting and saluted a brave sportsman.

1957

MANCHESTER UNITED were the first Football League club to enter the European Cup. Chelsea had been thwarted in their attempts a year earlier but manager Matt Busby would have no such dictats prohibiting his team. United began their campaign in Brussels where they comfortably beat the Belgian champions, Anderlecht, 2–0 and then in the second leg, played at Maine Road while United's new floodlights were installed, ran up a 10–0 victory. In the next round they faced the German champions, Borussia Dortmund, and in front of 75,598 at Maine Road won 3–2 after leading 3–0. The second leg was a goalless draw and United were through to the quarter-finals. Atletico Bilbao were their opponents but with United unexpectedly going down by five goals to three in the mud and snow of the San Mames stadium all looked to be lost. The Busby Babes, however, were not to be discounted and in a famous second leg, again played at Maine Road, United notched up a stunning 3–0 victory to give them a semi-final place against European champions Real Madrid.

The first leg played on Thursday April 11th in front of 120,000 in Real's magnificent Bernabau stadium sealed United's fate as they went down by three goals to one. Tommy Taylor scored United's only goal with a typical piece of poaching but Real were already two up and Mateos soon put them further ahead. The newspapers were not overimpressed by Real. 'Murder in Madrid' roared the *Daily Mail* as it blamed bad refereeing and a disallowed penalty for United's failure.

But the second leg played a fortnight later drew an altogether different response. Just over 61,000 crammed into Old Trafford as the new lights were switched on to greet the European champions. The game ended in a 2–2 draw with United going out on aggregate but drew accolades from the press. Real went on to beat Fiorentina in the final and were well on their way to winning the trophy five years in succession. Perhaps this game more than any other was to mark the turning point when the press finally realised that English football teams had no divine right to victory and heralded a transition from jingoism to admiration of foreign talent.

MURDER IN MADRID

Manchester United–hacked and slashed–end 2 goals down in the European Cup

Daily Herald, 12 April 1957

OUR CHAMPIONS GO DOWN FIGHTING

From Frank McGhee
Manchester, Thursday.

Man. Utd. 2, Real Madrid 2

THE dream is dead. Manchester United's bid to win the European Cup has ended in semi-final failure.

Brave failure. Fighting failure. Glorious failure . . . but that doesn't make it taste any less bitter to those who cherished a proud illusion that in United, England had the greatest football team in the world.

They are not. Real Madrid are the real McCoy.

Lesson

They gave Matt Busby's League champions a lesson in the basic arts and crafts of the game at Old Trafford tonight.

They had the edge in skill and stamina. And above all they had a man called Alfredo di Stefano, probably the greatest player I shall ever see.

Daily Mirror, 26 April 1957

RIGHT: *Glorious failure: United draw 2–2 with Real Madrid in the European Cup semi-final*

FOOTBALL STAR IS SOLD for £70,000

By FRANK McGHEE

JOHN CHARLES, the 6ft. 2in., twenty-five-year-old Leeds United centre forward, is to join an Italian club for the highest-ever transfer fee in British Soccer—about £70,000.

The deal between Leeds United and Juventus—of Turin—was completed yesterday.

About £60,000 of the fee will go to Leeds United, the rest to Charles, who is a Welsh international.

Daily Mirror, 20 April 1957

LEFT: *John Charles' popularity knew no bounds: a poll in* La Gazetta Dello Sport *voted him best player in the Italian league for 1958. Presenting the award is former Italian soccer star Giuseppe Meazza*

BELOW: *John Charles makes his debut for Juventus in a friendly at Biella*

BOTTOM: *Charles, the 'Gentle Giant', dominated Italian football just as he had the English game*

THE TRANSFER of John Charles, the giant Leeds United centre-forward, to the Italian club Juventus caused a sensation in Britain. Not that he was the first league player to leave our shores for more lucrative pastures. Perhaps the most prominent was Neil Franklin, the Stoke and England centre-half, who back in 1950 had joined the Colombian side, Santa Fe. Others also joined Franklin in the exodus to South America though many resisted the tempting offers. Eddie Firmani, the Charlton forward, had also signed up with another Italian club, Sampdoria of Genoa. But Charles was at the height of his career and one of the most popular characters in the game when he moved.

The massive £70,000 transfer deal which was twice the British record and not far short of the highest price ever paid in the world staggered the pundits. The Welsh international was set to receive £10,000 just for signing on and then a wage of £60 per week, four times the maximum permissable in the Football League. There were those who argued that Charles's transfer would either signal the end of the League's maximum wage policy or would lead to a spate of transfers to the rich European clubs. In the event it was the maximum wage policy which went, although Charles would be followed by a steady trickle of fellow exports.

Charles himself had played 297 games in the Football League with Leeds, scoring 151 goals before joining Juventus. In Italy the popular Welshman soon became known as the 'Gentle Giant' and went on to help the Turin club win three championships and two Cups. In August 1962 he returned to Leeds, but after only 11 games moved back to Italy, this time to Roma where he remained for a season before ending his days with Cardiff City in the second division. During the 1953/54 season Charles netted 42 goals for Leeds and scored 30 during the following season. He won his first cap for Wales in 1950 at the age of 18 and made his thirty-eighth and final appearance for his country 15 years later in 1965.

1957

THROUGHOUT THE 1950s, Cup Final after Cup Final seemed to be cursed by injury. In 1952 Wally Barnes of Arsenal limped off with a wrenched knee while, a year later, Eric Bell of Bolton was the victim with a torn muscle. In 1954 Jimmy Meadows, the Manchester City right-back, was injured and, in 1956, City's German born goalkeeper, Bert Trautmann, broke his neck. In 1957 it was a goalkeeper on the receiving end again as Manchester United's Ray Wood collided with Aston Villa's flying winger Peter McParland and had to be stretchered off the field. He returned on the wing, though only for a short period while Jackie Blanchflower deputised between the posts. With no substitutes allowed, that injury almost certainly cost United the Cup – and with it the Double.

Only 24 hours before Cup Final day the FA had met to discuss the question of substitutes but once more rejected the idea. Peter Wilson writing in the *Daily Mirror* laid the blame squarely on the shoulders of the Football Association. 'Obstinacy, sheer damn pig-headed, old-fashioned obstinacy. That's what's wrong with British sport,' he raged, revealing that 'the Football Association have again voted against the use of substitute players.' It was campaigning journalism, in which the *Mirror* excelled, at its best. But it did little good. The following year United were back at Wembley and again it was their goalkeeper, Harry Gregg, who was injured after being bundled into the back of the net with the ball. And a year later Roy Dwight of Nottingham Forest was carried off with a broken leg. In 1961 Len Chalmers of Leicester City wrenched a knee to reduce his team to ten men. The campaign for substitutes continued but it was not until the 1965/66 season that the FA and League finally relented and allowed their introduction. In the meantime a decade of Cup Finals had been virtually ruined by injury as ten men would inevitably find themselves battling against the odds on the jinxed Wembley turf.

Showpiece game became a farce, but— CUP FINAL SPECIAL

By PETER WILSON

F.A. SAY IT AGAIN: 'NO SUBSTITUTES'

BELOW: *Ray Wood (left) and Peter McParland lie prostrate after their collision in the 1957 Cup Final*

OBSTINACY. Sheer dam' pig-headed old-fashioned obstinacy. That's what's wrong with British sport.

It was revealed yesterday that the Football Association Council have again voted against the use of substitute players.

They did so on Friday—only twenty-four hours before the Cup Final—one of sport's showpieces—was turned into a farce because of the injury to United's goalkeeper Ray Wood.

The Council decided not to support an International Football Federation resolution proposing the use of substitutes in competitive matches.

THE FOLLY

Their decision will have to be confirmed at the F.A. annual meeting next month. If this happens, then England will vote against the resolution when they discuss it with Scotland, Wales and Northern Ireland at a meeting of the home international board later in June.

But how the folly of banning substitutes was spotlighted at Wembley!

Imagine it. A crowd of 100,000 had paid only £184 under £50,000 to see eleven men of Manchester oppose a like number from Birmingham.

Instead, for long periods they saw ten against eleven and never more than ten and a half against a full side.

SENTENCED

From the sixth minute onwards, sentence had been pronounced.

And only Manchester's heart and occasionally Aston Villa's ineptitude caused a stay of execution for something like sixty minutes—which, incidentally, was anything but Villa's "finest hour."

WHY, I ASK, should a massed crowd paying a rajah's ransom, be robbed of value for their tens of thousands of pounds?

WHY, I ASK, should the greatest club team this country has produced for a decade be so unfairly hamstrung?

WHY, I ASK AGAIN, should the winners' victory be tarnished for all time?

Daily Mirror, 6 May 1957

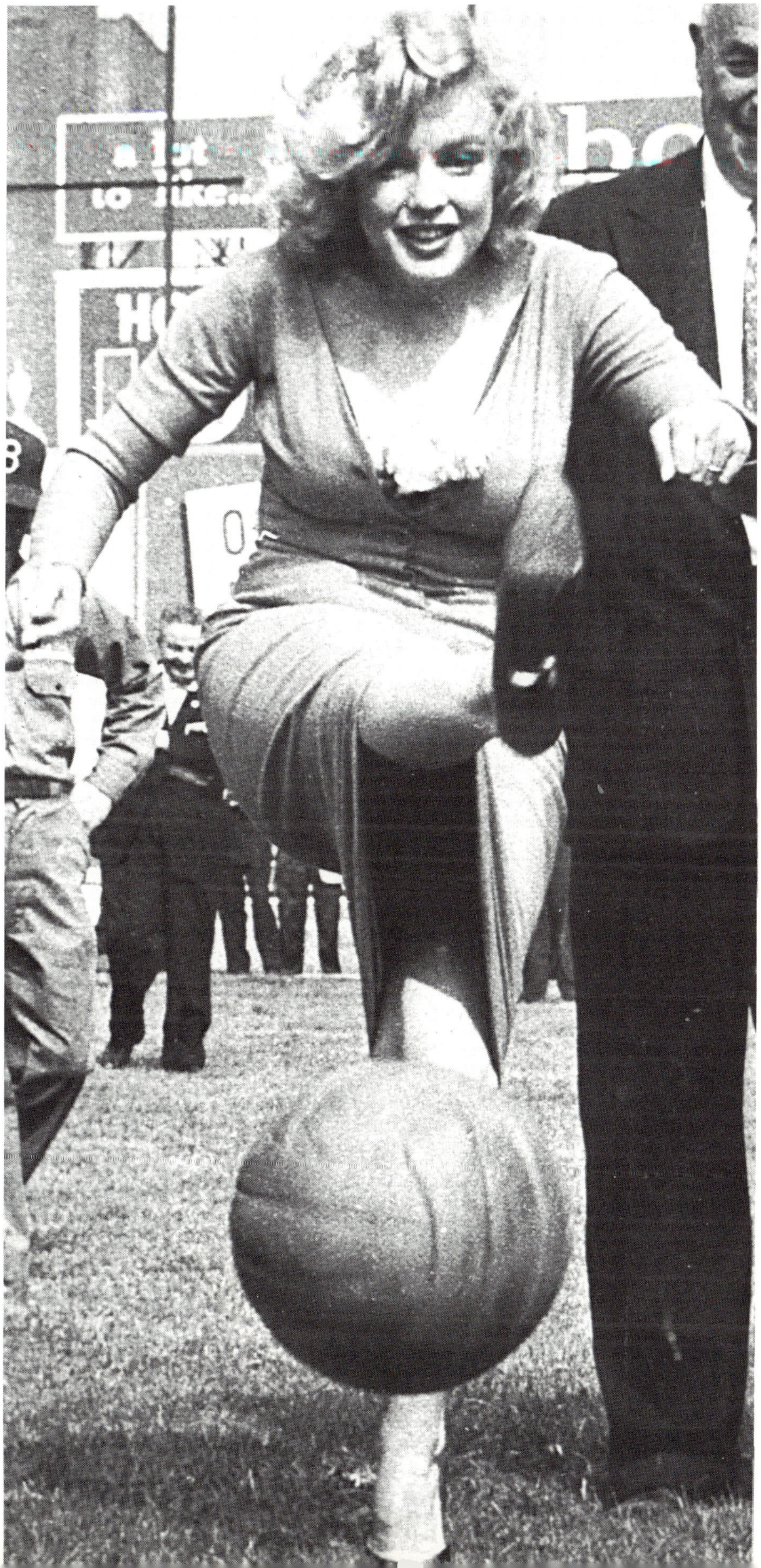

1957

Pin-ups and sport have long been vital ingredients for the successful tabloid. And if the two can be combined, it produces a winning formula.

In 1957, Marilyn Monroe was the sex symbol of the era, having recently married American playwright Arthur Miller after divorcing New York Yankees baseball star Joe di Maggio. Hardly a day passed without her photograph adorning some page of the tabloids. So, when the *Daily Mirror* snapped the Hollywood star kicking off a game between an Israeli and American soccer team in Brooklyn, it was always destined for the back page. By today's standards it seems tame, but twenty years ago it marked a watershed that would eventually lead to even more pin-ups on the sports pages as well as 'page three' girls.

The idea of scantily-clad women appearing on the sports pages, other than as competitors, would have been unthinkable to the proprietors of the *Athletic News* or the *Sporting Chronicle*. But by the 1950s, sex was beginning to regularly invade the tabloids and it would not be long before pin-ups drifted from the inside to the back pages.

LEFT: *Football gets the Hollywood seal of approval as sex symbol Marilyn Monroe kicks off a match between teams from Israel and America*

It's Marilyn!

THE elegant leg giving that football a hefty kick (above) belongs to—wait for it . . . Marilyn Monroe. She kicked the ball to start a game between Israeli and American teams at Brooklyn, New York, yesterday.

FOOTnote: Marilyn left the field limping.

Daily Mirror, 13 May 1957

1958

IT WAS IRONIC that the first papers to break the tragic news of the Munich air disaster should be Manchester's own *Evening News* and *Evening Chronicle*. The late final edition of the *Evening News*, on Thursday February 6th 1958, carried the chilling headline 'United Cup XI Crash'.

'At least 28 of the 40 aboard were killed,' it revealed, adding that 'some reports said that higher casualties were feared.' But there was little other information. The names of the dead were not known and the circumstances of the crash were a mystery. But by the following morning Fleet Street would be carrying the full horror of the disaster and its victims on their front pages. The whole nation was stunned.

Shortly before 3 pm the BEA Elizabethan airliner carrying the United party back from Belgrade after their 3–3 draw with Red Star in the European Cup quarter-final taxied ready for take off on the main runway at Munich airport where it had stopped to refuel. It was bitterly cold outside and sleet was lashing across the tarmac but they were on time, scheduled to arrive in Manchester at 5 pm. Twice, the plane attempted to take off only to turn back as the weather worsened. Then

ABOVE: *The Busby Babes shortly before they were decimated. From left to right, back row: trainer Tom Curry, Duncan Edwards, Mark Jones, Ray Wood (survived), Bobby Charlton (survived), Bill Foulkes (survived), Matt Busby (survived); front row: John Berry (survived), Bill Whelan, Roger Byrne, David Pegg, Eddie Colman*

Manchester Evening News LATE FINAL

THURSDAY FEBRUARY 6, 1958

UNITED CUP XI CRASH: "28 DIE"

Plunged into houses at Munich, exploded

SURVIVORS SAVED in BLAZING WRECKAGE

ONE of the greatest disasters to befall British football struck Manchester United this afternoon when the plane carrying the £350,000 wonder team crashed at Munich. At least 28 of the 40 aboard were killed; some reports said higher casualties were feared.

Manchester Evening News, 6 February 1958

BELOW: *The crashed BEA Elizabethan lies wrecked in the snow at Munich airport*

at 3.04 pm the Elizabethan revved its engines for the final time as it roared down the runway to disaster. Within a few moments Matt Busby's famous team lay destroyed in the sludge and chaos at the end of the runway. A public inquiry later blamed ice on the wings but no amount of blame could bring back the team that had twice been champions and Cup runners-up. The final roll call was less than originally feared with 23 dead, but included many of United's greatest talents – Roger Byrne, Tommy Taylor, Duncan Edwards, Eddie Colman, Mark Jones, Bill Whelan, Geoff Bent and David Pegg. Coach Bert Whalley and trainer Tom Curry were also among the dead. Eight football writers, who had been following United's fortunes also died, including the former England goalkeeper Frank Swift, then working with the *News of the World*, Henry Rose of the *Daily Express* and Tom Jackson of the *Manchester Evening News*. The sports page of that fateful late final edition carried Jackson's final report, filed from Belgrade when he looked forward to United's European Cup semi-final prospects. He ended his piece: 'United will never have a tougher fight than this'. Sadly he was to be wrong.

1958

THE 1958 World Cup finals heralded the arrival of Pele and the magical Brazilians. It was a new era of football that would delight and mesmerise spectators everywhere, and which for the first time was shown live on television throughout Europe. Third in 1938, runners-up in 1950 and quarter-finalists in 1954, the Brazilians came to Sweden with a proven track record but with not too many other pointers in their direction. By the end of the tournament, Brazilian football had conquered.

For the first time all four home nations qualified for the finals. Scotland contrived to finish bottom of their group while England – in the same group as Brazil – were forced into a play-off with the Soviet Union for a place in the quarter-finals. They failed, going down to the only goal of the match. Wales and Northern Ireland were also forced into play-offs but both managed to squeeze through. Nevertheless, it was short-lived with Wales losing 1–0 in the quarter-finals to the Brazilians while Ireland were easily beaten 4–0 by the French. In the semi-final Brazil overwhelmed the free-scoring French by five goals to two, to give them a place in the final against the host nation, Sweden.

It was a final billed as the Old World against the New and for the first time a team from another continent was set to capture the trophy. Yet after only four minutes, it looked as if Sweden might surprise everyone as they stormed into a one-goal lead. But within five minutes Vava had struck, sidefooting Garrincha's impeccable centre into the back of the net to level the scores. Twenty-three minutes later he scored an identical goal to give the Brazilians a slender half time lead. There may not have been much to choose between the two teams at the interval but once play was underway again, the incomparable Brazilians swept into control. Ten minutes into the second half Pele swerved past three defenders to make it 3–1, and then Zagallo struck a fourth before Pele ended the rout of the host nation with a score of 5–2.

Even the King of Sweden, hopeful of a home victory, had to admit to the superiority of the conquerors from the New World as he handed the Jules Rimet trophy to Didi who, as the linchpin of the Brazilian team, was universally acclaimed man of the match. But the youngster who had turned the Swedish defence one way and then the other, upside down and then inside out, was an eighteen-year-old by the name of Pele. It was Europe's first glimpse of the crown

ABOVE: *Pele sweeps past Swedish defenders to score the third goal for his country*

Champagne and tears as Brazil's bewildering blue shirts win the World Cup

FOOTBALL FABULOSO

Swedes swamped by ball-juggling wizards

From PETER LORENZO: Brazil 5, Sweden 2

STOCKHOLM, Sunday. — Fabuloso . . . magnifico . . . fantastico! In any language this scintillating 90-minute fiesta spells fabulous . . . magnificent . . . fantastic.

In the steamy jungle heat of the Rasunda Stadium here this afternoon, those 11 brilliant, bewildering, blue-shirted Brazilians took just 54 minutes to so deservedly snatch the World Cup prize which has eluded them for 28 years

The hands of the giant clock overlooking the ground had ticked to five minutes past four when 18-year-old inside-left Pele, a wriggling shadow of black lightning with the ball jugglery of a circus star, volleyed in a superb goal to make it 3-1.

That was the moment of doom for Sweden — the moment of justice for bubbling Brazil. You could have flashed it to the whole world then that the Jules Rimet trophy was Brazil's The remaining 36 minutes of this Soccer showpiece became scintillating, exhibition football from the world's finest craftsmen.

THIS WAS FOOTBALL FIT FOR A KING AND THE LUCKY MONARCH TO SEE IT WAS KING GUSTAV OF SWEDEN, PERCHED HIGH IN THE ROYAL BOX.

Sacramento! What a richly merited triumph for these superb Soccer senors. They conquered the Swedes, the soggy ground conditions, their own suspect temperament . . . and they crushingly silenced the hysterically partisan crowd with the finest display of ball-playing magic I have ever seen.

Sweden, the team George Raynor built, with everything in their favour—including the hope-zooming tonic of a great four-minute goal—weren't in the same Soccer world.

MESMERISED DEFENDERS

Millions of T V viewers saw for themselves the superlative mastery of these 1958 world champions.

● **THEY SAW** the fabulous Garrincha, the dusky right-winger with the magic of Stanley Matthews and the speed of Jesse Owen, lay on the first two goals.

● **THEY SAW** the towering Black Prince of inside-forwards, Didi, master mind his way through the whole 90 minutes.

● **THEY SAW** his 18-year-old inside-left apprentice Pele ever snaking, ever wriggling, and ever leaving a trail of mesmerised, head-shaking Swedes in his wake.

● **THEY SAW** the commanding Brazilian captain and centre-half, Bellini, emerge like a dominating giant to bolt up the middle.

● **THEY SAW** the superb Santos full-backs, coal black Dojalma on the right and his swarthy moustachioed namesake Nilton on his left, tackle and almost terrify Sweden's danger-wingers Hamrin and Skoglund out of the game.

Daily Herald, 30 June 1958

prince who would one day assume Stanley Matthews' mantle. At the final whistle, the young apprentice was overwhelmed with tears. Fleet Street basked in his performance. 'Ever snaking, ever wriggling and ever leaving a trail of mesmerised, head-shaking Swedes in his wake,' wrote Peter Lorenzo in the *Daily Herald*. One or two papers reminded us that England alone had managed as much as a draw with the new world champions, so we couldn't be all that bad!

BELOW: *Eighteen-year-old star of the 1958 World Cup Final, Pele, meets the Swedish goalkeeper in mid-air*

1959

9 CLUBS IN POLIO DRAMA

Daily Mirror, 25 March 1959

AFTER three operations to combat the effects of polio, surgeons battling to save international Soccer star Jeff Hall, pictured above, reported last night:

"HE IS VERY CRITICALLY ILL, BUT HOLDING HIS OWN."

Jeff, 29, Birmingham City full back whose transfer value is estimated at £25,000, was taken ill on Sunday.

Daily Mirror, 25 March 1959

Battle for life of £25,000 Soccer star Jeff

ONE SUNDAY in early March 1959, Jeff Hall, the Birmingham City and England full-back, suddenly fell ill. The following morning, still complaining of a sore throat, he failed to turn up for training at St Andrews. Five hours later he was paralysed and rushed into hospital where doctors diagnosed polio. He was immediately placed in an iron lung but despite three throat operations to relieve his breathing, his condition slowly deteriorated and two weeks later, one of England's finest defenders was dead. It was a tragic story that reverberated through the Football League.

As soon as his illness had been diagnosed, doctors warned that anyone who had had contact with Hall during the previous week should see their doctors immediately. There was a brief panic with Birmingham's three Easter games called off straight away while other Midland clubs and recent opponents anxiously gave medical checks to all their players. The Football League also advised every club to have its players vaccinated while the publicity surrounding the case led to a rush at clinics up and down the country with worried parents sensibly seeking vaccinations for themselves and their children. If a fit and healthy 29-year-old footballer could contract the disease then it was possible for anyone to be stricken down. In hindsight, the newspaper publicity which surrounded Hall's illness and death not only highlighted the danger of polio but led to the mass vaccination of the nation and may well have helped stem the spread of the killer disease.

Jeff Hall had made his debut for Birmingham in 1951 and played 227 games with the Midland club before his death. He had won the first of his 17 England caps in 1955 against Denmark and had the distinction of never being on the losing side in an England shirt. He was widely regarded as one of the most stylish left-backs in the business, always ready to skilfully play his way out of trouble rather than thump long aimless balls upfield. And although his death was much mourned throughout the football world, it possibly saved the lives of many others who sought vaccinations.

RIGHT: *Jeff Hall, whose football career tragically ended at the age of 29*

1959

THE WOLVERHAMPTON Wanderers and England centre-half Billy Wright became the first footballer in the world to win a century of international caps when he led his country out against Scotland at Wembley on April 4th. And England duly celebrated the occasion by defeating the Auld Enemy by a single goal, struck by Bobby Charlton.

But the biggest celebration had already occurred. On the Sunday morning, just hours before the England team was announced, Wright's wife, the showbiz star Joy Beverly, gave birth to their first child. Wright's marriage to one of the Beverly Sisters had thrust this private man from the back pages of the popular papers and onto the front pages. Wherever the couple went, they were followed by photographers and gossip columnists. Not surprisingly, the following morning virtually every Fleet Street paper carried the story of Wright's double triumph on their front page, complete with the inevitable photograph of the England star with his two famous sisters-in-law.

Wright had won his first cap immediately after the war when England hammered Northern Ireland 7–2 in Belfast. That day he played alongside legends such as Raich Carter, Tommy Lawton and Frank Swift while thirteen years later he was leading a new generation of players like Bobby Charlton, Johnny Haynes and Ron Flowers. He gave magnificent service to his country with 70 of his caps won consecutively, and helped Wolves to three league titles and the FA Cup in 535 league and Cup games. For a short period he stepped into football management with Arsenal, but was not wholly successful and finally quit to start a career in television.

BELOW: *Wright celebrates his 100th cap*

100th cap —and a baby girl

EVERYTHING went right for Billy Wright yesterday. An 8lb. 1oz. baby girl, and his hundredth international Soccer cap.

By JACK HARRIS

And there was a pleasant postscript to the day when I reminded him that although born right at the end of the income tax year the baby gains for Billy a whole year's child allowance rebate — £100.

The baby wasn't expected until the end of this week. But at dawn yesterday he decided to drive his wife, singer Joy Beverley, to the London Clinic.

Billy was waiting around at 8 a.m. when the baby was born.

"She was eight minutes old when I was allowed to hold her," he said.

Then later in the day he heard he had been chosen to play for England against Scotland next Saturday—his 100th international cap.

"I could not be happier," said the Wolves' 35-year-old captain. "It's my day all right."

The baby is to be called Victoria Ann. "Joy's mother was Victoria, mine was Ann," he said. "The baby's got fair hair like the Beverley family, but my nose. She's going to have a lovely voice, just like her mother's.

"We didn't mind whether it was a boy or a girl, but as I left Joy said: 'Let's have a son next time.' Oh, yes, we're planning a next-time all right."

The other Beverley sisters—Teddy and Babs—called to see Joy and the baby, bringing with them a six-inch model of a baby's cot, which had been blue (for a boy) when they bought it, but which they had hastily painted over in pink (for a girl).

Daily Herald, 6 April 1959

BELOW: *Billy Wright and the Beverley sisters – pictured in 1958 when his engagement to Joy was just a rumour*

1960

THE EUROPEAN CUP Final between Real Madrid and Eintracht Frankfurt was probably the finest exhibition of football ever seen on these shores. The game, played at Hampden Park on a warm May evening before 127,000 spectators and millions more TV viewers, mesmerised the nation and led to lashings of praise in the press the following morning. And it was two 33-year-olds who had inflicted all the damage on an Eintracht team which had managed to put 12 goals past Glasgow Rangers in the two legs of the semi-final. The 'galloping major', former Hungarian international Ferenc Puskas, hit four goals while his partner up front, the balding Argentinian Alfredo Di Stefano, struck the other three as Real went on the rampage.

Eintracht had begun well, even shooting into a dramatic lead after just 19 minutes, but that only seemed to inspire Real's famous forward line into action. Within minutes they were 2–1 ahead as they quickly grabbed control of the game. In the second half Real switched on the skills with Di Stefano hitting a memorable fourth goal that would compare with any ever seen at Hampden. Eintracht were not disgraced, they were simply overwhelmed. As the final whistle blew, 127,000 spectators stood and cheered the Spanish and European champions. The *Herald* spoke for the nation when it said, 'Thank you gentlemen for the magic memory.'

Sadly it was to be the last time Real would lift the European Cup for another six years. They reappeared in a final two years later with Puskas, Di Stefano, Del Sol and Gento still in tow but by this time their illustrious stars were beyond their best. The new champions, Benfica, had in Eusebio found a player to match any in Europe. Real had won five European Cups in a row and against Eintracht were probably at the height of their skills. In capturing the trophy that season they had scored 31 goals in just seven games. Their commitment to brave attacking football was incomparable and in their five victorious seasons they had stormed across Europe scoring 112 goals in 37 games. They will live in the memory as the finest club side to have ever graced a football pitch, with their greatest achievement that spring evening at Hampden Park.

SOCCER AS SHE IS PLAYED

Daily Mail, 19 May 1960

BELOW LEFT: *Di Stefano of Real Madrid scores one of his three European Cup-winning goals at Hampden against Eintracht Frankfurt, in front of a delighted Scottish crowd*

BELOW: *Centre-forward Alfred di Stefano (centre) looks ready to pounce as the Spanish side trounce Eintracht 7–3 in a memorable European Cup Final at Hampden Park*

by DON HARDISTY

Real Madrid .... 7 Eintracht 3

THE bald patch gets a little balder each year, but beneath it the football brain of Di Stefano remains priceless. The waistline grows more unwieldy, but the Puskas shot is still as lethal. And, of course, the European Cup remains with Real Madrid.

Hampden Park last night witnessed the systematic, ruthless slaughter of Eintracht, the excellent German champions, by the overlords of European football.

As I watched the 33-year-old aristocrats from Argentina and Hungary complete Real's fifth year of European dictatorship—Puskas hit four goals, Di Stefano three—I cringed as I remembered England's under-25 youth policy.

I felt sorry for the 127,000 spectators and the millions of viewers who have to return to English and Scottish League football next season after this dream of a game.

I can only hope the England selectors present got the point—that it doesn't matter how old you are if you can play.

The fast and fit Germans played British-style football, even to the extent of having a Tommy Docherty in right-half Hans Weilbocher to close-mark Di Stefano. It didn't matter.

Eintracht even scored first, in the 19th minute, when Weilbocher pushed the ball up to centre-forward Stein on the right wing, and outside-right Kress drove it home.

Kress, the German's best forward, incidentally, is 34!

The Germans remained cool and confident even when Di Stefano equalised in the 27th minute and even when the ambling Alfredo scored again within three minutes.

Paradise

But the slaughter really began just before half time as we were all wondering where Puskas was hiding. He answered the query by following up as the German defence cleared a breakaway by inside-right Del Sol, and made it 3—1.

Puskas added No. 4 after 54 minutes—a harsh penalty award for right back Lutz's charge on Gento. He added No. 5 later after Gento flew down the left wing and centred on the Hungarian forehead.

If this was ecstasy for the Hampden thousands, paradise was to follow with four goals in four minutes—No. 4 from Puskas (70th min.); a superb drive by Stein to make it 6—2; Di Stefano's third straight from the re-start, and two minutes later Eintracht's third from the ever-eager Stein.

The rest was superb exhibitionism—and Glasgow roared its delight at the fantastic ball control of Real.

No wonder not a soul stirred from Hampden until the Spaniards had completed their tour of triumph with the cup which they never looked like losing.

Eintracht: Loy; Lutz; Heofer; Weilbocher, Eigenbrodt, Stinka; Kress, Lindner, Stein, Pfaff, Meier.

Real Madrid: Dominguez; Marquitos, Pachin; Vidal, Santamaria, Zarraga; Canario, Del Sol, Di Stefano, Puskas, Gento.

1960

We won't play in new competition, say glamour clubs

BIG FIVE SHUN LEAGUE CUP

Daily Mail, 18 June 1960

The League Cup was not always as popular as it is today. When its introduction was first announced in June 1960, it brought an immediate outburst from the leading clubs with three of the previous season's top four from the first division all refusing to participate. Tottenham manager Bill Nicholson blasted League officials, accusing them of demanding far too much from players and in turn called for a smaller first division with less games. In all, five clubs shunned the first League Cup, Wolves, Tottenham, West Bromwich Albion, Arsenal and Sheffield Wednesday, and consequently the competition was hardly a success.

Aston Villa was the first name to be engraved on the trophy after a two-legged final which could only draw 43,428 spectators over the two games. The following season was even more of a disaster as a host of first division clubs opted out and it was not until the League hit upon the idea of having a single game final, played at Wembley, that the trophy began to take on a profitable look. That first Wembley Final in 1967 was an enormous success with a near capacity crowd of 98,000 watching third division QPR beat first division West Brom by three goals to two. Gate receipts were £57,000 and the following season everyone participated. The Cup quickly went on to establish itself as one of the highlights of the footballing calendar with gate receipts for the final soon hitting the £1 million mark.

There's too much Soccer already insist Tottenham

By ROY PESKETT

FIVE crack First Division clubs have told the Football League : "Count us out of your proposed new League Cup competition." They are Wolverhampton Wanderers, the Cup holders, Tottenham, West Bromwich Albion, Arsenal, and Sheffield Wednesday. Without these five star-spangled teams the competition will, inevitably, lose much of its glamour.

Daily Mail, 18 June 1960

BELOW: *Villa with the League Cup*

1960

ABOVE: *Peterborough United's £100,000 grandstand. The 'Posh' won their place in the fourth division by scoring 134 goals in 46 games after a wait of 20 years*

The 'Posh' are in after 21 years

by ALAN HOBY

FOR 20 years Peterborough United have been trying to break into League football. And for 20 years "The Posh"—as they are called by their proud and patient fans—have had their application thrown out by the shameful "jolly old pals" act of the League clubs.

But yesterday—at the 21st time of trying—Peterborough enjoyed their "finest hour."

For at 11.41 a.m. the big clubs, at their annual meeting in London, elected the brave and indomitable "Posh" to membership of the Football League.

As the applause at Peterborough's magnificent and so richly deserved success rippled through the packed conference room, I caught a glimpse of Peterborough manager, Jimmy Hagan, who, in his England heyday, played alongside such all-time masters as Tommy Lawton, Stanley Matthews, Wilf Mannion, and Raich Carter.

'MY DREAD . . .'

Hagan, who was wearing the broadest smile of his life, told me afterwards: "It's wonderful news.

"Before the meeting I was half-pessimistic, half-optimistic! You never know what they are going to do and we have had so many bitter disappointments.

Sunday Express, 29 May 1960

AT THE twenty-first time of asking, Peterborough United were finally elected to the fourth division of the Football League in 1960. And if ever a team deserved their promotion it was Peterborough who, season after season, had demonstrated with their gallant cup runs that they had class and quality to compete with the best of the lower divisions.

Peterborough were known as the 'Posh' because of their stylish London Road ground with its five star facilities. They compared with those of any other club in either the third or fourth divisions and were considered superior to most. The ground held 30,000 with 16,000 of those under cover, they had first-rate offices and dressing rooms, and under ambitious manager Jimmy Hagan, had erected floodlights and drawn up plans for a new stand.

A non-league side since they had been formed in 1923, they had been fully professional for 26 years, playing in the Midland League when the call finally came. But it was their Cup record which had most impressed league officials and other clubs. In 1954 they had battled their way through to the third round of the FA Cup before losing 3–1 to first division Cardiff. Three years later they were back, this time beating second division Lincoln 5–4 after a 2–2 draw before going out in the fourth round to Huddersfield Town. In 1959 they lost by the only goal of the match to a Fulham side on the verge of promotion. Their greatest success as a non-league side came the following season when they travelled to second division Ipswich and came away with a 3–2 win, only to lose 2–0 in the next round to high-flying Sheffield Wednesday.

1961

WHAT A WAY TO RUN A SPORT!

IDIOTIC is the word for the Football League's latest move in their dispute with the players.

Faced with a strike on Saturday, the League yesterday told the clubs to play Saturday's matches on Friday.

Even if the players agree, how on earth can this gimmick help achieve Soccer peace?

Time and again during this long wrangle, League spokesmen have made statements which suggest they know **NOTHING** about labour relations.

What is the good of League President Joe Richards telling the players that he has said "his last word"—when he changes his mind almost at once?

Right after saying this last week, Richards agreed to another meeting at the Ministry of Labour.

Get Down To It!

League Secretary Alan Hardaker objects to other trade unions giving their support to the Professional Footballers' Association.

But British unions have been supporting each other during disputes for half a century and more.

Tomorrow the League meet the players at the Ministry of Labour.

The strike can still be stopped—**IF** the League bosses realise that a serious industrial row **CANNOT** be handled by provocative dodges.

—But ONLY by real give-and-take.

Daily Mirror, 17 January 1961

IN 1961 STRIKE action threatened to bring the Football League to a standstill for the first time in its 73-year history. But, typically, at the last minute the strike was averted as the two sides reached an amicable agreement over sandwiches at the Ministry of Labour on January 18th. The dispute had predictably been about money and contracts. The maximum wage policy had been in force for sixty years and in 1961 stood at £20 a week. It was not a great deal of money, although it allowed footballers a comfortable living compared with many. But with John Charles and others already lured abroad by astronomical salaries, English football faced the prospect of losing many more stars. That particular dispute was settled on January 9th when after considerable haggling the maximum wage was abolished, but the League still refused to budge on player's contracts. What was in dispute here was the right of a player to demand a transfer at the end of his contract. The players called it a 'slave contract' which bound them to a club for life, but the clubs argued that few footballers had been refused their requests. At the centre of the row were two players: George Eastham of Newcastle United, who had been refused a transfer and who was challenging his club in the courts, and Jimmy Hill, chairman of the player's union, the Professional Footballers' Association.

There was considerable bitterness on both sides with the PFA poised to take strike action on January 21st. Being an industrial dispute, the story soon showed up on the leader pages

BELOW: *PFA chairman Jimmy Hill lashes out at the League's continuing refusal to abolish the maximum wage*

Daily Mirror

[illegible] Thursday, January 19, 1961 • No. 17,757

SOCCER STRIKE OFF

By BILL HOLDEN

THE football strike is OFF. . . . Saturday's Football League matches are ON. And this week's Pools are ON, using the normal fixture list.

This dramatic news follows last night's vital "peace" meeting in London between the Football League and the 2,000-member Professional Footballers' Association.

'Slavery' Goes

The League agreed, after nearly five hours of talking, to **SCRAP** the "slavery" contract which binds footballers to clubs for life.

The League have already agreed to end the present £20 a week maximum wage. They have also agreed to a new minimum retaining wage ranging from £12 in Division IV to £15 in Division I.

Daily Mirror, 19 January 1961

ABOVE: *George Eastham finally signs for Arsenal after a long battle to secure his release from Newcastle*

RIGHT: *The strike is off. Jimmy Hill and Minister of Labour John Hare emerge from talks with the League*

with the left-wing *Daily Mirror* backing the players in a hard-hitting editorial. 'What a Way to Run a Sport,' it barked, slamming League Secretary Alan Hardaker for his incompetence. With the Tory press taking a similar line the League was isolated, and with just 48 hours to go, it backed down shame-facedly. For the two leading actors, the dispute had extraordinary consequences. George Eastham won his battle and left Newcastle for Arsenal where he enjoyed a successful career, winning 19 England caps, while Jimmy Hill, who had argued the players' case so convincingly in front of the news cameras was immediately offered a job on television.

1961

SATURDAY APRIL 15th 1961 was the most humiliating day in Scottish footballing history and for goalkeeper Frank Haffey, playing in only his second international, it would be a day he would always want to forget, as Scotland ended their annual tussle with the Auld Enemy, beaten by nine goals to three.

Bobby Robson had opened the scoring for England who by half time had gone into a 3–0 lead. Within two minutes of the resumption Scotland had pulled a goal back and four minutes later the score was 3–2. But after that Scotland fell apart as Jimmy Greaves led the storming of the Scottish goal. In all the Chelsea forward hit three goals, with Bobby Smith of Spurs and Johnny Haynes of Fulham striking two each, and Bryan Douglas the Blackburn winger netting the other.

The combination of Douglas, Greaves, Smith, Haynes and Charlton up front was devastating. 'It was the finest English forward line I have ever seen,' wrote Alan Hoby in the *Sunday Express* the following morning. In five consecutive internationals England had struck 32 goals as they beat Northern Ireland 5–2, Luxembourg 9–0, Spain 4–2 and Wales 5–1 before hammering the Scots. As if that was not enough, in their next game they thrashed Mexico 8–0 to give a grand total of 40 goals in six games. Hoby was right, this was probably the most devastating spell English international football had ever known. There may have been high scoring England teams in the past but that hardly compared with a time when international competition was much tougher. And Scotland, boasting such fine players as Denis Law, Ian St John, Billy McNeill and Dave Mackay, were hardly a soft option.

Poor Frank Haffey – the Celtic goalkeeper who had been a late replacement – walked away from Wembley a disgraced man, never to wear

ABOVE: *Bobby Robson scores the first of his three goals against Scotland*

ABOVE: *The unfortunate Haffey allows goal number four to sweep past him*

THE MAN WHO LET 9 GOALS THROUGH

Greaves dazzles in rout of Scotland

ENGLAND 9 SCOTLAND 3: by ALAN HOBY

SCORERS: Robson, Greaves (3), Douglas, Smith (2), Haynes (2): Mackay, Wilson, Quinn.

THIS was slaughter in the spring sunshine. Dancing and prancing across the matchless Wembley turf, the white-shirted Wizards of England not only slammed their highest-ever score against Scotland—7—2 to England in 1955 was the previous best—but they shattered all goal-scoring records at Wembley. England—wonderful England—have now hammered the fantastic total of 32 goals in five internationals.

Sunday Express, 16 April 1961

It was the finest England forward line I have ever seen. Drilled and disciplined, turning the pace on and off in the best Real Madrid style and spraying the ball man to man in a stream of pinpoint passes, England enjoyed their finest triumph.

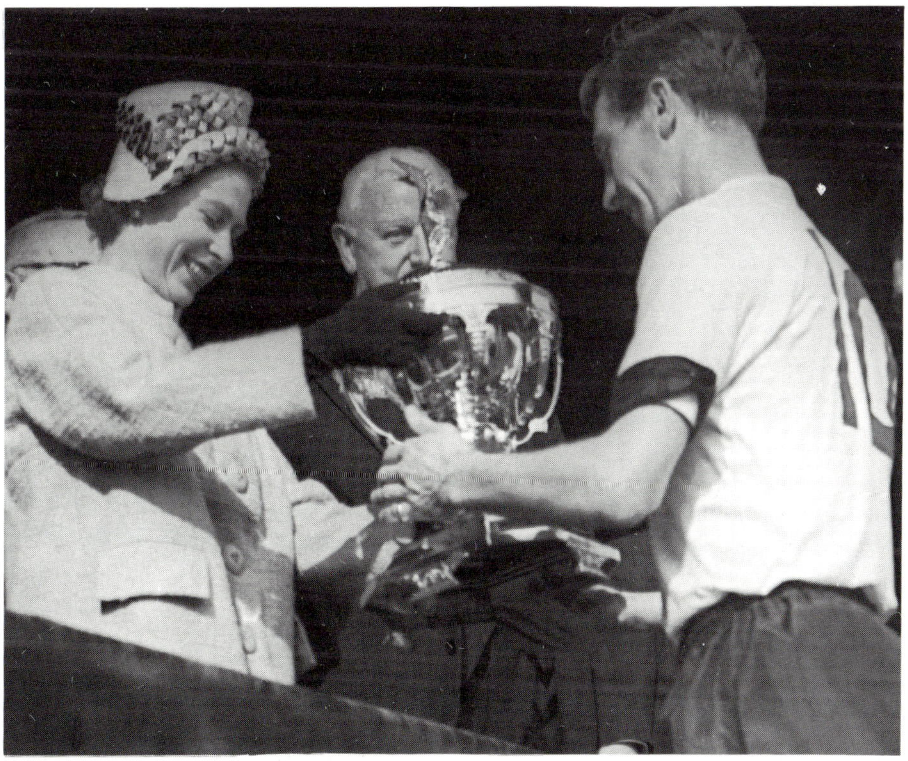

ABOVE: *Johnny Haynes receives the trophy after England's 9–3 victory*

the famous colours of his nation again, though he could hardly be blamed for all nine goals. The *Sunday Express* recorded each moment of English glory and Scottish shame with nine separate photographs showing Haffey stretching, fumbling, and askance as each goal ripped past him. Other papers preferred to simply capture him at the end of the match walking dejectedly towards the Wembley dressing rooms, head bowed, cutting a lonely and broken figure.

1961

NOT SINCE the gas-lit Victorian days of 1897 had any team achieved the magic double of FA Cup and league championship. But on May 6th 1961, Tottenham Hotspur, guided by their genial Irish captain Danny Blanchflower, beat Leicester City 2–0 at Wembley to become the first team since Aston Villa all those years ago to lift the two trophies in the same season. And what's more, it was a team fully deserving of the honour and a team which could stand proudly alongside the Preston 'Invincibles', Sunderland's 'team of all the talents', the Huddersfield Town and Arsenal sides of the 1920s and 1930s respectively and the Wolves and Manchester United teams of the 1950s.

At the back of their defence stood the imposing figure of Scottish international goalkeeper, Bill Brown, while in front of him, full-backs Roy Henry and Peter Baker sternly punished any adventuring forwards. Danny 'the Lip' Blanchflower, the towering Maurice Norman at centre-half and the awesome Dave MacKay at left-half, equally ensured that few attackers braved their fearsome tackles. But it was up front where Tottenham's greatest strengths lay, Out on the left wing Terry Dyson, all of 5 feet 3 inches (and said to be smallest man to have played in a Wembley final), regularly squeezed his way to the by-line while on the opposite flank Welsh international Cliff Jones could mesmerise and slip his way through the tightest defences. And the three men inside, the elegant John White, Les Allen and the bulky England striker Bobby Smith, supplied most of the 136 goals that Spurs had rattled up to win the Double. Leicester may have been

A WONDER GOAL—AND SPURS TAKE CUP AND DOUBLE

Sunday Express, 7 May 1961

ABOVE: *After a goalless first half, Bobby Smith's 69th minute goal put Spurs on the road to victory*

struck by injury – put down to the so called Wembley 'hoodoo' jinx – but even with their full complement of players they could never match Spurs' formidable line-up. It was a side dedicated to attack with 31 league victories and only seven defeats all season. The following year they reached the semi-finals of the European Cup only to lose narrowly to the eventual winners, Benfica, but they did retain the FA Cup with a 3–1 victory over Burnley. Having won three trophies in two seasons and they were still not finished as they added the European Cup-Winners' Cup to their collection in 1963.

Injury hoodoo shakes the Leicester rhythm

TOTTENHAM HOTSPUR 2 (Smith, Dyson) LEICESTER CITY 0

H.T. 0—0 Attendance 100,000 Receipts £49,813

AT exactly 4.45 yesterday afternoon an ear-splitting racket of sound rose from the giant grey bowl of Wembley Stadium. It was a roar full of triumph and joy and it came from the mighty host of Tottenham fans in the 100,000 crowd. For at that moment—as Referee Jack Kelly's whistle shrilled "Time"—Tottenham Hotspur became the first club of the century to win the fabulous Cup and League double

Sunday Express, 7 May 1961

ABOVE: *Danny Blanchflower, captain of the first Double-winning side since 1897, proudly holds the FA Cup*

1962

FOR 64 SEASONS, Headington United had quietly played on the outskirts of Oxford, including 11 in the Southern League. Then in 1960 the directors decided to change the club's name to Oxford United. It was an inspired decision which along with other initiatives dramatically changed their fortunes. The following two seasons they were champions of the Southern League and with Accrington Stanley dropping out of the fourth division in 1962 after just 33 games, Oxford applied to take their place. At the League's annual general meeting on Saturday June 2nd, Wigan Athletic were their only opponents for the spare place in the fourth division. The league clubs duly cast their secret vote and Oxford romped home with 39 votes against Wigan's five. 'I think the club has a fair future,' said manager Arthur Turner humbly. It was to be an understatement.

They finished in eighteenth place in their first two seasons in division four, before winning promotion in 1965. Oxford were on their way and after just two seasons in the third division they were champions and bound for division two. But the success story came to an abrupt halt and a couple of seasons later Oxford found themselves slipping back into the third division. In 1984, however, they were promoted again and the following season finished as champions of division two. Twenty-three years after joining the League they had made it to the first division.

OXFORD IN THE LEAGUE NEXT SEASON

Sunday Express, 3 June 1962

ABOVE: *Oxford United 1964. A year later they were champions of the fourth division*

1963

NOT SINCE the end of World War Two had Britain shivered as it did during the dreadful winter that struck during January and February 1963. Temperatures dropped to well below freezing and football slid to a standstill. On Saturday January 5th only three third round FA Cup games were played. Television cameras, slithering up and down snowbound Britain to find a game that was certain to be played, ended up at unglamorous Prenton Park, home of Tranmere Rovers, where the fourth division side were playing Tommy Docherty's Chelsea. The following Saturday turned out to be the bleakest day in league football with all but a couple of games called off. On the 19th January only eight matches were played and a week later with conditions worsening again, just six pitches were playable.

The pools companies had never experienced such chaos as three coupons in a row were declared null and void with the dividend passed on to the following week, promising a bumper jackpot for someone once football began again. But with prospects of a fourth week's cancellation, the pools companies latched on to the idea of a panel of experts forecasting the results. And so, on Saturday January 26th, Tom Finney, Tommy Lawton, Ted Drake, George Young and the former referee Arthur Ellis were closeted away to choose the draws. And for this leisurely task each was paid £100.

Although the notion of a pools panel was a novel one, it did not win universal acclaim. 'Soccer Fans In Storm Over Phantom 12X' ran the headline in the *News of the World* as it reported that 'people were calling it a farce'. The panel had selected seven draws, eight aways and 23 homes, leaving one punter richer by hundreds of thousands of pounds. The panel however had restored weekly fun for millions who each Wednesday or Thursday would sit down to select their eight draws and hopefully win a fortune.

BELOW: *'I can't agree there Tommy. I think Preston would have been hammered!' Making the pools panel decisions are ex-Arsenal and England forward Ted Drake, former referee Arthur Ellis, Tom Finney, Tommy Lawton and George Young*

POOLS RUMPUS

Soccer fans in storm over phantom 12X

By FRANK BUTLER

FURIOUS arguments broke out among pools fans all over the country last night over the phantom results selected by the five football experts.

One thing is certain. Nobody is going to end up rich. The dividend forecast for 24 points on the 2d. treble chance is £3,850.

This shows at least that the five experts, Tom Finney, Ted Drake, Tommy Lawton, George Young and Arthur Ellis, kept pretty well to form. They selected seven draws, eight aways, 23 homes.

The rumpus began after millions of fans watched Lord Brabazon, chairman of the panel, announce the results on TV.

Unsuccessful pools fans were naturally disgruntled and called the whole scheme a farce. But many people thought the panel did well.

Lord Brabazon commented: "I think the results, in view of the climatic conditions, were well received but I am only an amateur and have no views on the results."

During the day there were rumours that huge fees had been paid to the panel. But a spokesman of the Pools Promoters' Association refused to say how much they received.

He told me: "The question of Lord Brabazon's fee was raised but he said: 'I regard this as a public duty. The pools have given me a lot of pleasure and this is where I can do a public service and pay a little back.'"

I understand the experts received about £100 each plus expenses.

"We were dead right on all the panel's selections—it was the games actually played that mucked us up!"

News of the World, 27 January 1963

1964

TOP SOCCER STARS BRIBED

They agreed to 'fix' a First Division match

They backed Sheffield Wednesday, their own team, to lose against Ipswich, and each won £100 in a betting coup

The People, 12 April 1964

Peter Swan

Tony Kay

David Layne

FOOTBALL FANS all over Britain woke up on the morning of Sunday April 12th 1964 to read about the biggest scandal in soccer history. On the front page of the *People* was a story linking three first division players, two of whom were England internationals, with a betting ring to fix matches. The story later led to the imprisonment of all three players after a long investigation and trial.

The story was in the best traditions of investigative journalism. Led by Mike Gabbert, later to become the controversial editor of the *Star*, the *People*'s reports were spread over several weeks, winning the paper a galaxy of reporting awards.

At the centre of the scandal were three Sheffield Wednesday players – Peter Swan, Tony Kay and 'Bronco' Layne. Swan, the Wednesday centre-half since 1958 had won 19 England caps. David 'Bronco' Layne had joined the club in 1962 from Bradford City for £16,000 and was already proving to be a natural goalscorer. The third culprit, Tony Kay, was no longer with Wednesday having been transferred to Everton for a record £55,000 in late December 1962. With six England under-23 caps, plus one at full international level, half-back Kay had just inspired Everton to the league championship.

All three were accused of having backed their own team, Sheffield Wednesday, to lose at Ipswich in a league fixture played on December 1st 1962. Ipswich had won the game 2–0 and the three players were said to have won £100 each on the bet.

The naming of the three first division players was merely the beginning, however. The rot went much deeper and was far more prevalent in the lower divisions. The *People* was assisted in its investigations by Jimmy Gauld, the former Everton and Charlton inside-forward who had turned informer after acting as go-between. On December 1st he had helped fix three games including the Wednesday fixture. The others were the third division match between Lincoln and Brentford, and the fourth division game at York where Oldham were the visitors. Bets were placed on three home wins and that was precisely how the results turned out.

The following week there were further revelations in the newspaper with the Scottish international goalkeeper, Dick Beattie, named. Also accused were Walter Bingley of Halifax, Jackie Fountain of York, Ron Howells of Walsall, Bert Linnecor of Lincoln, Peter Wraggs of Bradford and Harry Harris of Portsmouth. The Football League took immediate action with most of the players suspended for life while others like Kay, Swan and Layne ended up in court where they received heavy prison sentences. It was one of the most shameful episodes in football history but without a press dedicated to digging up the facts, corruption in the game might have gone on much longer.

1965

STANLEY MATTHEWS was a national institution but there had to come a time when the old maestro would finally hang up his boots. So after 33 years of treading the football pitches of Britain, he finally quit at the end of the 1964/65 season. His last league match was played on Saturday February 6th 1965 when he helped Stoke beat Fulham 3–1 in front of nearly 30,000 at the Victoria Ground. It was his first appearance of the season and though nobody knew it at the time, it was also to be his final league game. Although the wizard failed to score, he set up Stoke's third goal and, according to the *Sunday Express*, showed all the old graceful touches.

A specially arranged friendly at the end of the season, to mark Matthews' retirement, gave Fleet Street their missed opportunity to wax lyrical. Peter Wilson, writing in the *Daily Mirror*, marked the occasion as if the King himself had passed on by inserting a thick black border around his piece. Probably no other footballer in history had ever warranted such an accolade. But Matthews, now Sir Stanley, was no ordinary mortal.

He had joined Stoke after leaving school at the age of 14 in 1928. A year later he was playing in the reserves and during the 1931/32 season made his league debut at the precocious age of 17. Stoke won promotion to the first division the following season and in 1934 the youngster was in the England team, winning the first of his 54 caps. Shortly after the war he left Stoke for Blackpool, played in three Cup Finals and in the memorable 1953 Final helped turn a 3–1 deficit into a 4–3 victory that gave Blackpool the Cup. In 1961 he nostalgically returned to second division Stoke and a year later the Potteries club were sensationally back in the First Division. In all, the maestro made 886 appearances in first-class matches, and became the oldest player ever to appear in a first division game when five days after his fiftieth birthday he beat Billy Meredith's record.

Farewell to this King of British sport . .

From PETER WILSON

Stoke, Wednesday

WHEN a King died, they used to print newspapers with thick black lines around the articles.

It was old fashioned—but I wish I could do it around this piece today*. For this is the farewell of the King of British sport.

Today, Wednesday, April 28, 1965, Stan Matthews — now officially renowned as Sir Stanley Matthews, CBE—appears for the last time on an English football field.

To be here today if you are of the same age as Stanley Matthews—he was 50 nearly three months ago so there is little more than eighteen months between us—is to die of pernicious anaemia.

NOT to have been here would have been to commit deliberate suicide.

In my lifetime, preoccupied with sport, we have had in this country so traditionally devoted to sport perhaps less than ten champions whose retirement or defeat signalled the end of an era.

Sir Jack Hobbs, Sir Gordon Richards Fred Perry, Jimmy Wilde, Henry Cotton, Joe Davis and Roger Bannister.

But even when you list those, you are still left with something less than Stan Matthews.

For Soccer is **THE** game in these islands.

You may not like it best. **I** may not—in truth I don't.

But we are democratic in sport and this is Britain's favourite sport.

And has there EVER been a player like Matthews, S., Stanley Matthews, Sir Stanley Matthews, CBE?

The progression of his nomenclature marks the changing pace of sport in Britain.

Tribute

Today, players, writers and—well, just let's call them friends—converged on Stoke on a typical wet English mid-week day.

Not just to pay homage to a genius, but to pay tribute to a man who has given so much to our most popular game.

And I don't care if he has, in fact I hope he has, made tens upon thousands of pounds out of it. **The sport is still in his debt.**

I'm not going into the old obvious stories — the Blackpool victory which will always be known as "The Stanley Matthews Cup Final," the return to Stoke on October 28, 1961, and what has happened to the Pottery club since.

Daily Mirror, 29 April 1965

Fit after my first game at 50—it was great to be back

NOW I'M READY FOR MORE!

Sunday Express, 7 February 1965

I enjoyed my tussles with Jim Langley

by STANLEY MATTHEWS

THE dressing room is silent. The crowd has gone home. And as I look back upon my 710th League game my first for more than 12 months—I can say: I am ready to play again whenever Stoke need me.

If they have any injuries I shall be in the background ready to help out. This week, if need be, for I felt as fit after the game against Fulham yesterday as I did when I ran out to face the crowd.

I always have "butterflies" before a match and never more so than on this occasion. But the fans helped to reassure me—it was simply wonderful to hear their roar of welcome again.

Some people have been wondering if I was wise to play League football again at the age of 50.

In my own mind I never had any doubts about my fitness. Stamina never worried me. I train regularly, and I would never have played had I not felt 100 per cent fit.

Some ask: Is it fair for a man 50 years old to play against defenders who may be inclined to lay off because of my age?

That's their argument, but I expect to be played as though I was any other winger. I am ready to take the knocks.

The maestro still shows his magic

by JAMES MOSSOP

Stoke 3 Fulham 1

THIS could have been a half-century gimmick. A day for old bones to rattle along the line a couple of times so that another entry might be scribbled in the record books.

But it wasn't. Stanley Matthews proved that he was right and the critics were wrong.

As City vice-chairman Albert Henshall said: "Fantastic. This man Matthews is incredible. We have written him off so many times and always he has bounced back to prove how wrong we have been. Now he has done it again."

RIGHT: *The maestro's final appearance against Fulham was to be his last*

1965

THE 'SWINGING SIXTIES' belonged to the city of Liverpool. The Beatles and a host of other scouse pop groups had taken Britain by storm, flooding the hit parade with their unmistakable sound. Everywhere, the music of Gerry and the Pacemakers, the Searchers, the Big Three, the Undertakers, the Swinging Blue Jeans and of course John, Paul, George and Ringo blasted from juke boxes and radios. It was hardly surprising then that the thousands who crammed into the Spion Kop at Anfield should adopt music to inspire their heroes every Saturday. 'You'll Never Walk Alone', a hit for Gerry and the Pacemakers, would eventually become the anthem of Anfield but before then, an old Liverpool children's skipping song, 'Ee-aye-addio', was adopted and adapted to suit every occasion.

When Liverpool reached their third Cup Final, the singing Kop accompanied Bill Shankly and his team down the motorway and for the first time brought the musical sounds of Merseyside to the terraces of Wembley. It was a memorable occasion even if the game itself did not live up to expectations. Liverpool, first division champions the previous season had finally climbed out of the ignominy of the second division but had yet to win the FA Cup. Their challengers, Leeds United, were similarly returning to the glory days. Runners-up in the league that season, their team was still maturing under manager Don Revie into what would eventually become one of the most formidable sides in soccer.

In a dour battle, that suddenly exploded in extra time when Ian St John hit Liverpool's winner, the rafters of the old stadium reverberated to the voices of singing scousers. And the chant that went up was 'Ee-aye-addio, we've won the Cup'. When the *Liverpool Football Echo* ran its own version of the song on the front page that evening – 'Ee-aye-addio, the Reds have won the Cup!' – it surely spoke for the whole of the city of Liverpool.

ABOVE: *Ian St John's extra-time winner*

LIVERPOOL 2 LEEDS UNITED 1

EE-AYE-ADDIO, THE REDS HAVE WON THE CUP!

By LESLIE EDWARDS

When Ronnie Yeats led his team out onto the lush Wembley pitch, Liverpool fans almost brought down the Wembley roof with their enthusiasm. With the sun failing to come through, it was not a spectacularly colourful Wembley, but the humour of Liverpool contingent more than enlightened the gloom. After the arranged community singing ended the chant "Ee-aye-addio we're going to see the Queen." The receipts were £89,000, and what they cost in aggregate including black market transactions, is anyone's guess.

The Duke of Edinburgh spent a few minutes in conversation with Ron Yeats and Manager Shankly and seemed to have particular attention also for the three match officials.

The side which defended the dressing room end would have the advantage of playing with the wind in the first half. Yeats won this advantage for Liverpool. Strong certainly started up in the right half position. Bremner left the field immediately before the kick-off to hand a ring to Revie at the touchline.

Stevenson was soon seen to be calming his colleagues in the first minutes in which no [illegible] produced anything [illegible]. The first foul was by Collins on St John, and Stevenson took it but a big clearance by left half Hunter removed all the danger.

Foul By Collins

Lawrence picked up a good length [illegible] from Reaney after Collins had found the full back going down the right wing like an express train.

Then Thompson came into the centre circle to start Liverpool's first real attack, which Collins ended with a heavy foul against Byrne who needed trainer's attention.

At teh same time, Hunter was having attention for a left leg injury he had received a moment or two before Byrne went down. Thus within the space of a few minutes both trainers had been on, and both sides had players suffering fairly severe knocks.

Bremner was now sandwiched by Byrne and Smith and was brought down heavily just outside the penalty box, Johanneson and Bell having initiated this first Leeds attack of any importance.

Bremner also needed attention. Leeds' free kick ruse with Bremner feinting to take the award, and in fact Collins doing so, came unstuck, and the game continued in its tentative vein.

Sharp Tackling

Charlton was dominant in the air but now he misheaded a big clearance kick by Lawrence, and yet the mistake cost his side nothing.

Charlton did well to nod for a corner a big right foot shot by Strong, and although Liverpool were inclined to play the ball across the field too much it was clear that they were prepared to shoot whenever opportunity offered.

Stevenson was unlucky not to be able to hold and control a very fine pass by St. John and then Lawrence came to the edge of his box to kick away direct, rather than chance fielding the ball with Johanneson around. Collins won a brave tackle against St. John, then dug the ball up in a cheeky reverse pass for Sprake.

Hunt made the best run of the game so far with an interchange of passes with St. John, and the pity was that his right foot shot at the end of it all should pass over the bar.

Leeds were rather pedestrian in their play and so far at least, there was no doubt that Liverpool had the edge on them.

Glorious Run

St. John made a glorious individual run and dribble [illegible] a final pass to Callaghan that invited him to score, and he most certainly would have I think, if Charlton had not taken the shot full amidships to turn it for a corner.

Not unexpectedly he was yet once more to need the trainer's attention. A bad foul by St. John on Johanneson, who was streaking away after the corner kick had been cleared led to referee Clements having a very stern word of caution with the Liverpool player.

Leeds covered up well in defence, and now started to play good constructive stuff for the first time, but Byrne and Stevenson between them [illegible]ded their good right wing attack. Neither Leeds back was slow to come up into the attack, and Bell now won a corner on the left.

Collins floated this one in splendidly, but when Peacock got his head to it he got too far under the ball which sailed innocuously over the bar. A fine cross field pass by Bremner just beat the head of Peacock by inches and went in for a goal kick.

Bremner was now in the wars, and Leeds United trainer came on yet again—surely the greatest spate of stoppages ever to afflict the continuity of a showpiece match like this. And now with the sky getting darker and darker, rain began to fall.

The Liverpool attack was playing with much greater fluency than Leeds, but a good number of their shots were crowded out by a defence which gave very little away.

Giles now came to the left wing to initiate with Collins one of Leeds best attacks, and after a rather shaky beginning, the Yorkshire side were now settling down to play some good closely linked stuff.

Sprake failed to grasp a fine centre from Callaghan, who had been found by St. John but happily for Leeds, right winger Giles dropped back and was there to pick up the loose ball and take it away.

St. John was much too bold with an attempt at a through pass, having brought the ball out of defence, and though Liverpool were having the better of it, they still had to make their superiority count.

Playing It Cool

Leeds made pretty poor use of the several freekicks they had been given so far. Lawler extricated himself from difficulty near the corner flag with Johanneson in attendance and the possibility of a reverse pass to Lawrence to dangerous to contemplate.

Sprake was able to pick up with time to spare, a tentative back header by Reaney. Liverpol were playing it coolly and safe in defence.

How They Lined Up

LIVERPOOL

Right Lawrence Left

Lawler Byrne

Strong Yeats Stevenson

Callaghan Hunt St. John Smith Thompson

Referee: Mr. W. Clements ● (West Bromwich)

Johanneson Collins Peacock Storrie Giles

Hunter Charlton Bremner

Bell Reaney

Left Sprake Right

LEEDS UNITED

Liverpool Football Echo, 1 May 1965

ABOVE: *Liverpool had waited 73 years for this moment. Finally Ron Yeats was able to show the travelling Kop what the FA Cup actually looked like*

1966

FOOTBALL HAS only rarely produced the lyrical prose which other sports such as cricket and boxing have attracted with more frequency. There is no football equivalent of Neville Cardus, C. L. R. James, Jack London or Norman Mailer and no football novels worth the mention. Quite why is difficult to explain. Perhaps the game lies too firmly rooted in its working class culture or its excitement remains visual rather than reported.

While there are no great literary figures, there are nevertheless some journalists who have laboured to capture its appeal and intensity. J. P. W. Mallalieu, the former Labour MP who during the post-war years wrote a regular column in the *Spectator*, set standards which others have endeavoured to emulate. Geoffrey Green in *The Times*, J. L. Manning of the *Guardian*, Ivan Sharpe and some years later Brian Glanville in *The Sunday Times*, and Hugh McIlvanney have all matched his eloquence. Between them they have set standards which contrast sharply with the average tabloid back page. Another was Michael Parkinson who cleverly combined good writing with humour, and possibly attracted a wider readership with his articles in *The Sunday Times*, *Punch*, and the *Daily Mirror* as well as his books.

Michael Parkinson, now a famous TV presenter, began a regular column in *The Sunday Times* on February 6th 1966 that catapulted him from regional obscurity into national fame. His weekly column was highly readable, skilfully composed and above all extremely funny. He returned shamelessly to the football of his childhood and re-lived those moments when he first stood on the terraces as a youngster. It was nostalgia at its best, which allowed him the licence to exaggerate and dream. He made writing look simple. Mostly he wrote about his beloved Barnsley of the early 1950s when wingers had bandy legs, centre-halves were giants, and full-backs had thighs the size of bacon slabs. In his very first column he reminded us of those days and introduced a name that has remained with us ever since – Skinner Normanton. The Barnsley half-back ('a Rocky Marciano of a player'), was as far removed from the modern defender as is conceivably possible. Normanton, forgotten by everyone other than the Barnsley faithful, rose again through the weekly column to become a legend. For the record, Sidney Normanton, born August 1926, played 123 games for Barnsley between 1947 and 1954 and scored just two goals before moving down the road to Halifax where he made 14 appearances. His name will always remain linked with that of Parkinson, Barnsley's two favourite sons.

Michael Parkinson

CUP-TIES were different from other games. If Barnsley won we went to the pictures in the best seats, but if they lost there was sometimes a punch-up and the old man would come home from the boozer with a skinful saying the beer was off.

Barnsley of course used to be a good Cup fighting side. They only won the Cup once and that was in 1912 but they've never forgotten it and many a team from a higher division has been slain by them on that ground with the muck stacks peeping over the paddock. The reason for Barnsley's success in the Cup was, more often than not, that their game remained unchanged throughout years of tactical innovation. The team was both blind and deaf to subtleties like the bolt defence, the wall pass, 4-2-4 and deep-lying centre forwards. Their game was founded rock solid on two basic principles best summed up by the exhortations of their supporters to "Get stuck in" or alternatively "Get rid."

During one spectacular Cup run just after the war when Barnsley had beaten a First Division side the old man held forth on the team's virtues on the bus going home. What he said was: "They'll take some stopping yon team." The bus agreed.

This love of hard combatative graft above all else was not in any way unique among the supporters who Saturday after Saturday had their week-end mood dictated by how their team fared. Their unanimous favourites were the hard men who got stuck in and got rid without thought for the game's niceties. The odd sophisticates who crept into the team were tolerated but never loved. Thus they will tell you even now that Danny Blanchflower once played for Barnsley, but that he wasn't a patch on Skinner Normanton.

Normanton, I suppose, personified Barnsley's Cup-fighting qualities. He was tough, tireless, aggressive, with a tackle as swift and spectacular as summer lightning. In the family tree of football his grandfather was Wilf Copping, his godson is Nobby Stiles. And just in case anyone is still uncertain about what kind of player he was, he could claim a distant link with Rocky Marciano. He was a miner and built like one. Billiard-table legs and a chest like the front of a coal barge. He was so fearsome that there are those who will tell you that naughty children in and around Barnsley were warned by their parents, "If you don't be good we'll send for Skinner."

Sunday Times, 6 February 1966

ABOVE: *'Skinner' Normanton – the fearsome Barnsley half-back*

1966

FOR A FEW brief months a small black and white mongrel called Pickles became as famous as Lassie and Rin Tin Tin. For it was Pickles who saved Britain's – and in particular the FA's – red faces after someone had walked off with the most glittering prize in soccer, the Jules Rimet trophy.

On a quiet Sunday afternoon in central London a crowd of around 200 had gathered for a Mothering Day service at the Methodist Central Hall in Westminster. Unknown to them a thief had walked into the building with the congregation and was now busily breaking into a room below where a £3 million stamp exhibition had been attracting numerous visitors. But the thief was not after stamps: he was looking for something far more important. On display alongside the stamps was the Jules Rimet trophy. Weighing barely nine pounds, the shining 12-inch trophy was worth little more than £2,000 even though it had been insured for considerably more. But its importance far outstripped its value.

Few thefts could have caused more headlines around the world. With the trophy about to be competed for in England, its disappearance could hardly have been more embarrassing. The exhibition organisers fidgeted uncomfortably, the Metropolitan police scratched their heads and the FA buried their red faces in their hands. Hurried plans had to be drawn up at Lancaster Gate just in case the trophy remained lost. Britain's pride was at stake.

Within the week however a culprit had been arrested after demanding a £15,000 ransom for the trophy's return. But the police soon discovered that he was a charlatan and the trophy's whereabouts still remained a mystery. Indeed it might always have done so had it not been for the engaging little black and white mongrel, Pickles. Exactly one week after the theft, Londoner David Corbett was out walking his dog through the leafy suburbs of Norwood. Darting into a garden, Pickles became absorbed in digging around behind the hedge, and when Mr Corbett came to drag him away, he found that Pickles had unearthed a brown paper parcel containing the World Cup. If it was a shock to Mr Corbett, it was a mighty relief for the nation. For weeks, Pickles was the toast of Fleet Street, until Bobby Moore finally lifted the Jules Rimet trophy for England – this time legally. And as the team celebrated at the Royal Garden Hotel in Kensington, Pickles was not forgotten, arriving just in time to lick the plates clean. Mr Corbett later received £6,000 in reward money, but the thief was never caught.

World Cup stolen

SIX MEN TO GUARD IT

Daily Mail, 21 March 1966

BELOW: *Pickles, who unearthed a rather unexpected buried treasure – much to the relief of the nation*

Intact—in London garden

WORLD CUP IS FOUND

Daily Express, 28 March 1966

1966

IT WAS hardly surprising that the Sunday newspapers of July 31st 1966 should devote most of their front pages to England's historic World Cup victory. It was like VE day all over again. 'It's Jubilation Night' roared the *Sunday Express* above a photograph of a beaming Bobby Moore and wife clinking champagne glasses at the celebration. England's triumph had rekindled the spirit of World War Two. The *Express*'s editorial picked up the theme, 'There's no use expecting others to make a supreme effort for the sake of the nation,' they preached, 'unless you really believe in the nation itself. If only we could see some of that ardent and united national spirit which glowed at Wembley spill over and inspire our public life, then we would lick the world. And not just at football.' The back pages of course were ecstatic though there was little analysis of England's questionable third goal and no mention by the football writers of their quickly-forgotten pre-World Cup predictions.

ENGLAND–CHAMPIONS OF THE WORLD

England (1) 4 West Germany (1) 2

Hurst 3, Peters — **Haller, Weber**

(After extra time; score at 90 mins., 2-2)

At Wembley — attendance 93,000

AROUND 5.15 p.m. YESTERDAY the most triumphant and tumultuous din I have ever heard rose from the stands and terraces of Wembley Stadium. From every side of what has been described as "this historic cathedral of football" a blaze of Union Jacks waved as people, unashamedly gripped by emotion and patriotism, danced, wept, and hugged each other.

Sunday Express, 31 July 1966

BELOW: *Geoff Hurst, scorer of three goals in the Final as England beat West Germany 4–2*

Not many of the papers had rated England's chances very highly, with Ramsey's laborious tactics winning him few friends on the back pages. But he was more than adequately served by the precocious Alan Ball and the subtle Martin Peters, while up front Roger Hunt and Geoff Hurst formed an effective spearhead. In defence Gordon Banks, George Cohen, Ray Wilson, Jackie Charlton and Nobby Stiles conceded only one goal on the way to the final, and with the experience and leadership of Bobby Moore and Bobby Charlton, England were worthy champions. As the trophy was lifted, all was forgiven and Ramsey was suddenly the toast of the nation.

BELOW: *A jubilant Bobby Moore and Nobby Stiles celebrate with Alf Ramsey*

Sunday Express Reporter

IT WAS LIKE a Coronation night when England's victorious World Cup footballers drove from their Hendon headquarters to a banquet and reception in Kensington last night to celebrate their 4—2 triumph over West Germany in the final at Wembley.

Banners and Union Jacks were strung everywhere along the route. Thousands stood on the pavements. Thousands more cheered from windows, from balconies, even from roofs as the team's bus drove by.

Sunday Express, 31 July 1966

IT'S JUBILATION NIGHT!

Sunday Express, 31 July 1966

1967

IT HAS been said that Scottish football, rather like Italian wine, does not travel well. But in May 1967 Glasgow Celtic pulled off Scotland's greatest international coup when they defeated the former European champions, Inter Milan, to win the coveted European Cup.

On a sunlit evening in Lisbon's national stadium, Jock Stein's green-hooped men held their nerve to overcome one of the tightest defences in world football. A goal down after just six minutes, when Mazzola converted a penalty, Celtic looked to be going the way of so many talented Scottish teams. To the surprise of everyone however, Inter decided to rest on their laurels and with eleven men holed up in defence sat back on their slender lead. For a side that was equally capable in attack it was a senseless and dangerous tactic. Wave upon wave of Celtic attacks hit Inter's brick wall as the Scots piled on the pressure, and in the 60th minute the vital breakthrough arrived when Tommy Gemmell pounced to slam home Jimmy Craig's back-heel. A stunned Inter now had little option but to reverse their tactics, but after an hour of sustained Celtic attacking it was not so easy, and as they threw more men upfield, so the gaps opened up in their defence. With just five minutes remaining a low ball from Tommy Murdoch was met by Steve Chalmers, and the impish Scot drove it home to win Britain the first of many European Cups.

The Celtic flags waved triumphantly in the setting sun as their army of more than 7,000 supporters began the victory celebrations. The party was said to have gone on long after Jock Stein and his team had returned to Glasgow. Even Willie Waddell, the former Rangers manager, put aside the sectarian divide and admitted for once that Celtic had done Scottish football proud. 'This was indeed the greatest day in our history,' he wrote magnanimously in the *Daily Express*. A slight exaggeration perhaps. The Scottish papers went overboard while the English press, keen to claim some credit, wrote up Celtic's victory as a British success rather than a Scottish one. It was a point which demonstrated how regional the back pages of the tabloids have

ABOVE: *Celtic celebrate Chalmers' winning goal in their European Cup Final win over Inter-Milan*

• The score that makes every Scot proud today

EUROPEAN CUP FINAL

CELTIC	2
Inter Milan	1

SALUTE CELTS—EUROPE MASTERS!

From JOHN MACKENZIE
LISBON, Thursday

Celtic 2, Inter Milan 1 (H.T. 0—1)
SCORERS: Celtic — Gemmell (63min.), Chalmers (85). Inter Milan — Mazzola (7, pen.).

MAGNIFICENT Celtic are the Soccer masters supreme of Europe.

In the National Stadium here tonight they came back from a desperately unlucky start to humble Inter Milan and bring the European Cup home to Britain for the first time.

What a fantastic night. What a heart-lifting occasion.

What a tremendous lift the wonderful men of Parkhead have given to Scottish football.

They not only beat Herrera's men. They sent the name of Celtic and Scotland ringing round the world.

They now rank alongside Real Madrid in giving a neutral public a wonderful night's entertainment.

LINE-UP

CELTIC	MILAN
Simpson	Sarti
Craig	Burgnich
Gemmell	Facchetti
Murdoch	Bedin
McNeill	Guarneri
Clark	Picchi
Johnstone	Domenghini
Wallace	Cappellini
Chalmers	Mazzolo
Auld	Bicicli
Lennox	Corso

Scottish Daily Express, 26 May 1967

become. English papers are not interested in Scottish football, nor for that matter are the Scottish papers concerned with events south of the border. Even worse, the English regional editions have become fixed upon their local teams almost to the exclusion of news from elsewhere. The London editions of the tabloids rarely feature Newcastle or Leeds United while the northern editions are equally not particularly bothered with happenings at Stamford Bridge or Highbury.

ABOVE: *A proud day for Scotland*

1968

TEN YEARS after the Munich disaster that had destroyed Matt Busby's dream of an English team lifting the European Cup, his own Manchester United rose like a Phoenix to finally conquer Europe. Although the nightmare of Munich would never be forgotten, the pain was eased as the new United achieved glory for their great predecessors.

FROM BRINK OF DISASTER

ABOVE: *A delighted Matt Busby is embraced by United players Bill Foulkes (left) and Pat Crerand*

THE MOST WONDERFUL THING IN MY LIFE—BUSBY

Daily Mirror, 30 May 1968

United's path to the European final began at Old Trafford with a 4–0 win over the Maltese champions, Hibernians Valletta, and a goalless draw in Malta. The next round took United to Sarajevo where they drew 0–0 with the Yugoslavs before winning 2–1 at home. In the quarter-finals they again faced tough East European competition when they drew Gornik of Poland, but a 2–0 win in the first leg at Old Trafford was enough to see them through in spite of a 1–0 defeat at Gornik. This left four teams in the competition, every one of them capable of lifting the trophy – Real Madrid, Juventus, Benfica and United. Whoever they drew, it would be tough and as luck would have it, United found themselves pitted against their old Spanish foes, Real Madrid. It had been the Spanish giants who had thwarted United back in 1957 but the current Real were a far different proposition from the team that had boasted Di Stefano, Kopa and Gento in its forward line. In the first leg at

Old Trafford, United squeezed home by the only goal of the game and looked set to go out in Madrid. But in the second leg, before a seething Bernabau stadium, United played their hearts out to clinch a 3–3 draw and a place in the final.

May 29th 1968 was a night of high emotion at Wembley as United faced the Portuguese champions Benfica, already twice winners of the tournament and vaunting skilful internationals such as Eusebio, Jose Augusto and Coluna. Ironically, it was none other than Bobby Charlton – the one survivor of Munich still playing – who set United on their way with a 52nd minute goal, but an equaliser from Graca soon left the teams on level terms again. As the match dragged on towards extra

. . MATT'S NIGHT OF GLORY

Daily Mirror, 30 May 1968

time, United looked the more weary side and it took a breathtaking last-minute save from Alex Stepney to stop the ubiquitous Eusebio from capturing the trophy for Portugal. With United's hopes barely alive, it seemed as if a league season that had seen them wind up in second place just two points behind neighbours, Manchester City, might have proved too tiring. Another runners-up spot looked to be beckoning, but United were not to be denied their moment of glory.

In the 92nd minute a long goal kick from Stepney was flicked on by the nineteen-year-old Brian Kidd to the mercurial George Best. The Northern Ireland international glanced up and, seizing his opportunity with all the coolness that made him the European Footballer of the Year, rounded the goalkeeper to put United back into the lead. Suddenly it was easy, and United's tired limbs regained their strength while Benfica's spirit deserted them. Within eight minutes United had scored two more through Charlton and Kidd. Fifteen minutes later, Busby's eleven-year dream had finally been realised as United captain Bobby Charlton handed him the coveted trophy.

ABOVE: *Manchester United celebrate their 4–1 victory after extra time*

European Cup Final

MANCHESTER UNITED. . . .	4
Charlton 2, Best, Kidd	
BENFICA	1
Graca	
After extra time	At Wembley

1968

ABOVE: *Charlton scores his second goal*

Three goals in extra time make United Europe champs

By KEN JONES

WHEN time has come to dim the emotion of this match, strong men will still remember it with tears in their eyes. Manchester United have the European Cup. Their illustrious manager Matt Busby has finally conquered his Everest.

We shall remember it for what it meant to a great club, a great manager and to British football.

Daily Mirror, 30 May 1968

ABOVE: *Kidd sends goal number three into the net despite the efforts of the Benfica goalkeeper*

1969

AS FLEET STREET'S circulation war hotted up during the late 1960s, so the back pages reflected more sensational, speculative stories. And football was always the most likely sport to be at the centre of any eye-grabbing exclusives. Players regularly swelled their wage packets by selling their life stories to the tabloids, though such 'scoops' of course always had to contain more than a little spice in order to make them attractive. And that usually took the form of telling dressing room secrets, criticising managers, or slamming incompetent referees and club directors.

Billy Bremner's efforts, billed in August 1969 – somewhat prematurely – by the *News of the World* as 'THE soccer story of the seventies', were typical. The former Leeds United captain had long been a hate-figure on the terraces and it was hardly surprising that he should eventually be contracted to tell a few tales. And the tales that he did tell were hardly revealing when they were published.

But Bremner was not the first and by no means would he be the last to append his name to a story which had been written for him by a tabloid journalist. As far back as 1928 the *Athletic News* had carried a front page exclusive by a 'mystery international' writing on the current state of English football. It was nowhere near as sensational as today's 'exclusives', and the player had been forced to hide his identity, but it set a trend that has culminated in some of the worst excesses of journalism. The stories, nearly always by 'ghost' writers, have contributed neither to our understanding of the game, nor to improving its tarnished image. Sadly, today's back pages have deteriorated even further as players openly hit out at each other with the most thoughtless comments and criticisms. It's all part of a hype, aided by players and managers and aimed at filling up the sports pages as well as selling newspapers.

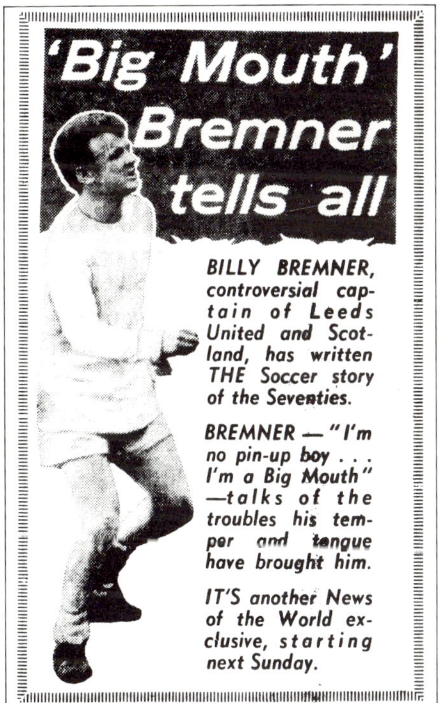
'Big Mouth' Bremner tells all

BILLY BREMNER, controversial captain of Leeds United and Scotland, has written THE Soccer story of the Seventies.

BREMNER — "I'm no pin-up boy . . . I'm a Big Mouth" —talks of the troubles his temper and tongue have brought him.

IT'S another News of the World exclusive, starting next Sunday.

News of the World, 31 August 1969

RIGHT: *The opening day of the 1966/67 season, and Leeds United hard man Billy Bremner pleads innocent – but in Dave MacKay of Spurs he meets his match*

1970

It's London's Cup after marathon replay

CHEERS, CHELSEA!

Daily Mirror, 30 April 1970

THE SUNDAY newspapers have traditionally had a monopoly on Cup Final reporting with the dailies forced to pick up the scraps for their Monday morning editions. But on Thursday April 30th 1970, the dailies had their first opportunity in 58 years to report the Cup Final ahead of the Sundays after Chelsea and Leeds had drawn at Wembley.

The replay was held at Old Trafford two-and-a-half weeks after the two teams had slugged out a 2–2 draw, the first since 1912 when Barnsley and West Brom had drawn 0–0 at the Crystal Palace. Leeds had always been favourites to take the Cup, but after failing at the first opportunity there was a growing feeling that Don Revie's team were about to lose out again. Late in the season Leeds had looked set to capture a unique treble. Top of the table, Cup finalists and semi-finalists in the European Cup, they were the most feared team in the land. But in March their dream turned sour as Everton sneaked ahead of them to take the league championship. Then, at the beginning of April, in a tumultuous tussle with Glasgow Celtic in the semi-final of the European Cup they lost both ties, the second in front of 134,000 at Hampden. Tired legs and weary limbs had taken their toll as the number of games mounted, but it required just one more superhuman effort to end the season with a trophy.

After 35 minutes, it looked as if Leeds might get their just rewards when Mick Jones shot them into a well deserved lead. But with just twelve minutes remaining, and Leeds beginning to think that luck was perhaps on their side, Peter Osgood snatched a headed equaliser for Chelsea. It was too dispiriting and from that moment Leeds were a beaten team. Webb finally ended their misery in extra time and Chelsea had won the Cup for the first time in their history.

Chelsea's Kings Road, the most fashionable haunt in the land, was said to be awash with dancing supporters as the celebrations extended well into the night. The popular dailies were making the most of this rare opportunity as they painted colourful pictures of the celebrations. They had no idea when the next opportunity might occur. But they had little to fear; it would be 11 years later.

ABOVE: *Chelsea captain Ron Harris and Peter Osgood raise the Cup after defeating mighty Leeds 2–1 at Old Trafford*

BACK IN 1970 everyone knew who 'Bobby' was. The *Daily Mirror* simply had to spread the name across the front page and it was quite obvious to all their readers whom they meant. Bobby was of course, Bobby Moore. Everyone also knew that the England captain was the impeccable Englishman and any suggestion that he might have stolen a bracelet was simply inconceivable. It was another dastardly act by those South Americans trying to frame him and unnerve the world champions prior to the World Cup Finals.

England had travelled to Colombia in May 1970 as part of their acclimatisation programme to prepare for the Mexico World Cup. They had already beaten the Colombians 4–0 in a friendly international and were about to depart for Mexico City when the police dramatically arrested Bobby Moore and charged him with having stolen a gold bracelet said to be worth £600. The theft was alleged to have taken place eight days earlier in a Bogotá jeweller's shop but only now had the salesgirl recognised the England captain. Overnight, salesgirl Clara Padilla became an international celebrity.

The incident caused a sensation in Britain as well as a major diplomatic incident with the Colombians. The First Secretary of the British Embassy in Bogota was sent dashing to the Colombian Foreign Minister to protest while the England team flew off to Mexico without their captain and key defender. And as Britain prepared to go to the polls to elect a new government, the affair threatened to become an election issue unless it was quickly resolved. Meanwhile, Moore was ordered to remain in the Colombian capital for a court appearance so that further investigations could continue. Then, just as dramatically as Clara had made her accusations, she retracted them, claiming she was confused. The charges were dropped, Moore was released and immediately put on a plane bound for Mexico City.

BOBBY

ENGLAND'S World Cup Soccer captain Bobby Moore was still under house arrest in Bogota, Colombia, last night after strongly denying that he stole a £600 gold bracelet.

Moore, 29, has told the investigating judge: "I know nothing about the theft. I have never seen that bracelet."

Daily Mirror, 27 May 1970

BELOW: *After the furore over the alleged stolen bracelet had died down, Bobby Moore is greeted by his relieved manager Alf Ramsey in Mexico as he returns to join his team*

1970

BRAZIL 4, ITALY 1

SUPREME VICTORY

BRAZIL reclaimed the World Cup here today in a frenzy of jubilation that echoed with cheers, drums and cannonade around the unforgettable sweep of the Aztec Stadium.

Here was the supreme triumph. The utter destruction of a vaunted well-organised Italian defence that had only been previously riddled in the muscle agony of extra time against West Germany in the semi-finals.

It was a vindication of the romantic ideals that Brazil have pursued throughout the competition.

The closing scenes were almost unbelievable as a wave of Brazilian supporters, hovering along the touchlines, broke out over the players.

Some players were stripped to their shorts, their shirts torn from their backs, stockings from their legs and boots from their feet.

Daily Mirror, 22 June 1970

THE 1970 BRAZILIAN team will live in the memory as one of the most gloriously skilful of all time. They compared with anything that had gone before or has been seen since. It was a side rich in artistry, with individualists who revelled in free-flowing football yet played intuitively as a team; they cared little for the vagaries of defensive play, relying instead on their instinctive attacking skills to win the hour. And usually they did.

Against Italy in the 1970 World Cup Final, Brazil faced the most resilient defence in world soccer. It was an iron wall of defenders reared on the traditions and discipline of Helenio Herrera's Inter Milan. Robustness, rather than flair, was the name of their game and if ever the attacking genius of Brazil would be tested, it was against Cera, Rosata, Facchetti and Bertini.

Brazil, the people's favourites, had stormed through to the quarter-finals with victories over the holders England, Rumania and Czechoslovakia before beating Peru 4–2. In the semi-finals they defeated the fancied Uruguayans 3–1 and then lined up before 110,000 in the Aztec stadium on a wet Sunday afternoon to face Italy for the coveted Jules Rimet trophy.

Within 18 minutes Rivelino had crossed for Pele to head Brazil's opening goal, but 20 minutes later Italy had equalised through Boninsegna. For the best part of an hour the old world matched the new as Europe's toughest grappled with South America's most graceful. But in the 21st minute of the second half Italy cracked. Gerson set up a one, two with the lightning Jairzinho, before the tall Brazilian received the return pass and turned to shoot Brazil into the lead. Five minutes later it was Gerson again as he slipped a forward ball to Pele who headed it down into the goalmouth, and in the scramble that followed Jairzinho smashed home Brazil's third goal.

LEFT: *With Pele in the vanguard, Brazil overwhelmed Italy to win 4–1*

That was the signal for the sambas. Italy were routed and for thirty unforgettable minutes Brazil arrogantly demonstrated the luxurious skills of Latin football. Their final goal came from the most delicately weighted pass which arrived fittingly from the magnificent Pele. Starting off on one of his loping runs, Pele cut diagonally towards the penalty area, stopping only to raise his head and then push a gentle pass into the open space on his right. Everyone watched and held their breath as Carlos Alberto arrived in full flight. There was never any question where his fiercely struck shot would end up.

Ken Jones, writing in the *Daily Mirror* the following morning, had no doubts that he had seen an incomparable display. It was Brazil's third World Cup victory and their most popular. The Jules Rimet trophy was duly handed to them for permanent display on their Rio sideboard and, one suspects, that is where it has always belonged.

1971

MOST PEOPLE learnt of the terrifying Ibrox tragedy through radio and television. Millions of football fans returning from matches heard the first news of a minor accident as they tuned into BBC Radio's Sports Report at 5 o'clock. By the time the programme ended an hour later the full horror was apparent.

It was Saturday January 2 1971 and 80,000 had been crammed into Ibrox for the annual New Year derby between Glasgow Rangers and Celtic. With just two minutes left and with Rangers a goal down, thousands of supporters began to pour out of the stadium to catch early buses home. Then, Rangers scored a dramatic equaliser and the crowd streaming down stairway thirteen turned suddenly to rush back up the stairs to see what the cheering was about. As they did so, they met hundreds more coming out. The result was a crush on the stairway; bodies fell and hundreds spilled down with 66 suffocated or trampled on. 140 others were injured with a hundred of those detained in hospital. It was the worst soccer disaster in Britain and for Rangers the second tragedy that had struck Ibrox. For Colin Stein, who had scored Rangers' last-minute equaliser, it was a goal that tragically would haunt him throughout his life.

The Home Secretary Reginald Maudling immediately set up an inquiry. Its findings and recommendations, published in the Wheatley Report, called for stricter crowd controls. It was a forerunner to the Safety of Sports Grounds Act of 1975 which severely curtailed crowd capacities, bringing sports grounds within the licensing system, like cinemas and other public buildings.

SOCCER DISASTER

66 die in big match panic

News of the World, 3 January 1971

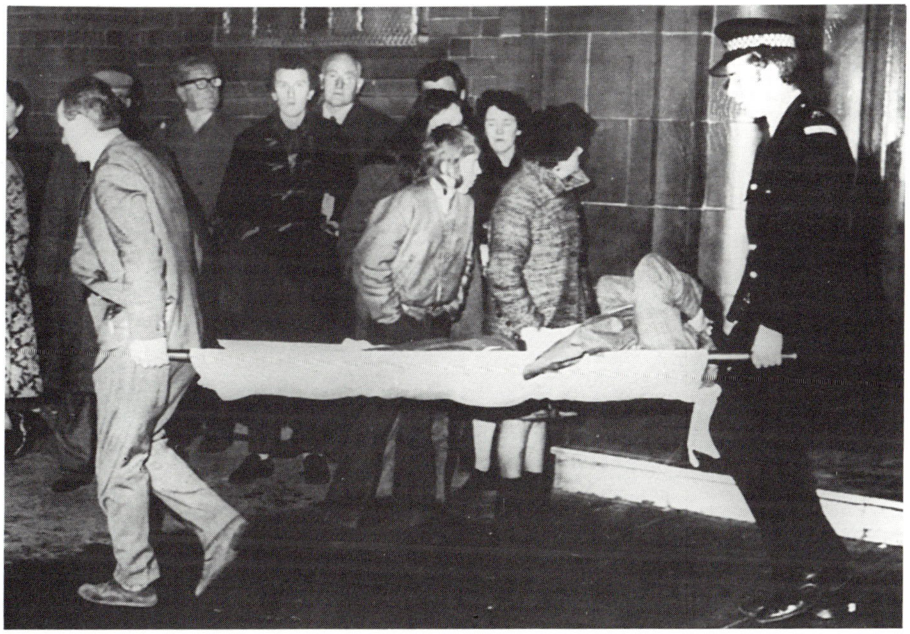

ABOVE: *The annual New Year derby between Celtic and Rangers ended in a catastrophe which caused the death of 66 fans*

ABOVE: *Officials examine the buckled steel barriers of stairway 13 at Ibrox*

1971

GEORGE BEST was British soccer's first genuine superstar. Young, handsome, rich, gifted, and single, he had all the necessary ingredients for the tabloids. His was a fame normally reserved for filmstars and pop singers, which during the sixties spread from the back pages into the news headlines. There was a time when it was almost impossible to open one of the popular papers without seeing George's half-shaven face and a story which romantically linked him with one pretty young girl or another. Sometimes it was hard to remember that he was a footballer. Fathers who had been reared on Len Shackleton and Dixie Dean would shake their heads at what the modern game had become. His home was besieged by young females, his Manchester nightclub was the trendiest in the north, his clothes came from the most fashionable boutiques and his E-type Jaguar was the target for much graffiti. If fame was thrust on George by Fleet Street, then he certainly did little to discourage it.

He arrived in Manchester a skinny, frightened 15-year-old Belfast boy but within a couple of years

STARTING TODAY

DOES he need a haircut or a halo, is he player or playboy, a giant of sport or an advertiser's fake—and do his friends think the worst of Best? Here are the answers in a sharp-edged assessment that strips away the myths. . .

BEST

SHORT OF ELOPING with Princess Anne or becoming chairman of the disciplinary committee, George Best can hardly surprise us more. His life is already an extravaganza in which Georgie, a footballer of magical talent, floats amid clouds of girls over mountains of money.

Fame came so fast (he's still only 24) that everything and yet nothing is known about him. The essential Best—withdrawn as Garbo, secretive as a cat—always evades the public eye.

The People, 17 January 1971

BELOW: *George Best, the way he will probably be remembered – surrounded by girls and bubbly*

AND HIS BIRDS

had taken the first division by storm, immediately thrusting United into title contention. The following season, 1964/65, United clinched their first championship since the days of the Busby Babes with Best's trickery down the left wing exciting crowds wherever United played. Within a couple of seasons he ranked alongside Eusebio, Cruyff and Pele as he weaved his magic skills around Europe. In 1967 United won the title again and the following year became the first Football League side to capture the European Cup with George named as European Footballer of the Year. Linking up with Charlton, Law, Crerand and Stiles, he was given the freedom to roam and exploit his talents as he wished.

BELOW: *George Best, the way he should be remembered – as a player of dazzling skill and ability who helped keep Manchester United at the top*

But there was another side to George. The pressure of continually being in the public eye had taken its toll. His fast-lane lifestyle was hardly conducive to fitness, and women, drink and other extra-curricular activities ate into his time. He began to skip training and in January 1971, for the second time, failed to turn up for a first division fixture. Fortunately for George, United won 2–1, their first victory in eleven matches, and manager Matt Busby tended towards leniency. But it was the beginning of the end. There was quiet resentment among his team-mates and his absences grabbed the front page headlines while his drinking bouts were now public knowledge. What was more serious, it began to show on the pitch as the old sparkle fizzed less frequently. The pressures of his playboy existence began to tell.

In 1972 Best walked out on United. He returned briefly the following season as his old team faced unimaginable relegation, only to storm off yet again, this time finally. He had played 361 games for United, scoring 137 goals and had won 32 caps for Northern Ireland.

To escape the spotlight of Fleet Street he ventured to America, playing in the NASL before returning to join, among others, Fulham and Hibernian. These were sad years as the one-time idol of the terraces took his circus act from club to club, dependent upon the highest bidder. But no matter where Best went he would always be remembered as the long-haired skinny left-winger whose genius could unravel the tightest of defences.

1971

THE *PEOPLE* described it as 'The Most Fantastic Result You'll Ever See' which was perhaps a slight exaggeration though it would certainly count among the half dozen most astonishing scorelines of all time. Colchester United of the fourth division, 3, Leeds United, top of the first division, 2.

It happened in the fifth round of the FA Cup in front of 16,000 impassioned fans crammed into Colchester's tiny ground at Layer Road. Colchester were enjoying an unusual run of luck in the Cup having disposed of non-league Barnet and Rochdale in the previous rounds. To draw mighty Leeds at home was by far the most romantic tie of the round – a David and Goliath clash.

Leeds arrived with no excuses. Their line-up included internationals like Jackie Charlton, Norman Hunter, Johnny Giles, Peter Lorimer and Allan Clarke. On paper, nobody would have given Colchester a chance yet with half an hour remaining Leeds were trailing by an unbelievable three goals.

Ray Crawford, the former Ipswich star began the assault, heading the fourth division side into an 18th minute lead. Six minutes later the same man collided with the Leeds keeper, Gary Sprake, and as they both tumbled to the ground, Crawford swept the ball into the net with his trailing leg. The small band of reporters who had journeyed reluctantly from Liverpool Street to write up yet another clinical Leeds triumph, suddenly found themselves with a real story on their hands. In a flash the telephone wires to Fleet Street were buzzing. At half time radio commentators and football ground announcers up and down the country had to repeat the scoreline to astonished listeners. But if the first half had been bewildering, then the second would prove even more breathtaking as Dave Simmons swept Colchester into a three goal lead in the 54th minute. Jubilant fans poured onto the pitch as a demoralised Leeds looked on in disbelief. What had happened to Don Revie's men of iron?

But the Yorkshiremen had not topped the league without reason. They had the true grit of fighters and within six minutes had pulled a goal back through Norman Hunter. Thirteen minutes later and Leeds had made it 3–2. That was the signal for Leeds to bombard the Colchester goal, but fortune smiled on the fourth division outfit that afternoon as they hung on grimly to their slender lead. When the final whistle blew it was Ray Crawford who was carried shoulder high around the ground. Colchester, who a few months previously had rescued him from the dole queue, revelled in their glory. Having beaten last season's runners up, they then drew the league champions Everton at Goodison for the quarter finals. Sadly that contest proved to be too much even for plucky Colchester. They went down by five goals to nil.

The most fantastic result you'll ever see

COLCHESTER 3 LEEDS 2

They DO come back.. Crawford proves it

The People, 14 February 1971

ABOVE: *Ray Crawford (on ground) hooks the ball past Leeds' goalie Gary Sprake and Paul Reaney to score his second goal, as Jack Charlton looks on*

FOOTBALL TOOK a sad turn for the worse during the 1970s as a new phase of hooliganism reared its ugly head. Although mob violence at matches could be traced back to the late nineteenth century, it was sporadic and had died away by the 1920s. But in the 1970s it emerged again in a new and more violent pattern. Although it is impossible to pinpoint a specific date, commentators tend to agree that April 1971 and Elland Road were the likely date and venue when the new social problem first hit the headlines.

Top of the table, Leeds United were two points ahead of Arsenal in the race for the title. They had played two more games than their nearest rivals and with only two more fixtures remaining, every match was crucial. When Leeds met West Brom at Elland Road on Saturday April 17th, few would have bet on the Midlanders to go home with both points.

West Brom had taken the lead in the 20th minute but Leeds were masters of the off-side game and when WBA's Tony Brown sprinted away with the ball in the 72nd minute the Leeds' defence pointed to Colin Suggett standing in an offside position. The referee Ray Tinkler waved play on however, claiming that Suggett was not interfering with play. Brown, who had himself paused, then fed a long ball to Jeff Astle, the West Brom and England striker who also appeared to be in an offside position. The entire Leeds defence stopped and looked to the linesman whose flag mysteriously remained by his side. The referee waved play on and Astle casually slammed home Albion's second goal. There was uproar. Leeds' players appealed to the linesman, then surrounded the referee in the centre circle, jostling him and arguing ferociously. Within minutes they had been joined by dozens of fans who swept angrily onto the field and the centre circle was soon a mass of fighting bodies as the police moved in to restore order. Twenty-three were arrested.

RIOT!

FANS, PLAYERS AND POLICE SCUFFLE . . . THE SCENE AT ELLAND ROAD

23 arrested as fans attack the ref

The People, 18 April 1971

ABOVE: *The punch-up in the centre circle*

To make matters worse, when play resumed Leeds pulled a goal back. Manager Don Revie was scathing of the referee's decision and reckoned the pitch invasion was justified. Even Albion's manager, Alan Ashman, agreed the goal was offside.

That defeat nudged Leeds off the top of the table and at the end of the season with just one point separating them from the new champions, Arsenal, they could justifiably claim that Tinkler's decision had robbed them of the title. Nevertheless, it quickly brought the wrath of the Football League on Leeds who were ordered to play their first four matches of the next season away. But it was only the beginning. Within a few years, there would be murders, knifings, mass fighting, more pitch invasions and police horses quelling riots in the penalty area. Football was about to face its sternest test. The report of the Leeds' riot was the first of many shameful stories and over the next 15 years Fleet Street would pour out thousands more words in repeated attempts to understand and solve the problem.

1971

ON A BRIGHT summer's day at Wembley in May 1971 Arsenal became only the second team this century to achieve the League and FA Cup Double when they defeated Liverpool by two goals to one in extra time. Their triumph had begun on the Monday before the final with a 1–0 win over north London rivals Tottenham at White Hart Lane that clinched the first division championship. Watched by 52,000 with as many locked outside, Tottenham – the only other twentieth-century Double-winners – fell to a late goal from striker Ray Kennedy. At one stage during the season Arsenal had been seven points adrift of leaders Leeds, but a late unstoppable surge left them needing to win their final two games of the season to lift both trophies.

It was a sterling effort and whereas many teams might have faltered in their final run-in, Arsenal seemed to gather strength. Manager Bertie Mee had built his side around the defensive skills of skipper Frank McLintock who was sternly supported by Rice, McNab and Storey, while upfront the attacking force of Kennedy, Radford and the ubiquitous Charlie George made them aggressive and formidable challengers.

Their rivals in the final had already won two league championships since their return to the first division in 1962, but Arsenal were not their luckiest team and memories of the 1950 final when Arsenal had beaten them were still vivid with many of their supporters.

The first 90 minutes ended goalless as the two tightest defences in the

Charlie's king of London

HE'S BEEN called conceited, peevish and arrogant. But Charlie George, a cockney boy of 20, won the Cup, clinched the double and launched North London last night on the biggest booze-up since the Coronation.

An extra-time pass by Radford just outside the penalty area set up string-haired George for his historic shot.

Liverpool's defenders, their stockings down on aching legs, their minds on a Tuesday replay at Sheffield, watched him wearily.

Maybe they forgot that George could strike a deadlier, faster, straighter ball than anyone in this deadlocked slog.

Or maybe they remembered, yet could do nothing about it.

For George's right foot became a rocket launcher, streaking the ball into the net. A deflection off Lloyd made it impossible for Clemence to anticipate.

Six days

So all in six days Arsenal have cleared the shelf—League championship, F.A. Youth Cup, Footballer of the Year for skipper Frank McLintock, and now the F.A. Cup.

And this is the side that finished last season in the wrong half of the First Division and were heaved out of the Cup in the third round by Blackpool.

It's a side managed by a physiotherapist whose footballing career was ended by injury before he could play even one League game.

A side with men who feared they were doomed never to be first up the steps at Wembley. Six of them had lost there twice, McLintock had been defeated there four times.

And when Heighway scored in the second minute of extra time that jinx fell on Arsenal like a sack of wet cement. Heads hung, bodies sagged.

Yet from the memories of a nearly invincible League season they dredged up the spirit to hurl themselves forward once more.

Forward towards a goal defended not only by the apparently impregnable Smith, Lloyd and Clemence but the banner-flaunting choirs of the Kop singing with heartless derision: "Poor old Arsenal, ain't it a bleeding shame."

No song

For Heighway, the Kop sing: "On him we look with great elation"—but they didn't sing it this time.

The People, 9 May 1971

RIGHT: *Charlie George celebrates with a victory somersault*

DOUBLE UP!

league stubbornly resisted all challenges. But as extra time kicked off, the game dramatically swung into life. After only two minutes, Steve Heighway skipped down the left wing to send a thundering shot past Bob Wilson and put Liverpool a goal ahead. But Arsenal battled back, and Eddie Kelly found himself in the right spot at the right moment to poke home an equaliser. The two teams turned around to face another gruelling 15 minutes in the sunbaked heat of Wembley and Charlie George with his socks dangling casually around his ankles seized the ball on the left and spurted towards goal, cutting in before arrogantly slamming a low shot beyond the flailing Ray Clemence. Arsenal had the Cup and with it the Double.

'King George' yelled the *News of the World*'s front page headline as it celebrated a London victory inspired by the 20-year-old Islington boy who had shot from obscurity to fame in just one season. But there was an alternative view. Many regarded Arsenal's football as dull and undeserving of the crown that Tottenham had so gloriously worn ten years previously. They could be negative, often winning by a single goal and the Final itself had hardly lived up to its pre-match hype. Maurice Smith in the *People* was scathing. 'Arsenal and Liverpool ... Cup Final of the decade, the clash of giants? The match worth £90 a blackmarket seat? Not on your flippin' nelly,' he wrote in an article certain not to win him many friends at Highbury. Nevertheless, Arsenal had achieved the Double and emulated Tottenham and nobody could take that away from them.

Sorry, lads— you're bores

MAURICE SMITH COMMENTS

The People, 9 May 1971

RIGHT: *King Charlie, pride of Highbury's North Bank, is crowned by George Graham*

BELOW: *Kelly (left) was accredited with Arsenal's equaliser but Graham (centre) still believes he had the final touch*

1972

FOR ALMOST a decade the satirical fortnightly *Private Eye* had been successfully needling the Establishment with its cutting comment and startling revelations. It had spoken where Fleet Street had previously been silent and had exposed the cosy world of politics and journalism. For a brief period in the seventies football also had its own satirical magazine which set out to do the same job on soccer as *Private Eye* had on politics.

To counter what was seen by some as a woeful deterioration in football reporting, a group of Cambridge undergraduates decided to launch a new soccer fortnightly. It was to be called *FOUL* and first appeared on the news-stands in October 1972. The aim was to redress the balance of Fleet Street cynicism and clichés. It was not there to repeat the outpourings of the boardroom or to boost the vanity of loud-mouthed, gold-chained managers but to parody and highlight the trough into which the tabloids, in particular, had fallen.

Behind the idea were Steve Tongue and Alan Stewart. They were later joined by Andrew Nickolds, Stan Hey, Peter Ball, Geoff McDonald and Steve Gleadall who between them succeeded in producing an attractive 'underground' newspaper against all the odds. Much of the money came from songwriter Tim Rice and for four years *FOUL* blossomed as its circulation rose from 6,000 to 12,000 copies per issue. But financial problems always loomed and after Mike Langley of the *Sunday People* had threatened to sue over an offending paragraph, which eventually had to be physically cut from each individual copy, *FOUL*'s days were numbered. The final issue, number 34, appeared in October 1976 and six months later the company was wound up.

ABOVE: *The first edition of FOUL*

At its best *FOUL* was scathing of Fleet Street's backpage mafia and was always committed to the fan on the terrace. At times, it repeated the sexism of the locker room and seemed to hold an unnecessary grudge against teams which won trophies. But it was always refreshing in an era when standards had slipped and its passing was mourned by many who wished to see their sporting papers return to the days of the *Athletic News* and *Sporting Chronicle*.

ABOVE: *Cartoon from the second edition*

1973

THE JUBILANT figure of Bob Stokoe, racing across the Wembley turf to greet goalkeeper Jim Montgomery, will always live as the memory of Sunderland's victory in the 1973 Cup Final. Leeds, the hottest Cup favourites in years, had been beaten by the sheer determination and grit of a second division side, urged on by its fanatical band of supporters.

Nobody expected Leeds to lose. In the top three of the first division for five years, they had triumphed at Wembley the previous season and fielded a team of international quality. Every player had or would represent his country, and manager Don Revie had instilled into them a discipline and steel that seldom buckled, even when under the most intense pressure. But Revie's famous dossier had not reckoned with Stokoe's travelling army. The Wearsiders, on their first visit to Wembley since 1937, were out to make the most of their trip and as the north-east chant of 'Ha'way The Lads' echoed around the rafters of the old stadium, there was a sense that something dramatic was set to happen.

And in the 31st minute it did. From Billy Hughes' corner, the ball swung dangerously into the Leeds box towards Dave Watson but the tall leaping centre-half could not reach it and the ball instead fell tantalisingly in front of Ian Porterfield. This was his moment, and pivoting on his left foot, he struck a thunderous volley into the Leeds goal. United, who had themselves been threatening to score until that moment, stood stunned.

Still, nobody expected Sunderland to be able to resist the surge of Leeds. They did, however – even though wave upon wave of white-shirted attacks plagued their goal – culminating in one of Wembley's finest goalkeeping moments when Jim Montgomery pulled off a second-half double save to keep them on course. And when the final whistle blew, Sunderland manager Bob Stokoe leapt off his bench to greet his hero, goalkeeper Montgomery.

W-U-N-D-E-R-LAND

For Stokoe's men a dream comes true

THE MIRACLE of Wembley hit the town of Sunderland like a red-and-white tornado last night. The whole place just exploded with incredulous joy.

The beer flowed like the waters of the Wear. They danced in the street. Cars trailing Sunderland banners drove round and round in aimless delight, their horns blowing.

Sunday People, 6 May 1973

ABOVE: *Bob Stokoe and Robert Kerr hug each other in delight after Sunderland's win over hot favourites Leeds*

1974

SUNDAY SOCCER arrived in England on January 6th 1974 and was generally acknowledged as a great success. For years commentators had urged the Football League to follow the Continental example. Attendances in Britain were on the decline and Sunday soccer was seen as a remedy to bring life back to the terraces. And so, with the country suffering power cuts as a result of the miners' strike, the FA finally agreed to give the go-ahead, on an experimental basis, for third round Cup ties to be played on a Sunday.

Nevertheless, there was opposition and football found its way unusually on to the letters page of *The Times* when the Bishop of Norwich replying to a *Times'* leader on the subject reminded people that Sunday was God's day.

Four clubs opted for the Sunday game – Bolton, Bradford City, Cambridge, and Nottingham Forest – with all reporting a near doubling of their normal gate. But there was a problem. Under the Sunday Observance Laws it was illegal to charge admission, so the clubs cunningly evaded the law by allowing spectators in free but instead charged them the usual admission price for the match programme.

A fortnight later Millwall Football Club broke further new ground by hosting the first Sunday league match. There were 15,000 at The Den, 5,000 more than usual and most clubs recorded higher gates. But despite all the high hopes, the novelty soon wore off and gates sadly slumped to their normal Saturday level.

Playing football on Sundays

From the Bishop of Norwich

Sir, I believe there are four clear grounds of objection to professional Sunday football, which are not fully drawn out in your leader last Saturday.

1 Family. Sunday draws many families together, at Church, at Sunday lunch and through family visits, "The family that prays together, stays together", and certainly Sunday lunches and 2 pm kick-offs are mutually exclusive! Your own leader and the BBC comment on Scottish football make the point that many footballers are against Sunday football and the strains on their family life should not be extended.

2 Social. Professional football is big business today, and Sunday football would seriously jeopardize the good social patterns of the day. Sunday excursion trains would be needed for away matches, with extra rail and coach transport for home games. More police, officials, caterers, and football staff would have to be on Sunday duty, and other major sports would soon be vying with each other for a financial cut of the commercial Sunday cake, and the breathless Continental and American Sunday would increase the already large amount of transport on the roads on a normal Sunday.

3 National. Doctor Dillistone's perceptive article on the same day as your leader, suggests that in England, social ethics and revealed Christian religion are less related than in earlier days in England. I believe Sunday is a vividly clear illustration of this. God created His world to work well, and from the start provided a rest or Sabbath Day, for the good of mankind, which is not narrowly restrictive, but is given by God as a day of rest, worship, refreshment, and family happiness. Above all, it is a Holy day, in which all men can remember their Creator, and in the words of one of my predecessors, Bishop Reynolds of Norwich, can thank Him "for our creation, preservation, and all the blessings of this life".

4. Christian. Your leader writer does not appear to have heard of away matches! It is quite unrealistic to imagine that Sunday football will not have an adverse effect on Sunday worship, and it is a retrograde step to feel that worship can be hurriedly crammed into a part of Sunday morning, so that the rest of the day can be used for matters of financial gain. The Lord's Day is an opportunity for worship, fellowship, prayer and instruction in the Christian faith, so that the basic law of God, "Remember to keep Holy the Sabbath Day", is worked out in the principles of Christian worship throughout that Day.

Yours sincerely,
MAURICE NORVIC:
The Bishop's House, Norwich.
January 28.

The Times, 2 February 1974

SUNDAY BEST
Crowds boom their message to F.A.

Daily Express, 7 January 1974

RIGHT: *The crowds turn out to watch Bradford City v Alverchurch, Sunday January 6th 1974*

IT WAS Denis Law, the one-time favourite of the Stretford End, who with what the *Guardian* described as 'the unkindest cut of all', sentenced his former team-mates to life in the second division. At Old Trafford on Saturday April 27th 1974, Law, then with Manchester City, sheepishly backheeled a ball from Francis Lee past Alex Stepney with eight minutes remaining, to give City a 1–0 lead over their neighbours. The unthinkable had happened and Law, always the professional, had plunged the final dagger into the body of United.

Not surprisingly Law's remarkable goal caused a pitch invasion which was initially quelled, but four minutes later, with United unquestionably doomed, the hooligans invaded Old Trafford once more and referee David Smith had little option but to take both teams off the field and abandon the game. Two hundred were ejected and 33 arrested in an afternoon United would always want to forget. Perhaps the invading fans had foolishly hoped their action would result in the game being replayed, but there was little doubt that when the Football League met a few days later they would confirm that the result should stand.

Law had begun his footballing career with Huddersfield Town under the legendary Bill Shankly. A skinny, bespectacled 16-year-old, he had arrived at Leeds Road from Aberdeen in 1956 and within two years had set the league alight with his razor sharp pace and skill, winning the first of his 55 caps in 1958. It was inevitable that Huddersfield would eventually be forced to sell their crown jewel and when Manchester City jumped in with a British record offer of £55,000 in March 1960, he was on his way to Maine Road. But even City were susceptible to money, and £100,000 worth of lira waved under their noses fifteen months later was enough to take Law to Torino. But it was a brief and unhappy affair that ended after just twelve months with his transfer back to Manchester and this time, to United. Here, under Matt Busby's careful tuition, Law, Charlton and Best helped spearhead one of the most exciting forward lines British soccer has ever moulded. The trophies rolled into the Old Trafford boardroom but the years were taking their toll as injuries plagued the fans' idol. He was even forced to miss United's night of glory in the European Cup Final and was eventually transferred back to Manchester City in 1973. But United could never have guessed that in his final league game he would score the goal that would consign them to the ignominy of the second division. He had never wanted to play in the game and later confessed that it was the most depressing weekend of his life.

Law's last sad word

ERIC TODD describes the scenes at Old Trafford

Guardian, 29 April 1974

ABOVE: *Et tu Brute? Denis Law's last league game was also his saddest*

1974

FOOTBALL KNOWS little loyalty and when Sir Alf Ramsey was sacked as the England manager in 1974, the glory of 1966 was but a distant memory. Fleet Street had ridiculed Ramsey's tactics prior to the World Cup triumph, then hypocritically lauded him on that victorious July day, only to revert to bitter complaining in 1970 and especially after the draw with Poland that had ended England's hopes of competing in the 1974 finals. The back pages were after his scalp. Ramsey had never enjoyed a close rapport with the press. He was considered aloof and secretive and his teams were said to reflect his own nature. Wingers were dispensed with, and caution rather than attack was the hallmark of his sides.

As the football manager grew in importance during the 1960s and 1970s, so Fleet Street's ability to create and destroy careers became keener. Ramsey was just one of many victims. And even *The Times*, a paper which until the 1950s had hardly found room to report football, now devoted space on its front page to announce Ramsey's dramatic departure.

Ramsey, the elegant Tottenham and England full-back who had played against the Hungarian team that had destroyed England at Wembley in 1953, had moved into soccer management to recreate some of the magic he had seen that day. Taking over unfashionable Ipswich Town of the third division south, he set them on a path that would take them to the first division title within six years. He succeeded Walter Winterbottom as the England manager in 1962, when English fortunes were at their lowest, and over the next twelve years his team played 113 games, winning 69, drawing 27 and losing only 17. They scored 224 goals with just 99 against. By comparison, Liverpool in their three successive championship years during the early 1980s played 126 games, won 72 and lost 21 scoring 240 goals with 101 against. Few, if any, modern teams or managers could compare with Ramsey's record. But for Fleet Street it was still not good enough.

ABOVE: *Ramsey may have had his critics in Fleet Street but there were few among his players*

Sir Alf Ramsey and England to part company

By Geoffrey Green
Football Correspondent

The 11-year reign of Sir Alf Ramsey as manager of the England football team is, it seems, about to end. Whether he has resigned or had the terms of his contract ended will be made known in an FA statement that may be expected today.

Whether Ramsey is to hand over the reins to a successor—and there will be further guesswork about his identity—at the end of the home international championship later this month, or at the completion of England's close-season tour of East Germany, Bulgaria and Yugoslavia in early June, remains to be seen. This, too, I gather, will be duly confirmed.

Since England's dismissal from the World Cup last October, and even for some time previously, Ramsey has been under attack from various quarters over his cautious, unambitious handling of the national side. Recently, when England faced Portugal in Lisbon at the beginning of April with five new caps, his outspoken criticism of clubs who withheld players for international action for one reason or another (mostly dishonest, in his opinion) met with considerable criticism in several places.

Sir Alf, as a man, a player and a manager, has proved himself. Short of speed, perhaps, he was yet the most thoughtful, constructive full back England has had for many a decade. Between 1949 and 1953 England stuck to him faithfully. He won 32 caps. Ironically, the last time he wore an England shirt was the historic day when Hungary became the first foreign team to win on English soil, beating England 6—3. He also played for Southampton and Tottenham Hotspur.

Cool and analytical in his performances, he also brought these qualities to his duties as a manager when he joined Ipswich Town in 1955. There he always worked on a financial shoestring, yet within six years, building a team from the cast-offs of others, he set a League record by winning the championships of the third, second and first divisions within six years. In 1962 he took over from Mr Walter Winterbottom as manager of England. Within four years he had won the World Cup, his team beating West Germany 4—2 at Wembley after extra time.

He succeeded in cementing a team spirit, equivalent to that of a successful club side, which had never before existed at a national level. It was this spirit, plus a new tactical formation which excluded the use of legitimate wingers, that took England to the top.

Elimination from the World Cup in 1970, by West Germany, and this year, by Poland, have been major setbacks. But from 1963 to 1970 he made England a deeply respected power in world football.

The Times, 1 May 1974

ABOVE: *Sir Alf Ramsey – no England manager has ever equalled his record*

1974

THE BACK pages, and in particular television, helped create the modern football manager. Prior to the 1960s only Herbert Chapman and Stan Cullis were well known names on the terraces but all that changed with the era of Busby, Nicholson, Shankly, Revie, Mercer, Allison and of course Brian Clough. The track suit managers suddenly became big news with the papers full of their post-match quotes, comments and quips. The newspapers also discovered that they could make or break careers as club directors searched for scape-goats when results turned sour and the vote of confidence on the back page from the chairman usually heralded the sack.

They were characters created by television and moulded by Fleet Street, and none more so than Brian Clough. After a distinguished goal-scoring career with Middlesbrough and Sunderland, Clough had gone into management with Hartlepool, and then joined second division Derby County. In 1969 a young Derby side romped away with the second division title and three years later were league champions. Clough had arrived. But following a row with the club in 1973, he and his partner Peter Taylor packed their bags and moved south to join Brighton. But it was a short-lived experience. England had just appointed Don Revie to succeed Alf Ramsey as the national manager, and Clough was invited to take over Revie's old job at Leeds. It was an awesome task and if Clough had known stormy days earlier in his managerial career, he was about to experience a hurricane.

He arrived at Elland Road on Monday July 22nd 1974 amid a blaze of publicity, and immediately began to stamp his no-nonsense personality on the club. New players were signed, some of the old guard transfer listed and a new authoritarian regime introduced. It was not to the liking of everyone and the reaction was there to be seen. Results were poor with only one win in eight matches, and the league champions found themselves in the unusual position of fourth from bottom with Clough being booed by his own supporters. There was much talk of crisis on the back pages, and as the pressure mounted it was inevitable that chairman Manny Cussins would wield the axe. And so, 44 days after joining the Yorkshire club, Clough was sacked and given a golden handshake worth £44,000. It was one of the biggest sports stories of the year and the *Daily Express* had the exclusive by Clough himself. Even Mrs Clough managed a few column inches as she talked of the heartache while Brian explained precisely why he had been sacked. Within 24 hours Leeds captain Billy Bremner was giving his version of the story while Clough was himself preparing a reply to those accusations. It may have all made good copy for the newspapers but it was yet another example of how managers and players were being unfortunately drawn into a back-page war of words that would not necessarily do them or the game much credit.

ABOVE: *Brian Clough's reign at Leeds United was a short one, his methods proving unpopular with players*

CLOUGH: WHY I WAS SACKED

They were frightened ... panic set in

Daily Express, 13 September 1974

1975

IF THERE is no serious or interesting news then the next best course of action is to make it up. That at least is the rule by which some newspapers live. And the easiest stories to conjure up centre on transfer speculation. Every big club is in the hunt for new players and there are always plenty around, particularly young ones, likely to move club. All you have to do is link the two. And, of course, the football fan likes nothing more than to read about his club bidding hundreds of thousands of pounds – or even millions – for some famous star or budding young starlet. The story that appeared on the back page of the *News of the World* in May 1975 was typical. It might well have been true but more likely it was speculation. Above all it concerned one of the biggest names in football – Alan Ball – and linked him with a move from one big club to another. It was the kind of story that would draw the attention not just of Leeds and Arsenal fans but anyone interested in soccer.

LEEDS MOVE FOR BALL

Arsenal star shock hits Swales

By REG DRURY

LEEDS are the surprise rivals to Manchester City to sign Arsenal's Alan Ball.

It's shock news for City chairman Peter Swales, who expected a clear field when the clubs return from end-of-season tours.

A definite offer was being made for the England skipper, who was transfer-listed at his own request. Now it could be a tug-o'-war battle with the European Cup finalists.

A move to Leeds would certainly tempt Ball, who has said he has finished with Arsenal and wants to join a club with more immediate prospects of success.

Nothing will be done until the end of the month. Ball's priority is captaining England in the Home Internationals; Arsenal are in the Far East and Leeds are preparing for the European Cup Final with Bayern-Munich.

But Leeds boss Jimmy Armfield is already thinking of next season, aware that veteran Johnny Giles is nearing the end of his playing career and an obvious candidate for a top managerial job.

Ball, 30 later this month, would be an ideal replacement for "general" Giles. His short-passing mid-field style would fit perfectly into the Leeds pattern.

Although a natural leader, Ball would have no objections to playing under Scotland's Billy Bremner next season—especially if Leeds are again in the European Cup.

Leeds wanted Ball nine years ago after he had starred for England in the 1966 World Cup triumph. Don Revie felt he had all the qualities required of a Leeds player and was bitterly disappointed when Everton stepped in to sign him from Blackpool.

It is ironical that failure to land Ball at that time led to Giles emerging from an average winger to the finest mid-field man in Britain.

The transfer fee of around £150,000 would present few problems to Leeds who have a surplus of saleable players. It is on the cards that £250,000 Duncan McKenzie will move during the summer.

Manchester City hope to raise the cash by parting with Rodney Marsh, who interests his old club Fulham, and could also be tempted by a worthwhile offer for ex-Sunderland striker Dennis Tueart.

News of the World, 11 May 1975

Ball was an England international and, although he was nearing the end of an international career which would eventually bring him 72 caps, he was still considered one of the hottest properties in the game. In 1966 he had helped England win the World Cup before leaving Blackpool for Everton, who paid a record British fee of £110,000 for the tenacious midfielder. At Goodison Park he linked up in a famous midfield with Colin Harvey and Howard Kendall, collecting a league championship medal and a Cup losers' medal before sensationally joining Arsenal for another record fee of £220,000. That was in 1972 and four years later he was on the move again, this time to Southampton in a £60,000 deal.

Ball's transfer had finally arrived 18 months after the *News of the World* had run their story. It may well have been that Ball was unhappy at Highbury in May 1975 and maybe Leeds did make an inquiry about him, but the story nevertheless had a strong whiff of speculation about it. No doubt it sold a few extra papers and excited a few Leeds fans as well as frightening some Arsenal fans at the thought of losing one of their heroes. Transfer speculation makes good reading yet it must be worrying for managers to find their players linked with other clubs, while many a player might be concerned to read that he is about to be shunted elsewhere in the merry-go-round of the transfer market.

LEFT: *Alan Ball in goalscoring action for Arsenal*

1976

THE MATCH programme billed it as 'the final act of the great first division drama'. The game was the final fixture of the 1975/76 season between Wolverhampton Wanderers, standing on the threshold of relegation, and Liverpool, poised to become champions. Wolves needed to beat Liverpool in order to hang onto their first division place – always provided that rivals Birmingham City were beaten at Sheffield United – while Liverpool needed either a low scoring draw or a win to clinch a record-breaking ninth league championship. No scriptwriter could have penned a more theatrical end to the season, and the drama of the occasion did not go unnoticed in Fleet Street.

ABOVE: *A determined Kevin Keegan pushes Steve Daly aside as Liverpool battle back after an early Wolves goal*

The game was played at Molineux just a couple of days after Southampton had thrillingly beaten Manchester United to win the FA Cup, and almost 50,000 spectators crammed into the old stadium with at least 25,000 having travelled down from Merseyside. Not since the visits of Honved, Moscow Dynamo and Real Madrid in the 1950s had Molineux seen such a clamour on the terraces. The tension seemed to be at bursting point as the two teams kicked off with second place Liverpool looking the more nervous. But if Liverpool were anxious then League leaders Queens Park Rangers, having completed their programme, must have been nerve-wracked as they sat at home listening to the commentary on radio.

With just thirteen minutes of the game gone, Steve Kindon sensationally scored for Wolves to send Molineux frenzied with excitement. They had been thrown a lifeline; now they had to hang on to it. At half time, Wolves still led by that single goal but were coming under mounting pressure as Liverpool searched doggedly for the equaliser. Into the second half Wolves found themselves increasingly penned back into defence as red shirted attack after red shirted attack laid siege on their goal. Another half hour ticked by and Wolves were still clinging desperately to Steve Kindon's goal while Liverpool were trying anxiously not to become too frustrated by the wall of defenders thrown up by Wolves. Finally with only 13 minutes remaining, the effervescent, diminutive Kevin Keegan pounced to hit the equaliser. Molineux erupted as thousands of Liverpool supporters raced on the pitch. The Merseyside club merely had to hold out now to be sure of the championship while Wolves had again to begin the despairing search for a goal. And as Wolves threw everything into attack, so glaring holes appeared in their defence. Within minutes John Toshack, Liverpool's giant Welsh striker, had exploited the gaps to secure a firmer grip on the league trophy and shortly before the final whistle blew Ray Kennedy gave Liverpool an unassailable lead and a stylish victory. Molineux was invaded by scousers while thousands of Wolves fans trudged home dejected to face a season in the second division. Ironically the result for Wolves

1976

never really mattered, as Birmingham clinched a draw at Bramall Lane to hold on to their first division spot. But Liverpool had shown yet again that they were at their finest playing under the most intense pressure.

Molineux match double decider

By DONALD SAUNDERS

THE most fiercely contested League championship for many years will be settled tonight, when Liverpool tackle Wolves at Molineux, while Queen's Park Rangers sit nervously at home awaiting the outcome.

Liverpool line up for their last domestic game of the season needing victory or a low-scoring draw to enable them to slip past Rangers and take the title on goal average or by a single point.

If they draw 0—0, 1—1 or 2—2 the Merseysiders will secure the place in next season's European Cup competition for which Rangers, Manchester United and Derby also have challenged strenuously during the past eight months.

Unless Wolves do them a good turn, Rangers will have to begin their European career in the UEFA Cup, alongside Manchester United and Derby! — who both seriously attempted the double and won neither championship nor FA Cup — and Manchester City, the League Cup holders.

Although Liverpool are past masters of the away draw their task is anything but a formality, since Wolves will be fighting for continued existence as a First Division club.

Wolves will be relegated unless they win tonight and then learn that Birmingham have been beaten at Bramall Lane by Sheffield United, who, like Burnley, are already destined for the Second Division.

European foray

Before announcing his team for this crucial match, Bob Paisley must make up his mind whether to rely on John Toshack, so often a match-winner, or give another chance to young Jimmy Case.

Crystal Palace also are delaying their choice of team for tonight's visit to Chester, which will decide whether they remain in the Third Division or clinch promotion.

Daily Telegraph, 4 May 1976

ABOVE: *John Toshack hits the goal that wins Liverpool their ninth League championship*

1977

THE BIENNIAL journey south of the border by the tartan army of Scottish football supporters for the England–Scotland clash at Wembley, ended in disgrace on Saturday June 4th 1977 when thousands of them poured over the wall that surrounded the pitch and began to tear Wembley apart. Since 1924 they had come, bagpipes, kilts, whisky and all with their fervent support always adding to the occasion. But during the 1960s their arrival began to take on an ominous dimension, with violent behaviour on the underground and hordes of drunken supporters swarming up Wembley Way and around London for days.

The mass invasion of Wembley in 1977 had been sparked off by a fine Scottish victory over a much depleted Auld Enemy. With Brooking and Keegan missing, England were no match for a Scottish midfield, inspired by Danny McGrain, which tore the heart out of England with goals from Gordon McQueen and Kenny Dalglish. It took an 87th-minute penalty from Mick Channon to bring some respectability to a scoreline that gave Scotland only their fifth triumph on English soil since 1938. But that was no excuse for what happened as the final whistle blew. The hordes charged across the pitch to congratulate their heroes, tearing down the goalposts and carving up Wembley's sacred acres to be carried off for souvenirs, and even today gardens all over Scotland still boast a patch of Wembley turf.

The scene after the game was one of devastation. More than £15,000 worth of damage had been caused with splintered goalposts, large bare patches around the goalmouth, and terraces littered with empty cans and bottles. Over the weekend 132 Scots had been arrested, and the cry was out that the Scots must never be allowed to descend on London for another Saturday international. As fellow Scot Hugh McIlvanney neatly called it in the *Observer*, it was 'the tribe that lost its head'.

The tribe that lost its head

HUGH McILVANNEY: England ...... 1 Scotland 2
Attendance: 100,000. *Receipts*: £309,000

Observer, 5 June 1977

ABOVE: *'Bonnie Scot-land, Bonnic Scot land, We'll support you evermoore!'*

LEFT: *Down come the goalposts, net and all, as the hordes invade Wembley*

THE ANTICS of George Best during the 1960s thrust the private lives of footballers onto the front pages. Suddenly, their romantic liaisons and drinking activities were the stuff of gossip columns, as familiar as those of film stars or pop singers. But it took another Manchester United employee, Tommy Docherty, to dramatically catapult the exploits of managers from the back pages into the same prominence.

Docherty had been manager of Manchester United since 1972, taking over the club after the disappointing reigns of Wilf McGuinness and Frank O'Farrell. Neither had lived up to their promise, and the presence of Matt Busby along with the memory of his famous sides, made life difficult for any successor. But Docherty was his own man; a powerful, buoyant personality with a wicked sense of humour and a proven knowledge of football management.

YOU AND YOUR HAIRDO PAGE SEVEN

DAILY EXPRESS

No. 23,955 Tuesday July 5 1977 Weather: Sunny spells 8p

Mary Brown

Punished for love affair, says Soccer boss as 'moral code' United tell him: You're sacked

Mrs Docherty

CLUB WIVES OUST DOC

Who will take over at Old Trafford? Back Page

Daily Express, 5 July 1977

Under Docherty, United had been unable to avoid the inevitable drop into the second division during his first complete season but had immediately climbed back as champions and the following season wound up in third place. The next May they beat Liverpool at Wembley to take the Cup and Docherty was the toast of Old Trafford. Six weeks later, the flamboyant Scot publicly announced that he was leaving his wife and four children to set up home with Mary Brown, the wife of the club's physiotherapist, Laurie Brown. Docherty's three-year-old affair with Mary Brown had been public gossip around Old Trafford and in soccer circles for some time. The footballing press all knew of it, yet had never chosen to divulge it. After all, it was the kind of liaison that goes on every day in offices and factories up and down the country and Docherty was not the only Old Trafford employee known to be having an affair. But when Docherty made his statement, the muck-rakers of the popular press could not resist and descended in their hordes on Old Trafford. Docherty's home was besieged and his love affair splashed all over the front pages. It was deeply embarrassing for United whose Catholicism was well known. A tormented Docherty pleaded that this was no casual affair and that the decision to leave his wife and family had been a painful and difficult one.

There may well have been sympathy at Old Trafford for Docherty and initially it looked as if the club would support him. But Fleet Street had the bit between its teeth and was clearly determined not to let this story die until it had reached its inevitable conclusion and United had sacked the manager. That would make it an even better story. The headlines ran for a week or more until on Monday July 4th, United took what they regarded as their only course of action. Given that it was the close season with no playing commitments, United might have been better advised to try and outlast Fleet Street. Sooner or later the waiting hacks would have become bored and packed their bags. Instead United bowed to the pressure.

In Docherty's place, United appointed the respectable and dependable Dave Sexton as manager. Docherty's humour was not heard for a while but if nothing else, he was a survivor and was soon back in football management with Derby County and later QPR. After a short spell in Australia, he returned home and is now happily married to Mary Brown.

BELOW: *Tommy Docherty in happier times*

1977

DON REVIE'S resignation came like a bolt out of the blue. Not always the most popular of England managers, Revie had been leading the national side since 1974. The former Leeds manager had guided England to 14 wins in 29 games with only seven defeats, yet had failed to take the international side beyond the qualifying stages for the European championships, while England's prospects of competing in the 1978 World Cup looked highly improbable. At one point England had gone six games without a win, their worst run in 19 years. He had produced a dour, unlovable side, and although his departure came as a shock, it was not universally greeted with dismay.

Capped himself six times by England, Revie had begun his playing career at Leicester before moving to Hull and Manchester City. He probably enjoyed his best days with the Maine Road Club, becoming Footballer of the Year in 1955, and in the same year was on the losing side in the Cup Final. A year later he was back at Wembley, this time inspiring City to victory with his 'deep-lying centre forward' plan. After City he moved to Sunderland and then Leeds before taking over the managerial reins of the second division club, then teetering on the brink of the third division. Under Revie the Yorkshire club went on to win two league championships and the FA Cup, and were losing finalists on three occasions. They also reached the final of the European Cup, only to be beaten by Bayern Munich, but in 1971 won the European Fairs Cup.

With England facing a crucial World Cup decider against Italy, there was considerable speculation about why Revie had chosen such a moment to resign. Much of it centred around Manchester United, themselves in search of a manager following Tommy Dochery's hasty departure only days before. But the truth, as revealed exclusively again by the *Daily Mail* the following day, was far more intriguing. Revie was off to the Persian Gulf with a £340,000 deal to manage the United Arab Emirates' national side. The British press were horrified that an England manager could turn his back on the country just for the sake of money. The FA agreed and slapped a ten year ban on him for 'bringing the game into disrepute', though he later successfully challenged it in the High Court.

MAIL EXCLUSIVE 'I sat down with my wife one night and we agreed the job was no longer worth it...it had brought too much heartache'

REVIE QUITS OVER 'AGGRO'

Daily Mail, 12 July 1977

REVIE HITS THE JACKPOT

WITHIN 24 hours of quitting as England manager, Don Revie is about to sign the most amazing contract in the history of soccer.

He has reached agreement in principle on a four-year deal worth a total of £340,000 tax-free to become football supremo of the United Arab Emirates.

Revie, whose decision to resign as England manager was revealed exclusively in the Daily Mail yesterday, has been negotiating with representatives from the group of oil states on the southern shore of the Persian Gulf.

Daily Mail, 13 July 1977

ABOVE: *Revie as England manager talks to Peter Taylor and Kevin Keegan*

1977

THE DAY after Don Revie's dramatic resignation as the England manager, the *Daily Mirror* came up with a novel idea for choosing his successor. The paper suggested that its own readers should decide and offered them the chance to vote in a poll with the result to be declared the following week.

With the co-operation of the bookmakers Ladbrokes, they drew up a list of candidates. Brian Clough of Nottingham Forest was rated the 9–4 favourite with Middlesbrough's Jack Charlton second favourite at 5–1. Also in the running and on the voting form were Jimmy Armfield, Jimmy Bloomfield, Les Cocker, Ron Greenwood, Bobby Robson, Ron Saunders, Dave Sexton and Terry Venables. The one name surprisingly missing was that of Bob Paisley, who in three years had taken Liverpool to two league titles, and wins in both the UEFA and European Cup finals. Quite why nobody ever considered the man who would soon become the most successful manager in the history of the Football League, is a mystery.

On Tuesday July 19th, having counted up all the thousands of voting slips which they claimed to have received, the *Mirror* declared that Brian Clough was far and away the People's Choice for the England managership. Eighty-four per cent had voted for him with only six per cent opting for Jack Charlton. The remaining eight candidates could pick up a mere ten per cent of the votes between them. It was much as the bookies had predicted. But neither the bookies, nor the *Mirror*'s readers had the final say, and the Football Association, which did, went for the unfancied outsider, Ron Greenwood of West Ham United. At least the Mirror could always say, 'we told you so…' years later when Greenwood failed to live up to expectations.

Mirror Sport

Tuesday, July 19, 1977 No. 22,850
Telephone: (STD code 01)—353 0246

The People's Choice for England boss

CLOUGH

Mirror's poll puts Forest manager in front by a mile!

BRIAN CLOUGH is the public's choice to succeed Don Revie as England manager.

Clough collected 84 per cent of the thousands of votes cast in Mirror Sport's poll last week.

The call for Clough comes as the official England Supporters' Union demand a say in the appointment of the national manager.

Mike Norton, secretary of the 50,000 strong Football Supporters' Union has written to Minister of Sport Denis Howell asking him to back the idea.

"The fans are always left in the cold. It's about time they had their say," he said.

Outspoken

"A ballot would be a democratic process if it were run on the lines of a general election—and the fans would feel part of the system. It wouldn't do any harm to at least give it a try."

Mirror Sport has already canvassed soccer fans and it's a landslide victory for Clough, a controversial and outspoken figure who has such an impressive managerial record at Derby and Nottingham Forest.

Only **JACK CHARLTON**, who resigned as manager of Middlesbrough at the end of last season, earned more than a mention in the count. He

By KEVIN MOSELEY

received 0 per cent. of the votes with the remaining 10 per cent. being split among other contenders.

The most significant aspect of what the man-on-the-terrace feels is the rejection of favourite Bobby Robson of Ipswich.

There is also a widespread condemnation of Don Revie, who quit to take a £340,000 tax-free job with the United Arab Emirates.

Like the Football Association, the fans say — and hundreds not only voted but wrote in expressing their views—how unhappy they were that Revie had walked out on the job. They say that Clough is the right man to take over. For, despite his outspoken comments, the average football supporter feels he speaks sound sense.

And certainly his record—leading Derby to the League championship after taking them over as a struggling Second Division side and then last season getting Forest promotion to the First Division — backs his claim.

Sir Alf

We gave ten possible candidates for the job, based on a bookmaker's list. You, the football supporter, produced some interesting additional names.

Perhaps it wasn't surprising that some asked for the recall of **SIR ALF RAMSEY**, who was sacked despite his World Cup success in 1966.

BILL SHANKLY, Liverpool's former manager and one of the most successful in the last 20 years, also won votes.

1—JIMMY ARMFIELD
2—JIMMY BLOOMFIELD
3—JACK CHARLTON
4—BRIAN CLOUGH
5—LES COCKER
6—RON GREENWOOD
7—BOBBY ROBSON
8—
9—DAVE SEXTON
10—TERRY VENABLES
11—

How 84% of you voted

Daily Mirror, 19 July 1977

ABOVE: *Clough was not the FA's choice*

1978

MILLIONS HAD been entranced by the delightful skills of the Argentinians during the 1978 World Cup finals as they stormed to a popular victory. But nobody guessed that within weeks two of their stars would be entertaining thousands every Saturday in the Football League. For that, English football had to thank two men. They were Keith Burkinshaw, the Tottenham Hotspur manager, and Harry Haslam, of Sheffield United, both of whom were wise enough to realise the possibilities and quick enough to seize the opportunity.

Even before the World Cup had begun, Haslam had established a scouting link with Antonio Rattin, the infamous Argentinian captain who had been sent off playing against England during the 1966 World Cup finals. Haslam, unable to afford the kind of transfer fees demanded in the English market, had tapped Rattin to feed him information on potential recruits at prices within his means. Burkinshaw was also on the lookout for players to strengthen his newly promoted side. He too had scoured the Football League unsuccessfully and sitting in the comfort of his home, watching the finals, he heard that the World Cup-winning team was about to be broken up as they all cast their eyes towards Europe. Within hours Burkinshaw was on a plane to Buenos Aires with a list of names scribbled on the back of an envelope. He may have been alone among English managers making the trip, but he had competition, particularly from the rich Spanish clubs.

But while some of the more obvious goalscoring talents were negotiating lucrative contracts to play in Spain, Burkinshaw concentrated on midfielders and on Monday July

ABOVE: *Tottenham's Argentinian imports Ricardo Villa (left) and Ossie Ardiles (right) evade Peter Withe of Nottingham Forest, as they display dazzling Latin American skills at their debut game against Nottingham Forest in 1978*

BELOW: *Three years later and the Argentinians are still going strong. Ricardo Villa (right), who scored two goals, is seen here with Garth Crooks after Tottenham's FA Cup Final victory at Wembley*

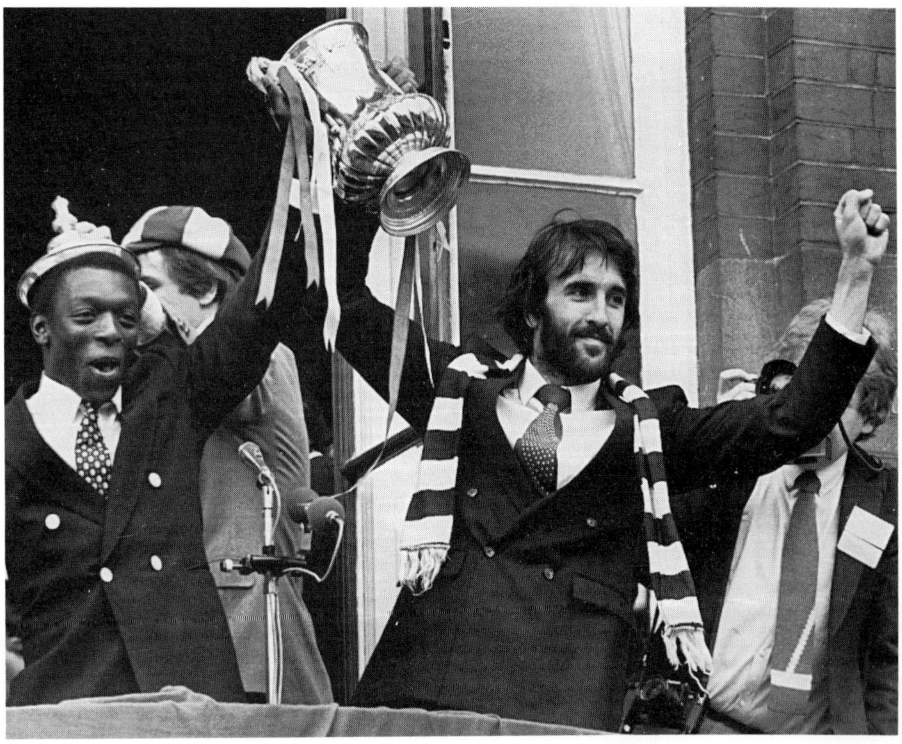

SPURS SCOOP THE WORLD

EXPRESS EXCLUSIVE

Ardiles and Villa sign in £750,000 double deal

By Malcolm Folley

TOTTENHAM manager Keith Burkinshaw yesterday signed two of Argentina's all-conquering national side — Osvaldo Ardiles and Ricardo Villa — in a £750,000 deal.

Ardiles masterminded Argentina's World Cup triumph in Buenos Aires last month.

But while the Italians drooled over his skills and the Spaniards awaited developments, Burkinshaw caught a plane to the Argentine capital.

By last night Tottenham's £1.500 investment in his airline ticket had reaped rewards which will make the North London club the focal point of British football.

Here on Sunday

Ardiles and Villa, both 25 and midfield players, had signed three-year contracts and begun to organise their travel arrangements to arrive in London on Sunday.

The whole transaction, which breaks shattering new ground in the British game, had taken just 72 hours to complete.

Daily Express, 11 July 1978

10th, just two weeks after Argentina had beaten Holland to clinch the World Cup, he was able to announce to the press that he had signed Osvaldo Ardiles and Ricardo Villa for a joint fee of £750,000. Ardiles, the lean, gaunt-looking midfielder with the Buenos Aires club Huracan, had been a regular member of the World Cup-winning side, while Villa from Racing of Buenos Aires had appeared only once. The deal took just 72 hours to complete and was heralded in the press as 'shattering new ground in the British game'. Fleet Street was ecstatic at the prospect of Argentinian talent gracing the first division and applauded Tottenham for their initiative. Most reckoned the slightly built Ardiles would have problems with the sticky, wet mud of an English winter whereas the powerfully built Villa would sweep his way to success. In the event, it was just the opposite. Ardiles brought new vision, coping admirably with the conditions while Villa laboured hard to find a spark that would set the first division alight.

RIGHT: *Keith Burkinshaw's recruits outside the Tottenham ground clutching their new club shirts*

Once Fleet Street had broken the story, half the first division's managers were on the next plane to Buenos Aires, clutching open cheque books. Harry Haslam remained one step ahead and within days of the Tottenham deal had signed the River Plate players Alex Sabella and Pedro Verde, while later Sunderland paid £320,000 for Claudio Marangoni of San Lorenzo. Sadly, this later influx of talent never really lived up to its reputation, and before long most had either moved to other league clubs or returned home. Only Ardiles remained, the one player who made the transition successfully and who won the admiration of the terraces.

1978

ABOVE: *Jimmy Hill prepares to introduce 'Match of the Day' for the BBC*

TELEVISED FOOTBALL has come a long way since the first experiment in 1937 when the *Daily Herald* predicted that a time would soon come when we would regularly watch football by the comfort of our firesides. After the early success of that first transmission from Highbury, the annual televised match for those wealthy enough to own TV sets was the Cup Final. Yet it was not until 1953, when the Coronation sparked off the mass purchase of cheap sets, that football really arrived in the average living room. And the Stanley Matthews Final of that year was the first sporting event to be seen in millions of homes. But for the remainder of the 1950s, televised football was generally restricted to internationals, Cup finals and the odd friendly.

Indeed, it was not until the 1960s that league soccer found its way onto the small screen, when a live fixture between Blackpool and Bolton was shown on the Saturday evening of September 10th 1960. But the game was a grave disappointment, and plans for regular live televised Saturday football were quickly dropped. Four years later, on Saturday August 22nd 1964, the BBC introduced edited football with highlights of the afternoon's clash between Liverpool and Arsenal shown that evening under the title 'Match of the Day'. Only 75,000 watched that first programme, transmitted on BBC 2, but once the series had been transferred to BBC 1, it soon became one of the nation's favourites with Saturday night crowds returning home early from pubs, dance halls, and cinemas for their weekly diet of David Coleman and Jimmy Hill. Appropriately enough, Anfield was also the venue for the first colour transmission of football when BBC cameras captured the action between Liverpool and West Ham for 'Match of the Day' on Saturday November 15th 1969.

Independent television's inaugural broadcast from a soccer ground came in January 1956, when the third round Cup replay between Bedford Town and Arsenal was transmitted in some regions, but ITV generally lagged behind the BBC whose years of experience had given them a near monopoly of sports coverage. It was not until 1978 that ITV really made its mark when it signed a lucrative contract with the Football League to guarantee edited soccer on the channel every Saturday evening beginning in August 1980, instead of in their traditional Sunday afternoon slot. The contract, stolen from under the noses of the BBC, was negotiated by Michael Grade of London Weekend Television and was said to be worth more than £9 million over three seasons. BBC chiefs who had automatically assumed that the League would again sign a deal with them were furious.

THE BIG SNATCH

ITV's £9 million deal wipes out soccer on BBC

THE BBC has lost Match of the Day . . . to ITV.

In secret negotiations, an ITV team has won exclusive rights to televise all English League and League Cup matches for three seasons.

London **Weekend** TV — representing all ITV companies—is believed to be paying £9 million for the deal.

Now the ITV companies will drop their Sunday Big Match to screen League matches on Saturday night—taking over from BBC's prestige Match of the Day.

Instead of Jimmy Hill and David Coleman of BBC, ITV's Brian Moore and his team will be dominating the football fans' screens.

Daily Mirror, 17 November 1978

FOOTBALL HAS remained surprisingly untroubled by drug scandals. Only a handful of cases have ever come to light, thanks usually to the tabloid press. In the mid-1960s Albert Dunlop, the Everton goalkeeper, claimed in the *People* that he had taken drugs and that on one occasion he was so totally confused towards the end of a match because of the number of stimulants he had swallowed that he had to be stretchered off the field. He also claimed that he was not the only Everton player involved in drugtaking, but after an internal investigation no action was taken by the Football League, either against the club or Dunlop.

Perhaps the most famous case was that of Willie Johnston, the former Glasgow Rangers and West Bromwich Albion winger who was sent home from the 1978 World Cup finals in Argentina after failing a drugs test. Johnston always maintained his innocence but the Scottish FA had been severely embarrassed before a watching world and Johnston who had played just one game in Argentina never played again in the blue shirt of Scotland.

Just a few months after the Johnston affair, Stan Bowles, the 28-year-old Queen's Park Rangers' striker went public in the *Daily Star,* claiming that he had taken drugs. He told the newspaper that he had tried amphetamines and valium and added that in his opinion some drugs should be legalised. Bowles however was a controversial character, well known for his gambling and drinking and the Football League did not appear to take his allegations too seriously. The following day Charlie George, the former Arsenal favourite, revealed that drug taking among footballers in America where he had played was widespread. But again with players either retired or with no specific or provable allegations it was impossible for the League to take much action. Bowles almost certainly touched on a scandal that went much deeper and it remains surprising that, even to this day, the press has continued to ignore investigations into an area which could offer some rich journalistic pickings.

Exclusive: Soccer ace Stan Bowles' amazing confession

YES, I TAKE DRUGS

Daily Star, 27 November 1978

ABOVE: *Stan Bowles*

1978

ENGLISH FOOTBALL entered a new era in November 1978 when Viv Anderson became the first black player to win an England cap. Though he was just one of many young black players emerging in the Football League, it was always likely that the Nottingham Forest full-back would be the first to gain international honours.

Anderson was chosen to represent his country against Czechoslovakia at Wembley when England's regular right-back, Phil Neal, was injured. He donned the number two shirt and gave a performance to fully justify his selection, as England ran out 1–0 winners. And although Neal returned to his spot immediately after injury, Anderson had put himself into contention and was soon forcing his way into the team. By 1987, he had gone on to win more than 25 caps and had been joined in the England squad by other black players such as John Barnes, Luther Blissett and Cyril Regis.

The *Daily Express* greeted his selection with appropriate applause, finely striking the right balance between recognising the historic moment while not appearing patronising. Most of the other papers followed suit, voicing their approval and acknowledging that this was a reflection of a changing Britain. In a society that was ridden with racial problems, they all agreed that it might help eradicate the racist abuse that was becoming so common on the terraces as well as give some pride to young blacks who for so long must have felt that their talents were not appreciated by a predominantly white society.

RIGHT: *Viv Anderson of Nottingham Forest in his debut game for England*

GREENWOOD NAMES ENGLAND'S FIRST BLACK INTERNATIONAL

SOCCER'S FOLK HERO

Viv, the world his stage now, says: I'm just another fellow doing a job

By David Miller

VIV ANDERSON has the world as his stage when tomorrow he becomes the first black player to represent England in a full Soccer international.

The supremely athletic Nottingham Forest right-back has the potential to achieve fame on two fronts as he steps out against Czechoslovakia at Wembley.

He can, I believe, develop into an attacking fullback comparable to the memorable Djalmar Santos of Brazil's 1958 World Cup-winning team.

And he can become a folk hero as socially significant to Britain's coloured population as champion athlete Daley Thompson.

If this weather doesn't warm up, England will be one black'un and ten blue'uns.

Daily Express, 28 November 1978

1978

BELOW: *Viv Anderson earned himself a place in the record books when he became the first black player to play for England, against Czechoslovakia in November 1978*

BELOW: *Phil Neal's replacement Viv Anderson takes the field followed by Tony Woodcock and Peter Barnes.*

1979

BRITAIN'S FIRST million pound footballer was always guaranteed to hit the headlines. It was just the sort of story Fleet Street relishes and so, when Trevor Francis left Birmingham for Nottingham Forest in February 1979, the headlines were predictable. 'Zip Goes A Million' yelled the *Guardian* while even the normally staid *Daily Telegraph* blared, 'Francis becomes Million Pound Man of Forest'.

Francis was always the man most likely to break the million pound barrier. He was one of a small number of players able to command such a fee and it was known that the young England forward was not happy at St Andrews. With City anchored firmly to the bottom of the first division and with second division soccer looming, Francis was eager to cash in on his talents as well as win medals. Likewise Birmingham, knowing they had a rare jewel in their hands, decided to realise their asset while the market was buoyant, and the word went out among the first division clubs that the England international was available at the right price. Although everybody showed interest, most clubs quickly dropped out of the auction when a one million pound price tag was attached, but Coventry under chairman Jimmy Hill and Brian Clough's Nottingham Forest battled it out to the end to secure his signature. Eventually, Clough won and lured the 24-year-old into his net, with the promise of lucrative football

FRANCIS BECOMES MILLION POUND MAN OF FOREST

By ROBERT OXBY

TREVOR FRANCIS became Britain's first £1 million footballer yesterday when he signed for Nottingham Forest. The transfer of the Birmingham and England striker doubles the previous record, set last December when David Mills moved from Middlesborough to West Bromwich for £500,000.

When V A T, the Football League Provident Fund and Francis's five per cent. cut are added, Forest have committed themselves to paying £1,180,000. In Mills's case the gross amount approached £625,000.

Francis, who spent more than five hours discussing the move with Brian Clough, the Forest manager on Thursday, made his decision after considering the matter overnight. He drove to Nottingham to sign at lunchtime yesterday.

The way was cleared for Francis to sign for the League champions when Mr Clough raised no objection to the striker spending the coming summer with Detroit Express of America, from whom he is expected to collect £80,000.

Trevor Francis . . . £80,000 from Detroit Express.

Daily Telegraph, 10 February 1979

ABOVE: *Mr and Mrs Francis, proud owners of the European Cup, after Forest's 1–0 victory over Malmo in 1979*

in America during the summer to supplement his salary.

Francis had been with Birmingham all his playing life, making his league debut while still a sixteen-year-old apprentice and had gone on to score 118 goals in 270 league games as well as collecting a dozen England caps. The deal that took him to Forest broke the previous record fee paid by West Bromwich Albion for Middlesbrough's David Mills by more than half a million pounds. At the end of the day, Francis was £50,000 richer and Forest £1,180,000 poorer after tax had been paid. But he was worth every penny to Brian Clough who, when he sold him to Manchester City two-and-a-half years later for another million pounds, could boast that Francis had scored the winning goal for Forest in the European Cup Final and had only cost them his wages.

If Francis had sparkled under Clough at Forest, he was something of a damp squib at Maine Road, playing in a mediocre team where his flowing talents were largely wasted. After just ten months he continued his wanderings, joining Sampdoria in the Italian League for £900,000 and eventually wound up a £250,000 buy at Glasgow Rangers. All told, Trevor Francis's wanderings around Europe had cost football more than £3 million.

BELOW: *Francis scores his first goal for Forest, against Bolton Wanderers on 31st March 1979*

1979

LIVERPOOL, THE 1979 European and league champions, became the first major British club to adopt the continental style of shirt advertising. In July 1979 they announced that they had signed a deal with Hitachi, the Japanese electrical giant, to wear the company's name on their shirts. The one-year deal was said to be worth £50,000 although the club added that if the hastily-applied TV ban on shirt advertising was lifted, the value of such deals would be worth at least a quarter of a million pounds a year. That immediately sparked off a campaign to abolish the ban and also alerted dozens of other clubs to a new source of income. Liverpool had made a profit of only £71,000 that season and was desperate to improve its finances. Liverpool's announcement offered the ideal photo-opportunity and the Liverpool captain, Phil Thompson, was the stooge who had to model the new shirt for the press corps along with the requisite pretty girl. While the press generally welcomed shirt advertising some papers warned that only the Liverpools and Manchester Uniteds of the first division would ever be able to attract sponsors, but their fears were unfounded. Within two years virtually every football club in the league was carrying a sponsor's name while television had reluctantly accepted the inevitable.

The vast majority of sponsors were private companies but some clubs, such as West Bromwich Albion, became associated with anti-smoking campaigns and others with local councils. But perhaps the most disappointed sponsor of all was Hafnia, a Liverpool-based corned beef company who backed Everton for some years. Finally tired of Everton's inability to win anything, Hafnia ditched the Merseyside team, whereupon Everton found new sponsors – NEC – and went on to appear in three Cup Finals and win two league championships.

OUT OF THE RED

Liverpool lead way with shirt 'ad' deal

Daily Mirror, 25 July 1979

ABOVE: *Kenny Dalglish – fitted with some Japanese electronic wizardry himself?*

1980

JUST OCCASIONALLY the seasoned football writers of Fleet Street can be deceived and surprised. Such a moment occured on Monday February 11th 1980, when the Southampton manager Lawrie McMenemy called a press conference at a country motel in Hampshire. Rising to address the waiting journalists he announced that he wanted to introduce 'someone who will play a big part in Southampton's future.' And to the astonishment of the gathered hacks, in walked Kevin Keegan.

There had been not a hint of a deal to bring the European Footballer of the Year back to Britain and the football pages – which always thrive on speculation – totally missed the biggest transfer story for years. McMenemy, the former Guardsman now in charge of the south coast club, had pulled off a coup which left most other clubs green with envy. He had been forced to maintain the utmost secrecy in order to stave off any attempt to lure Keegan elsewhere. Southampton were not a particularly wealthy club and unable to compete in the million pound market but at £400,000 Keegan could be considered the bargain of the season. But even before the deal could be signed with Hamburg, McMenemy had to secure the agreement of Keegan's former employers, Liverpool, who had a first-option clause in their contract with the German club. Keegan, however, informed the Liverpool manager, Bob Paisley, that he did not wish to return to Anfield and so the league champions lost the opportunity of linking Keegan with his Scottish replacement, Kenny Dalglish, in a deal which would have cost them a mere £200,000.

The *Daily Mirror*, along with the rest of Fleet Street, may have missed out on any transfer speculation but they made up for it with a post-signing exclusive in which McMenemy detailed the events that led up to the deal. But it was a tale which also showed how football reporters hunt in packs, rarely digging around for a story themselves. Instead, many are spoon-fed by clubs, players and agents, rarely asking awkward or embarrassing questions for fear of offending and losing a contact. Having failed to get their story by proper reporting, the *Mirror* bought their exclusive and were able to look forward to months of mutally beneficial revelations.

Kevin Keegan finally arrived at the Dell in July 1980 in time for the new season and immediately began to set the Football League alight again. By the end of the season, Southampton had climbed to their highest ever position in the first division, finishing in sixth place, just one point behind Liverpool. In retrospect, McMenemy had been wise to maintain a silence and hide his activities from his friends on the tabloids. Fleet Street may have been conned by the genial manager of Southampton but they had to smile at the style with which he had done it.

HOW I MADE KEVIN INTO A SAINT!

By LAWRIE McMENEMY

EXCLUSIVE!

KEVIN KEEGAN telephoned me on Sunday night to confirm that he would sign for Southampton.

Do you know what he said? "Another 5-1 win, then," he remarked – we had beaten Brighton by that margin the previous day.

"Well," he added, "I don't mind sitting on the substitutes bench for a few weeks." And I believed him, for he is that kind of man.

I have always tried to be straight and honest. I like honest people around me, and who can be more honest on and off the field than Keegan.

I knew Keegan was considering a return to England. That was what prompted me to try to get him.

Nothing is impossible. I've always thought. Who would have given Southampton a chance of winning the F A Cup a few years ago when we were in the Second Division? Who would have thought I had a chance of getting Keegan?

I saw him last week when he was over to play for England against Eire at Wembley.

We went into a room and I immediately locked the door. I just told him the plans and ambitions of Southampton and myself.

At the end of three hours talking he had agreed to join us. But there were still problems, although when I watched Keegan at Wembley on Wednesday—when he scored those two goals—I felt like shouting out: "He's my player." But I had to keep quiet. It was difficult.

We were waiting for confirmation from Hamburg of the transfer and we also had to get approval from Liverpool, who had first option on Kevin if he returned to this country.

I was still sweating it out on Sunday. To ease my worries I went for a cycle ride with my 16-year-old son Sean and 11-year-old daughter Alison around the country lanes near my home. My wife Anne, as in all moments of stress, started baking cakes.

It was a similar situation to last year, when I was offered the job at Leeds, and I then drove around the Bournemouth area trying to make up my mind. Now, at 43, trying to keep fit, I cycle.

We managed to contact Liverpool chairman John Smith, who was playing golf, and I had nothing but admiration for him when he rang back and said that Keegan was ours.

He said he had spoken to Kevin and there was no doubt in his mind that Southampton was the club he wanted to go to.

Now everyone here hopes that we will have a stadium to match our team. With the local council's approval, we will be able to build a brand new stand at the Dell or even move into a completely new sports complex.

Surely we've proved we deserve one, and while Kevin isn't banking on it, he shares those ambitions.

This is a wonderful moment for me, for the club and for the city. And who can doubt now that we intend to compete with the Liverpools, Manchester Uniteds and Nottingham Forests of this world?

LAWRIE McMENEMY was talking to KEVIN MOSELEY

Daily Mirror, 12 February 1980

ABOVE: *Keegan in action for Southampton*

1980

ABOVE: *Malcolm Allison welcomes Kevin Reeves to Manchester City*

Norwich ace set for City

£1m REEVES

By John Bean

KEVIN REEVES, Norwich City's England striker, is set to join Manchester City today for £1 million.

Maine Road chairman Peter Swales last night telephoned his Norwich counterpart Sir Arthur South with a firm bid.

Daily Express, 7 March 1980

1979 AND 1980 were the crazy years when transfer fees went through the ceiling and left a number of clubs wishing they had never let their managers loose with a cheque book. The million pound tag, even for mediocre players, became common currency and any young player stringing half a dozen useful games together could easily fetch a quarter of a million pounds or more. Brian Clough was one manager not afraid to dig into his pockets though at least his deals were always shrewd. But the blame for sending transfer prices spiralling rests with two men – the Manchester City managers Malcolm Allison and John Bond.

The transfer of the 22-year-old Norwich City striker, Kevin Reeves, to Manchester City in March 1980 brought manager Malcolm Allison's spending, in a little over 12 months, to almost £4.5 million. Reeves, at £1.25 million, arrived at Maine Road hard on the heels of Steve Daley, a £1.5 million import from Wolverhampton Wanderers. And just ahead of him in the queue for introductions was the largely unknown Michael Robinson who had joined City from Preston North End for a staggering £750,000. In a little over a year Allison had turned over £7.1 million.

As a coach Malcolm Allison had enjoyed considerable success at Manchester City under manager Joe Mercer. Between them they had won the league, the FA Cup, the League Cup and the European Cup Winners' Cup. Mercer and Allison were a winning formula. Allison had an early spell as manager of City after Mercer had left, but his position did not last long and after eight months he too was on his way. He returned, like the prodigal son, in January 1979 and began a clearout that made Maine Road look like Piccadilly Circus. Out went nine players including Brian Kidd, Peter Barnes, Asa Hartford and Mick Channon with £2.6 million pouring into City's coffers. But that was easily gobbled up by the £4.5 million which he spent on another ten players. Neither was it money wisely invested, as City found themselves glued to the bottom of the first division. That spelt the end for the outspoken Allison and in came another big spender, John Bond.

Bond had carefully guided Norwich City to first division security on one of the tightest bank balances in the league. When City hired him they must have reckoned that his astute budgeting at Carrow Road was precisely what they required. But Bond turned out to be almost as embarrassing as Allison.

Although the team quickly settled under Bond, climbing steadily off the foot of the table and winning their way to a Wembley final, the former West Ham colleague of Allison clearly placed little value on some of his expensive purchases. Out went seven players, including Steve Daley for a mere £450,000 — £1 million less than had been paid for him. Trevor Francis was bought for £1.2 million and sold not long after for £1 million. The Allison spending fever was catching as Bond managed to spend £3 million while recouping £1.8 million from the players he sold. The transfer market which Allison had helped inflate had now collapsed and ironically, City would be the biggest losers. In four years the two men had turned over almost £12 million. For Manchester City the days of champagne and cigars were at an end and even today, City remain millions of pounds overdrawn, still counting the legacy of Allison and Bond.

Comings and goings

ALLISON

BUYS	£	SALES	£
Silkman	65,000	Kidd	150,000
Robinson	765,000	Watson	150.000
Shinton	300,000	Owen	450.000
Stepanovic	140,000	Hartford	450,000
MacKenzie	250,000	Barnes	748.000
Daley	1,437,000	Channon	200,000
Lee	80,000	Robinson	400.000
Reeves	1,000,000	Futcher	130,000
		Silkman	50.000
	4,037,500		2,728,000

BOND

Hutchison	47,500	Henry	125,000
MacDonald	250,000	Gow	75,000
Boyer	220,000	O'Neill	125,000
Gow	175,000	Hutchison	free transfer
Bond	350,000	Daley	450,000
O'Neill	275,000	Palmer	70,000
Hartford	350,000	Francis	1,000,000
Francis	1,200,000		
Baker	225,000		
Cross	free transfer		
	3,092,500		1,845,000

As always transfer figures are unreliable, and these figures slightly underestimate Allison's deficit (said by the chairman to be "around £1m") and perhaps slightly overestimate Bond's (said to be "around £1m").

The Times, 12 April 1983

The ghosts of City's past are still haunting Maine Road

BELOW: *John Bond and another £1 million signing, Trevor Francis. But the spending failed to bring results and Francis soon left for Italy*

1980

IN EARLY 1980 the investigative eye of ITV's award-winning 'World in Action' turned its usual attention away from war zones and dirty deals in the City of London, and instead focused on some shady goings-on in football. The programme, entitled 'The Man Who Bought United', alleged financial irregularities involving the Manchester United chairman, Louis Edwards. A highly respected figure in league football, Edwards also ran a meat packaging company and the Granada TV programme accused him of share dealings in the club that had produced substantial profits for his family as well as a controlling interest. The programme, which had taken 12 months to compile, also claimed that a special slush fund existed for bribing the parents of schoolboy players. It was serious stuff and was splashed across the front pages the following morning.

The Football League, the FA and the police began immediate inquiries. Local MPs tabled questions in the House of Commons and there was even speculation that United might be thrown out of the League. Louis Edwards denied all the allegations but within a month, and before he could try to clear his name, the 65-year-old chairman suddenly died following a heart attack. Not surprisingly, there were bitter recriminations. Edwards' son, Martin, who assumed the position of chairman of United, accused Granada Television of killing his father. With Edwards dead the Football League and the police decided to drop all their inquiries and no more was heard of the allegations.

There was a mixed reception from the press, with most papers reluctant to test the story and at least one commentator – John Junor of the Sunday Express – saw it as the ideal opportunity to attack Granada TV and its own chairman Lord Bernstein. Nobody seemed to be concerned with actually examining the facts and discovering whether or not they were correct. The cosy relationship between Fleet Street and football clubs stood exposed, with the press reluctant to damage any partnership that from time to time had given them facilities as well as the occasional exclusive. Indeed, the United story had been originated not by the newspapers but by television.

The story also demonstrated the dilemmas local papers face as they rely on their neighbourhood clubs so much for news. If they expose corruption, humbug and lies they are liable to be blacklisted, and in the past a number of famous club have shamefully refused access to some newspapers because they have written offending items. All too often, the friendly partnership between football clubs and newspapers, where club and paper feed off each other, becomes unhealthy with a reluctance to 'dish up the dirt' in case it affronts the chairman, manager or players. It is a lobby system which does not always work to the benefit of the public or the game.

ABOVE: *Manchester United chairman Louis Edwards, who died just weeks after ITV's accusations*

SOCCER BOSS IN PROBE

Accused chairman says: My conscience is clear

Daily Express, 29 January 1980

FANTASTIC ON PLASTIC

Rangers pitch looks like a big hit

Daily Star, 2 September 1981

1981

PLASTIC FOOTBALL arrived with the opening of the 1981/82 season. And it was a second division side, Queen's Park Rangers, who pioneered the new artificial turf at their Loftus Road ground in West London. It was laid during the close season at a cost of £300,000, with QPR anticipating a quick return for their investment by hiring the ground out regularly for sporting and other events, without any damage to the turf.

With QPR away from home for their first Saturday fixture, the press were forced to wait until midweek before they could cast their eye over the new turf. And when they did give their opinion, it was unanimous. Plastic football was here to stay. Bob Driscoll in the *Star* had no doubts. 'As a milestone in British soccer history, it was perhaps the most important this century,' he wrote adding rather frivolously that, 'if you thought soccer was a kick in the grass – you'll reckon it's fantastic on plastic.' But as we all know, he was wrong.

QPR's experience encouraged other league clubs – Luton Town, Oldham Athletic and Preston North End – to follow suit but there was considerable criticism from players who found the bounce of the ball and the speed at which it flew off the surface not to their liking. There was also talk of burns and muscle injuries. Some of the most skilful sides and players were unable to master the new technique and criticism slowly began to mount. And so, the revolution that Bob Driscoll had predicted never happened.

As far as QPR were concerned plastic had mixed fortunes. They may have lost their first league game on the new surface to Luton but by the following season they were topping the second division and bringing in vital revenue as Loftus Road became the venue for hockey internationals, world title fights, and pop concerts. But with so few clubs following suit, particularly in the first division, QPR decided to rip up their artificial turf at the end of the 1987/88 season and revert to – yes – natural grass.

RIGHT: *'There have to be some weeds somewhere.' Manager Terry Venables inspects the new plastic pitch at Loftus Road*

ABOVE: *The 'faultless' artificial turf after its installation. It may have been a hit to begin with but seven years later QPR ripped it up*

1981

IF EVER a city adopted a son, it was Liverpool with their adulation of Bill Shankly. And, as with Manchester and the Munich air disaster, it was the city's own newspaper, the *Liverpool Daily Post* which was first with the sad news of his death.

Shankly had been taken ill at his home on the Saturday afternoon of September 26th. It was immediately diagnosed as a heart attack but there never seemed to be any fear for his life. Indeed, the day before he died, doctors were predicting an early recovery. But then, on the evening of Monday September 28th, he took a turn for the worst and just after midnight died in the intensive care unit at Broadgreen hospital. The 3 am edition of the *Liverpool Daily Post* carried a simple front page: 'Shankly Is Dead'. Some of the other tabloids with late editions also managed to carry the news but the *Post* pulled together an astonishing series of features in a short space of time which made one wonder if they had not anticipated his death. The following day a special twelve-page paper was available, packed with the memorable quips that had made the man so famous.

Shankly had arrived at Anfield in December 1959 from Huddersfield Town, following a distinguished career as a player with Preston North End and Scotland. Already five times champions, Liverpool were a slumbering giant who had been languishing in the second division since 1954. But Shankly saw the potential and quickly began to mould a team around Scottish imports Ron Yeats and Ian St John. To them he added others such as Roger Hunt, Peter Thompson, Gordon Milne, Gerry Byrne, Willie Stevenson and Tommy Smith.

In three seasons Liverpool were back in the first division and well on their way to their sixth championship. Under Shankly they won three championships, two FA Cups and the UEFA Cup. He bought cleverly, introducing players such as Kevin Keegan, Ray Clemence, Emlyn Hughes, Steve Heighway, Ian Callaghan and John Toshack to first division football. And at Anfield he established a system that would see the club in good stead for many more years to come. It was little wonder that the man born not far from Glasgow should soon become the city's favourite adopted son. 'Some say football is more than life and death,' he once joked, adding, 'It's not. It's much more serious than that.' The people of Liverpool knew precisely what he meant.

ABOVE: *'Some say football is more than life and death. It's not, it's much more serious.' Shankly and his beloved Kop*

DAILY POST

Tuesday, September 29, 1981 — Price 12p

Former football manager Bill Shankly died at 01.20 today in Liverpool's Broadgreen Hospital.

How the news which shattered the football world was broken by the Press Association.

SHANKLY IS DEAD

Bill Shankly—one of the soccer greats.

by Daily Post Reporters

BILL SHANKLY lost his fight for life early today.

The former Liverpool manager (67) died in the Intensive Care Unit at Broadgreen Hospital.

Early today a hospital spokesman said: "Mr Shankly suffered a cardiac arrest at 12.30 a.m. and was certified dead at 01.20.

News of his death rocked the football world and tributes immediately began to pour in.

The legendary 'Shanks' had been battling for life since he suffered a heart attack early on Saturday morning.

He had been making good progress until his condition suddenly deteriorated yesterday morning and he was transferred from an open ward to the Intensive Care Unit.

His wife Nessie was by his side when he died.

Worried fans calling to check his condition had jammed the hospital switchboard ever since details of his illness were announced.

His special relationship with Merseyside was reflected in a service held last night to pray for his recovery at Liverpool Parish Church.

In his 15 years as Liverpool boss, Shankly steered the Reds to three League championships, two F.A. Cup victories, and a UEFA Cup triumph.

He stunned Liverpool fans when he announced his retirement as manager in 1974.

His career—Page 3; Thanks, Shanks—Pages 12-13; Comment—Page 12.

Among the first to pay tributes to the great man were three members of the famous side he built up in the sixties.

Ron Yeats (former skipper and centre-half) said: "He was like a second father to me. He will be missed more than I can say.

"He was a great man. You could not talk to him, you just listened.

"His motivation could move mountains."

Ian Callaghan (winger, England international) added: "He's a one off. There has never been anyone like him.

"It's all down to him. He put Liverpool on the map. They broke the mould when they made him."

And Roger Hunt (the striker who holds Liverpool's goal scoring record) added: "He built the dynasty. I was there when he arrived and he transformed the club to what it is today.

"He was dynamic. If you lost a game, you lost to rubbish, if you won, you had beaten a great team.

"Anyone who was flash or who cheated was out. He made sure there were no shirkers in the Liverpool team."

Such was the mystique of the man that the day he stepped down in July 1974, shortly after the teams Cup Final victory at Wembley, supporters in tears jammed the club's switchboard hoping it was all a hoax.

Even a local factory threatened to go on strike if he did leave.

Shortly afterwards he received the OBE and the Queen told him: "You have been in football a long time". He replied: "It's been 42 years".

INSIDE

Well fed

Why there is no magic key to dieting: Day 2 of an intriguing series on family health—Page 6

Well read

Why Elizabeth Smart, the poet who waned, is now waxing lyrical again—Page 7

Deadlock

Union chief blasts Fleet Street employees in Times dispute.

Page 5

Attack

Army swoop to hold seven men after rocket attack in Ulster

Page 8

Blast

Children hurt as terrorist bomb kills 11 in Lebanon.

Page 10

Shock

Dual Derby winner Shergar has run his last race.

Back Page

INDEX

WEATHER: Early fog, sunny later. Outlook: Unsettled, warmer. Round-up: Page 22.

1982

ROCKETING TRANSFER fees, rising salaries and declining attendances all added up to a financial crisis for many clubs during the early 1980s. As if all this was not enough, Wolverhampton Wanderers had a further problem. In 1978 they had committed themselves to building a new £10 million stand when as a first division club they were enjoying healthy gates in the optimistic climate of the time. Four years later in the wake of relegation, gates had fallen dramatically and their magnificent new stand was now an empty and costly memorial to better days. With interest charges rising day by day, Wolves – original members of the Football League, three times champions, four times Cup winners, and twice League Cup winners – were bankrupt with debts of £2.5 million. On top of the £10 million they had paid out for a new stand, they had also joined the transfer merry-go-round, splashing out a record British fee of well over a million pounds for Andy Gray. A ground that had once held 61,000 now averaged rather less. Past extravagances had caught up with Wolves.

Wolves were finally saved with just hours to spare before the deadline set by the Football League expired. And the man who came to their rescue with a £2.5 million takeover was none other than their one-time star, Derek Dougan. The Irishman had put together a package deal acceptable to both Wanderers and the League and another club had been fortuitously saved from extinction. But they were not alone. Chelsea, Charlton Althletic, Tranmere Rovers, Burnley, and Middlesbrough have all faced the threat of liquidation or closure in recent years. Yet thanks to takeovers, creative accounting, and the official receiver, all have avoided the fate that would have forced them out of league football.

Charles Burgess

Time running out for Wolves

SOCCER

The Football League are growing increasingly anxious about the situation at Wolverhampton Wanderers, who may go out of business at the end of the week if no one makes a bid for the club, who are £2.5 million in debt.

The League are worried about the dent to confidence in League football should Wolves go under and are also worried about the club's ability to start the coming season's fixtures on August 28. The League secretary Graham Kelly said yesterday: "We are watching the situation very carefully and we cannot leave it much longer than a month before the season starts before deciding what has to happen. By the end of next week we will be approaching any deadlines we might be thinking about."

Guardian, 21 July 1982

ABOVE: *The £10 million new stand at Molineux*

'STREAKER' WAS one of those words conjured up by the press that was to soon become common currency in the English language. Like most slightly zany activities, it began in America but soon made its way across the Atlantic. And as the tabloids degenerated into a battle of showing more bust and buttock in order to increase their flagging circulations, photographs of near naked females running down streets or dancing in discos became a cheap alternative to the more expensive professional model.

It didn't take long for sport to experience its first streaker. The most famous of all was Erika Roe who stripped during a rugby international at Twickenham before a live audience of 50,000 with millions more watching at home on television. Erika quickly found fame on the back pages though perhaps not solely for the reasons she might have imagined. Football invariably followed suit and a week after Erika had thrilled the nation, a mystery streaker escaped from the packed terraces of Highbury and bared all to the gawping fans of Arsenal and Tottenham. The following day she appeared on page three of the *Daily Mirror*, in the spot normally reserved for scantily clad women, and inevitably faced comparison with Erika. For the record Arsenal won 3–1.

BELOW: *This particular shot of the Highbury streaker was tame compared with most of the photographs in the following morning's tabloids*

Anything Erika can do, I can do BIGGER!

By STEVE ATKINSON

SOCCER'S answer to rugby streaker Erika Roe made her dashing debut yesterday. The busty brunette burst into the big league at Highbury, where Arsenal were playing their North London rivals Tottenham.

Only six minutes of the match remained when the girl climbed on to the pitch and peeled off her jumper and bra.

Her performance was the one bright spot for Arsenal fans. Spurs won 3-1.

Waitress Variania Scotney, 17, of Mottingham, South London, will appear in court on Thursday acused of insulting behaviour.

Daily Mirror, 13 April 1982

1983

Tottenham Hotspur plc

(Incorporated in England under the Companies Acts 1948 to 1981 – No. 1706358)

Offer for Sale

by

Sheppards and Chase

of

3,800,000 new ordinary shares of 25p each at 100p per share payable in full on application

Financial Times, 3 October 1983

ABOVE: *Whatever happened to football's cloth cap image?*

TOTTENHAM HOTSPUR may well have had their measure of back page headlines – even hitting the front pages when they won the Double – but never before had they, or for that matter any other football club, made the headlines on the business and financial pages. On Friday October 14th 1983, Spurs caused a minor tremor on the stock exchange when they announced in the *Financial Times* that they were to go public. It was an unprecedented move, aimed at raising £3.8 million while at the same time giving the ordinary supporter the chance to have a stake in their club and maybe make a small profit on the investment.

The full prospectus was advertised in the *Financial Times* on October 3rd covering six full pages and was repeated in the club's next home programme. Assets – including details of all the first team squad and honours – were listed, along with financial details of the club's estates at Cheshunt and White Hart Lane. Spurs were offering 3,800,000 25p shares for £1.00 each with a minimum investment of £200. When the day arrived for the public quotation, Tottenham were able to proudly announce that the application had been oversubscribed four and a half times.

As soon as the stock market opened on Thursday October 13th with the share quoted for the first time, there was a rush of activity. The shares immediately shot up with one and a half million changing hands in 20 minutes before they began to slump. At one point they dropped to 94p but rose slowly to close at £1.00. Since then, the shares have proved a good buy, rising to well over £2.00 at their height though falling again following the stock market crash in October 1987.

It was a brave venture by Tottenham, inspired by the new young breed of business executives on their board but frowned upon by many fellow soccer clubs and even questioned by some accountants. Other clubs have talked of following suit but only the few rich clubs could possibly survive the rigorous scrutiny the stock market applies. At the final count, the stock market is more interested in profits than trophies and although both often go hand in hand, clubs could still be forced to sell players at the end of a financial year in order to balance the books and satisfy the hungry investor. But at least Tottenham have been determined to keep their financial house in order and not to overstretch themselves like so many clubs.

1984

ROBERT MAXWELL (born Jan Ludwig Hoch)

All over in week after bid of £10m.

‘Only the best is good enough for him’

The man who wants to be Mr United

Daily Mirror, 8 February 1984

BELOW: *Robert Maxwell and Oxford manager Ian Greaves. Maxwell however already had his sights set on a far more glamorous club*

THE MILLIONAIRE publisher and owner of Oxford United Football Club was a well known figure in the boardrooms of the first division but nobody suspected that he was secretly nurturing an ambition to run the most famous football club in the league. But in the late editions of his own newspaper, the *Daily Mirror*, on Friday February 8th, the back page broke the news that Robert Maxwell had made an audacious bid of £10 million for Britain's most glamorous club, Manchester United. The news shook the footballing public who had always assumed that the giants of division one were immune from any temptations.

Maxwell, a Czechoslovakian emigre and former Labour MP had paid just £130,000 for his own home club, Oxford United, in January 1982 when it was floundering in the third division. Under his chairmanship the club had rapidly risen up the divisions and at the time were candidates for promotion from division three. But that was clearly not sufficient for Maxwell and given that he was in the market for another club, where better to begin than with one of the best. For two weeks the takeover battle raged. Just over half the United shares were owned by chairman Martin Edwards, with his brother Roger holding a further 20 per cent. Between them they toyed temptingly with the idea of selling while United supporters watched on, amazed that the family which had owned United for so long could even consider parting with their jewel. But money talks and Edwards let it be known that if Maxwell would increase his offer to £15 a share, the club was his. Maxwell however was not prepared to haggle and on Valentine's Day, with the Edwards family still not prepared to sell at £10 million, the bid was called off. But that was not the end of Maxwell and his takeover bids. Years later he was back, this time with a bid that would be successful, for Derby County. And in 1987 he attempted to buy Elton John's stake in Watford but was denied by the Football League whose growing concern at the number of clubs he owned brought a sudden halt to his dealings.

1985

SUNDAY TELEGRAPH

IN COLOUR MAGAZINE
Country house life between the wars

No. 1251 May 12, 1985 Price 35p

40 dead in soccer inferno

More feared killed, 200 hurt, as fire sweeps stand at Bradford

TOP OF the league and celebrating their promotion to the second division, Bradford City took the field against Lincoln on Saturday May 11th 1985 to the rapturous cheers and applause of their supporters. It was the last match of the season and a large crowd of 11,000 had turned up at Valley Parade. Three-quarters of an hour later, thousands of them watched horrified as an inferno swept through the packed stand and left 55 dead.

The disaster began as a small flame which burned its way along the wooden floorboards of the main stand and then dramatically engulfed the entire stand, turning it into a red-hot furnace. Supporters poured over the seats and onto the pitch but for those who headed for the rear entrance there was no escape. Fathers and sons, separated in the blaze, never saw each other alive again while whole families were wiped out in the devastating fire. Yet, there were still heroes who braved the heat to pull supporters from the flames. More than 200 were treated in hospital with burns that evening as Bradford became a city in mourning. Photographs and television pictures left their indelible image of the horrific disaster. Less than three weeks later tragedy would strike again, and once more the world would watch in dismay.

LEFT: *Countdown to disaster. Within seconds, what seemed at first like a small fire took a hold and swept through the wooden stand, to become a blazing inferno that cost 55 spectators their lives and injured over 200 others*

Soccer hits the ultimate depths

BLOODBATH

Daily Mail, 30 May 1985

1985

ABOVE: *Police survey the scene of devastation around the collapsed fence*

IT SHOULD have been another night of glory for Liverpool Football Club as they faced Juventus at the Heysel stadium in the 1985 European Cup Final. Instead, it turned into a nightmare that left 39 dead and almost 450 injured, most of them supporters of the Italian club. The image of English soccer, and in particular that of Liverpool, lay in tatters alongside the crushed bodies and carnage that littered the terraces.

Millions throughout the world turned on their TVs to watch an eagerly-awaited Cup Final. Instead they were transfixed by live pictures of marauding Liverpool fans shamefully smashing down the flimsy wire fence that separated them from Italian fans on the terrace known as Sector H. They saw terrified Juventus supporters turn and run for an escape route. But for many there was no way out. Hundreds were crushed in the corner of the terrace, as panicking fans trampled over bodies and a wall collapsed, spilling hundreds more on top of each other. It was a disaster that was splashed across the front pages of every European newspaper the following morning.

There were many disagreements among the press, with page after page devoted to analysis. Some argued that the Heysel stadium was too old, that it was ill-equipped for such a major fixture, that drink should never have been so freely available outside the ground, that opposing fans should never have been on the same terrace, that the barrier separating them was inadequate and that the police could not cope. Fortunately, the British press did not shirk from pointing out that no matter what the excuses, opposing fans should never riot. The responsibility ultimately lay with Liverpool fans and in handing out its punishment, UEFA condemned English football to an indefinite ban from European competition with Liverpool given an additional sentence of three extra years. For Joe Fagan, the retiring Liverpool manager, it was the saddest night of his distinguished career. He had hoped in his final match to lift Liverpool's fifth European Cup, but returned instead with tears, shame and a bowed head.

THE FINAL SHAME

Daily Mirror, 30 May 1985

1985

SAINT PATRICK'S NIGHT

Super Jennings checks England

Daily Mirror, 14 November 1985

ABOVE: *Irish hero Pat Jennings, with more than 1,000 first-class games and over 100 caps to his credit*

AT THE grand old age of 40 and with more than 100 Irish international caps to his credit, Pat Jennings performed one more great feat for his country when he held the England attack at bay to give Northern Ireland a place in the World Cup finals. It happened on a chilly November night at Wembley stadium where the Irish needed just one point to qualify for the Mexico finals. It was a night made for sentiment as Jennings time and again foiled the English forwards. And in the dying minutes, when a Kerry Dixon header looked set to defeat them, Jennings appeared from nowhere to scoop it over the bar and earn Ireland a much deserved draw. Even though the man had not played first team football for a year, there was no way England would ever score against him that night. It was, as the *Daily Mirror* dubbed it, 'St Patrick's night'.

Born in Newry, County Down in June 1945, Jennings joined third division Watford in May 1963, and won his first cap the following year. By June 1964 however, after just 48 games with Watford, he was on his way to White Hart Lane where he would become a regular fixture between the posts until the summer of 1977 when he sensationally joined north London rivals Arsenal. He had played 472 league games for Spurs picking up an FA Cup winner's medal in 1967, two League Cup winner's medals, a UEFA Cup winner's medal and well over 60 more caps. At 32 many considered him too old to give much service to the Gunners, but that was to underestimate the genial Irishman who went on to play 237 more league games for the Highbury club and win another FA Cup winner's medal. In the summer of 1985, Tottenham rectified their earlier mistake by re-signing the great goalkeeper on a free transfer, and although his appearances were rare he was still worth a few more international honours.

With his long fashionable sixties hairstyles and giant hands he was one of the most popular figures in league soccer, becoming Footballer of the Year in 1973. He once saved two penalties in front of the Kop at Anfield, to win the undying admiration of the Koppites, and scored for Tottenham in the Charity shield match against Manchester United when his 100-yard goal clearance went, first bounce, into the United net.

After taking Northern Ireland to the World Cup finals, his international career fittingly ended in Mexico when he won his 119th cap against Brazil on his 41st birthday, to make him the most capped player in world football. When the final count was made he had played in 1,098 first-class games over 24 years that had taken him to all corners of the earth and into most competitions. It was an astonishing record.

1986

I'LL SIGN CATHOLICS! says GRAEME SOUNESS

Ibrox boss in team vow

by ANDY McINNES

GRAEME SOUNESS yesterday pledged to bridge the religious divide that has kept Glasgow Rangers from signing Roman Catholics.

Ibrox's new player-manager, married to a Catholic, said he would not have taken the job unless he had a guarantee he could sign Catholic players.

Announcing an end to the club's 113-year Protestant-only tradition, Souness said:"How could I possibly have taken on this task if I could not have signed Catholics? I am married to one and share my life with one. I could not have returned to Italy and told my wife I had the job but there was a problem with Catholics.

"The best players will be signed, no matter what they are. It is not a thorny question as far as I am concerned. Perhaps previous managers have been unable to find Catholic players good enough for Rangers."

Souness must play three more games for Sampdoria before he begins his Ibrox duties.

He added: "To say I have been thrown in at the deep end is an understatement.

Envious

"But I am envious of what Kenny Dalglish has done at Anfield and I want to follow in his footsteps.

"I believe I have taken on a harder job than he did because Liverpool were already a winning side.

Souness, 33 next month, will cost Rangers £400,000 in transfer fee and compensation and could earn £100,000 a year at Ibrox.

He added: "I see this club as second only to Manchester United in Britain and bigger than Liverpool, Tottenham, Arsenal and anyone else."

Daily Star, 9 April 1986

BELOW: *Controversial new Rangers boss Graeme Souness strides forth in the famous blue shirt following his dramatic appointment as player-manager of Glasgow Rangers*

ONE HUNDRED and thirteen years of history and Glasgow Rangers had still not played a Catholic. But when Graeme Souness, the former Liverpool and Sampdoria midfield iron man took over at Ibrox, he pledged to end the ban against signing Catholics. Souness, himself a Protestant, was quick to point out that his wife Danielle was Catholic and that his only concern was in signing the best players no matter what their religion.

For a century, sectarianism in Glasgow football has flourished in a hothouse of bigotry. Celtic themselves for many years shunned Protestant players but finally broke with tradition in the 1960s. Yet Rangers continued to resist, encouraged by their die-hard, anti papist supporters. Investigations by the Scottish FA and FIFA have either been carried out with little enthusiasm or have never been able to prove a difficult case, although the General Assembly of the Church of Scotland strongly condemned Rangers for their 'sectarian bias'. In October 1976 Willie Waddell, then General Manager and vice-chairman of Rangers, declared in the *Daily Express* that 'we will try to buy a Catholic player when we find one up to our standards'. It was just one of many such pledges made over the years that have never been carried out.

The response of the press has generally been mixed. None, certainly in recent years, has supported Rangers' policy; yet equally some papers, particularly the Scottish editions, have hardly raised their voice above a whisper. One who did was John Mann in the *Daily Star*, who argued for many football lovers when he wrote after the Souness appointment that 'It is astonishing in these enlightened times that any kind of discrimination – of race, creed or colour – should be allowed to flourish in football, or in any other walk of life.' Following his momentous statement, Graeme Souness signed a Jewish player and a black player, but in August 1988 Ibrox still awaited its first Catholic recruit.

1986

AS FAR as Merseyside was concerned this was the game to end all games. Almost one hundred years of rivalry had led to a fitting climax. Everton, runners-up in the league and the previous year's champions, faced their neighbours and current champions Liverpool in the FA Cup Final at Wembley. Victory for Liverpool would make them only the third team this century to achieve the Double and to achieve it at the expense of rivals Everton gave an added incentive to the men in red.

The two teams had met only once before at Wembley, in the 1984 Milk Cup Final when a dreary game played beneath rain-sodden skies petered out into a goalless draw. But May 1986 was different. The sun baked down on the famous stadium as coachloads of Merseyside fans began to arrive. It was like an old-fashioned final, with rival fans pouring from the same buses, cars and trains, to march side by side up Wembley way with never any fear of trouble. The dividing line of Merseyside football is neither geographical nor religious. Over the years it has split families and friendships – fathers from sons, brothers from brothers, mates from mates – without any recourse to violence or ill-feeling. Together, the two sets of fans marched to the game, separating only at the twin towers and then re-linking for a few pints before the journey home.

And just for a change, the game itself lived up to all expectations. Everton soared into a 28th minute lead as a flat-footed Liverpool defence failed to grapple with Gary Lineker. Bruce Grobbelaar in the Liverpool goal threw out an arm to stifle the England international's initial shot but Lineker, fast as a dart, seized upon the rebound and the score was 1–0. For the next half hour Everton dominated, throwing men forward and delightfully stroking the ball around their midfield, yet failed to capitalise on their one-goal lead. Liverpool were in disarray, their front runners demoted to the role of watchers rather than workers.

It took a moment of unusual anxiety in the Liverpool defence to suddenly snap the league champions

BELOW: *Gary Lineker, in his final game before joining Barcelona, puts Everton into an early lead*

Liverpool rush on to double delight

DERYK BROWN reports from WEMBLEY

Everton .... 1 Liverpool 3

LIVERPOOL'S Cup. Liverpool's Cup and League double. Although at half-time they were struggling mightily, and trailing to a goal from Lineker, the men from Anfield did it. From nowhere Rush and Johnston scored goals around the hour, and later Rush added a third.

If pressed on team selection, Kenny Dalglish is liable to say, "Ach, the wife picks the team." Well, it was 1.55pm yesterday before Mrs Dalglish allowed the waiting world to know that Gillespie was unfit and that, surprisingly, MacDonald would play and McMahon would be substitute.

This late declaration was one more unusual aspect of the first all-Merseyside FA Cup Final which kicked off in fleeting sunshine. Everton were at full complement, their one doubt, Mountfield, soon easily holding off Rush. Nevertheless it was Liverpool who made the initial running, as, indeed, was to be expected because they were much the form team.

Beglin soon put in a centre from which Rush headed down, but without power. Then the unexpected MacDonald, thin and curly, unexpectedly found himself well forward twice within a minute, and almost on the end of something. Next, Beglin again, after a Liverpool corner misfired, but his header was monstrously wide.

Wembley looked a shade too green after a wet English spring, and the grass was cut long, which might have explained the lack of fight in some of the early passing. Certainly it took 20 minutes for Everton, despite that lovely midfield balance of theirs, to mount a telling attack.

This finally came with Sharp, as lean and hungry as ever, racing into the penalty area with Nicol, the two of them tumbling down, but Mr. Robinson predictably refusing the Everton howls for a penalty.

Not discouraged, Everton began to use their width and Reid's clever pass set up an excellent test of pace between the Lineker and Lawrenson. Fortunately for Liverpool, Lawrenson's galloping legs were just long enough.

But, just inside the half hour, the blue portion of Merseyside had a goal to cheer. It came when another typical Liverpool probe broke down. Everton, in the person of Reid, seized the chance with an accurate through ball down the middle. This time Lineker's speed was just enough to take him beyond Hansen.

Grobbelaar carried Lineker's first shot, but, such is often the luck of that goalkeeper, the ball fell for Lineker to bury sweetly.

Now this all-scouse affair had noise to go with its colour, mingled together as the red and blue was on the terraces. But still Liverpool could not find the rhythm which, only a week earlier, had carried them to the League championship.

Admittedly, there was danger in the way that Rush brought the ball down near goal, despite Ratcliffe's close attentions. But Everton ended the first half with their customary bubble.

So far the Final [illegible] had lived up to its name, with the exception of one tackle by Mountfield on Dalglish which the referee decided not to punish with a caution. It would be fanciful to say that this shook King Kenny, but he was having an unhappy Wembley, now being slow and dispossessed a moment later, putting the highest shot of the day over Mimms.

Johnston: joyful scorer

And, into the second half, Everton's greater poise and confidence were putting them far ahead of their rivals in terms of points. Sheedy burst through Lawrenson and Hansen for a shot (right foot, unfortunately), which flew just wide. Immediately afterwards, it was Sheedy again, forcing Grobbelaar to push wide.

Grobbelaar is normally the most affable of fellows, but even he lost his patience with a dithering defence, playing merry hell with Beglin as that player messed about by the by-line.

But just as Liverpool's great day looked like crumbling, they equalised from nowhere. The goal began when Stevens inexplicably gave the ball away. Whelan pushed to Molby who had time and room to feed Rush. Rush took the ball in his stride to slip it past Mimms, previously untroubled, for 1-1.

Seven minutes later, the match was turned completely on its head. This time Rush started the move to goal, passed to Molby, and Molby's crisp cross found Johnston, previously quite out of the game, who buried the ball at the far post.

The second goal was the knock-out, and [illegible] ting the ball against Mimms, suddenly emphasised Liverpool's new confidence. The last goal, eight minutes from time, came from more sweet Liverpool passing. It was scored by Rush, the climax to a memorable Final.

Everton (4-4-2): Mimms, Stevens, Ratcliffe, Mountfield, V den Hauwe, Steven, Reid, Bracewell, Sheedy, Sharp, Lineker.

Liverpool (4-4-2): Grobbelaar, Nicol, Hansen, Lawrenson, Beglin, Johnston, Molby, MacDonald, Whelan, Rush, Dalglish.

Referee: A Robinson (Hampshire).

Sunday Times, 11 May 1986

into action, as Grobbelaar and his young Irish full-back Jim Beglin visibly exchanged flashing glances and harsh words. Two minutes later they unexpectedly equalised when a sloppy pass out of the Everton defence was seized upon by Beglin. His pass to Jan Molby was pushed into the penalty area, and striker Ian Rush arrived to finish the job. Six minutes later Liverpool were sensationally ahead, when Craig Johnston on the far post sidefooted Molby's centre home, and with just seven minutes remaining Ian Rush made Liverpool's Double certain when he slammed in a Ronnie Whelan pass.

At least one-half of Merseyside was delighted and Kenny Dalglish, in his first year as player-manager, had achieved a remarkable Double to expunge a little of the shame that had fallen on the club a year earlier in the Heysel stadium. In Soho that evening victorious Liverpool fans helped their brother Evertonians drown their sorrows.

RIGHT: *Ian Rush's two goals clinched victory and the Double for Liverpool. A year later he joined Juventus*

1986

JUST FOUR years after the Falklands War, England found themselves pitted against Argentina in the Mexico World Cup Finals. Ever since the draw for the tournament, it had looked likely that the two nations would find themselves facing each other in the quarter-finals. England had reached that stage of the competition after finishing runners-up in their group and having then impressively beaten Paraguay 3–0 in the second round. The Argentinians had topped their group over Italy, Bulgaria and South Korea and then followed that up with a methodical 1–0 win over Uruguay.

The confrontation with England was scheduled for midday on Sunday June 22nd at the Aztec Stadium in Mexico City. Not surprisingly the British press – which during the Falklands Crisis had excelled itself in vitriolic hate and jingoism – seized the opportunity to vent some more spleen on the Argentinians. 'High Noon' ran the headline in the *Daily Mirror*, which claimed that 'reports that Argentine thugs are planning to infiltrate the crowd and cause trouble are being studied by the Mexican authorities.'

If the High Noon clash could be narrowed down to two individuals, it was a gunfight between Argentina's Diego Maradona, the world's most expensive player, and Gary Lineker, leading scorer in the competition and about to become the latest English export to Europe. Since his transfer from Leicester to Everton, Lineker had matured into the most exciting England striker since Jimmy Greaves. In 200 games at Leicester he had scored 100 goals and in just one season at Everton had struck 30 league goals before he attracted the attention of Spanish giants Barcelona. Equally prolific on the international scene, Lineker had already netted five goals in the World Cup Finals.

Sport often heals old wounds but as the two teams nervously lined up to kick off in the midday heat of the Aztec bowl, neither Lineker nor Maradona could have guessed that after 90 minutes England and Argentina would be as divided as ever.

ABOVE: *Gary Lineker, star of the England team, v Paraguay*

WORLD CUP CRUNCH

IT'S ENGLAND v ARGENTINA

HIGH NOON

Falklands shadow over showdown at mid-day

Daily Mirror, 19 June 1986

DURING THE Falklands War the *Sun* had produced one of the most controversial frontpages in the history of newspaper publishing when it conjured up the headline 'GOTCHA!' to report the sinking of the Argentinian battleship *The General Belgrano*. Torpedoed by a British submarine, more than 350 Argentinian sailors died as a result, and the *Sun*'s tasteless headline caused a furore. It was probably inevitable that the *Sun* would find a variation on that headline to report the England–Argentina clash. Had England won, the front page would no doubt have read 'GOTCHA AGAIN!'. As it was, England lost and instead the headline turned out to be 'OUTCHA!'.

The controversial manner of England's dismissal, however, still allowed plenty of scope for attacking the Argentinians. And in the thick of it all was the world's finest player, Diego Maradona, who stood accused of scooping the ball into the net with his hand to score Argentina's opening goal. 'CHEAT!' was the word emblazoned across the backpages of most newspapers the following day. Slow-motion replays of the goal and blurred photographs clearly showed that Maradona had handled the ball and his failure to admit it was, the press alleged, just the kind of slyness to be expected from Argentinians. The incident had done nothing to bridge the gulf between the two nations even though Maradona's second goal was one of the most stunning ever seen in the history of the World Cup. England were out, beaten 2–1, although Gary Lineker with a total of six goals was the leading scorer in the competition. Argentina went on to win the World Cup in style, beating West Germany 3–2 in the final. Maradona however would always be remembered by the English for his blatant cheating, and when the Argentinian captain appeared at Wembley a year later for The Rest of the World against England, the booing supporters on the terraces would not let him forget.

Elsewhere it was different. After a disappointing World Cup in 1982, Maradona had at last shown his true potential as a player in the mould of Pele, Eusebio, and Crayff.

OUTCHA!

Argies get their own back on us

BRAVE England last night failed to prevent the Revenge of the Argies.

The South Americans knocked us out of the World Cup to get their own back for the hammering they took in the Falklands war four years ago.

Sun, 23 June 1986

ABOVE: *The 'hand of God' intervenes and Argentina take the lead*

1987

SPONSORSHIP TOOK a new and controversial twist in November 1987 when the *Daily Mirror* exclusively revealed that the FA Cup was set to be sold in a £12 million sponsorship deal with Foster's lager. Over the years the sagging fortunes of football had already led to the sale of the League Cup and the League itself. But sponsorship of the FA Cup was a totally different proposition that brought the wrath of Fleet Street on the Football Association.

The rot had begun during the 1970s when a deal negotiated by new FA secretary, Ted Croker, with the sportswear firm Admiral led to a new England strip almost every season. That was followed in 1982 with the League Cup renamed the Milk Cup and four years later renamed the Littlewoods Cup. The Japanese electronic company Canon had been the first to sponsor the league, in a three-year deal. They then handed over to the newspaper *Today* who subsequently pulled out to pass the league contract on to Barclays. And then of course there was the Freight Rover Cup, The Texaco Cup, The Simod Cup, the Bell's Whisky awards and so on.

Given that Fleet Street had already been involved in football sponsorship, it was perhaps surprising that they should have given such a hostile reception to the FA Cup deal. Some of the criticism however was levelled at the notion of breweries sponsoring football when so much violence on the terraces had been caused by drunkenness. Following the *Mirror* story, Fleet Street unloaded its venom on the deal. 'A national institution undermined,' wrote Patrick Barclay in the *Independent*. He regarded it as 'crass commercialisation,' adopting the ethics of Thatcherism. 'The FA Cup already has a sponsor,' he continued, 'It is called the British people'.

Within a couple of weeks the Football Association had taken the hint and the deal with Fosters lager was quietly shelved. The *Daily Mirror* claimed a great victory. But just how long it stays on the shelf, remains to be seen.

Trouble brews as Cup goes up for grabs

Independent, 19 November 1987

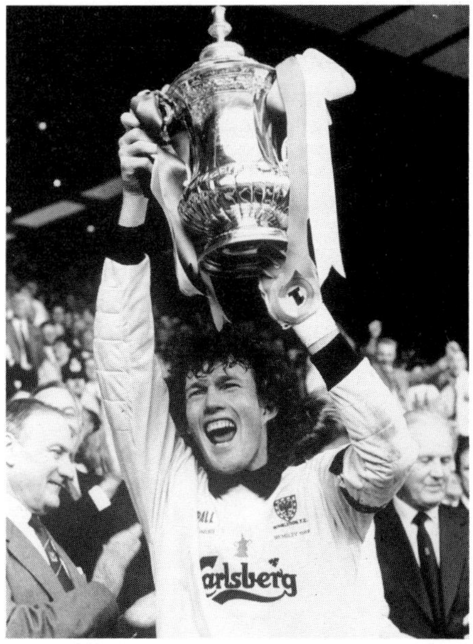

ABOVE: *Dave Beasant lifts the FA Cup. But how much longer before a sponsor's name is splashed across the well-loved trophy?*

A national institution undermined

THE FA Cup already has a sponsor. It is called the British people. Every season, nearly two million watch the world's oldest and best knock-out competition for clubs, contributing more money than any company could provide. If the Cup's name were sold, they would have every justification for withdrawing their support.

Already the FA have gone too far in even considering the crass commercialisation of the game's most cherished institution. They may have embraced the values of the Conservative Government, whose recently appointed Sports Minister, Colin Moynihan, has lent the idea swift and enthusiastic backing, but such insensitive behaviour is stretching the supporters' loyalty threadbare.

The time has come to say: no more. For the FA Cup has a mystique that must be protected from the tarnish of association, a quality that only a cynic would fail to appreciate.

PATRICK BARCLAY argues that the FA must revert to their old standards

A cynic, according to Wilde's Lord Darlington, is a man who knows the price of everything and the value of nothing. Such men have gone unchallenged in football for too long.

The deterioration in standards began in the Seventies with the selling of the England strip, the infamous Admiral deal, arranged by Ted Croker in one of his early acts as FA secretary.

Clubs followed suit, and their colours have become, like England's, a so-called fashion item, changed with varying degrees of subtlety every two years or so. There is no aesthetic thought behind it: only the intention of increasing turnover in the replica-kit market through the coercion of parents and others.

Then there was the sponsorship of the League/Milk/Littlewoods Cup. Fair enough; a competition with such a short history could hardly have its tradition bruised. The League sponsorship that followed was, however, different.

After Canon's three highly successful (for them) years, the void left football looking vulnerable; something the League had done without for the best part of a century was suddenly deemed necessary if it were to prove its virility in a god-forsaken, commerce-worshipping world.

And so the League took *Today* newspaper to its breast, a brief and mildly damaging union. It remains to be seen whether Barclays do the game as much good as they do themselves or whether, like Canon, they simply use it as a convenience. Why should they be any different?

A more pertinent question is: why should football feel such a desperate need for financial infusions that read impressively but, once dispersed among 92 clubs, are almost insignificant?

Of course the FA need money to keep the game's roots fed. Of course they, and the League, must be commercial. But they must learn from the Americans, the masters of sports salesmanship, that identities are not for hire. You don't get Budweiser Leagues over the Atlantic.

By all means let the FA do deals, gain additional help with the School of Excellence and the Charity Shield (that could have a million sponsors; the more money it raises the better) but let them also remember the public.

Several years ago, when the League sponsorship was announced, I asked Croker if the FA Cup would follow. Only over his dead body, he said. It was part of the national heritage. He is due to retire in 18 months. More recently the FA chairman, Bert Millichip, also expressed opposition.

So who, I wonder, was the mysterious, all-powerful force behind the recent negotiations? Unless he is brought forward in evidence, we shall be driven to the conclusion that the FA hierarchy has changed its mind. And we shall then have to ask why.

Independent, 19 November 1987

SPURS BOSS CAUGHT IN VICE SWOOP AGAIN

Another Sun exclusive

Sun, 23 October 1987

EL TEL'S THE MAN FOR SPURS

Sun, 23 October 1987

LIKE POLITICIANS and showbiz stars, football managers have become public property. It is not so much that the press have become the keepers of the nation's morals but more to do with a tabloid war that has waged through Fleet Street since the late 1970s.

ABOVE: *May 1986. David Pleat joins Tottenham from Luton. Eighteen months later the smiles had turned to tears*

The classic example hit the headlines in October 1987 when the *Sun* alleged that Tottenham manager David Pleat had been cautioned by police for kerb crawling in the West End. Pleat was not the first manager to see his private life splashed across the front pages – Tommy Docherty and Manchester City's John Bond had both suffered a similar indignity.

The Pleat *exposé* had begun in June 1987 when the *Sun* led with a story about the new Tottenham manager being cautioned by police while still managing Luton. The Tottenham management took a dim view at the time but as the incident related to his former club, Pleat remained in his job. But when a similar accusation was made four months later, Pleat was on his way.

What made the *Sun* story a classical piece of tabloid 'journalism' was that they devoted the front page to the news story and then ran a sports exclusive on their back page speculating that Terry Venables would be taking over the reins at White Hart Lane. And all this was even before Pleat had resigned or Venables had been approached.

1987

BEFORE THE early 1970s, only a handful of black footballers had ever played league soccer in Britain. But a new generation of young blacks – born of parents who had arrived in this country during the 1950s – suddenly matured into fine footballers twenty years later.

They tended to be concentrated in those clubs from areas where Commonwealth immigrants had settled, such as West Bromwich Albion, Nottingham Forest and West Ham. They were among the first to give an early welcome to this new generation but their reception on the terraces was not so generous. There was fearsome barracking, particularly at away grounds, with players insulted, spat at and struck with banana skins. To their credit, most coped admirably with the abuse and Viv Anderson of Nottingham Forest initiated another breakthrough when he became England's first black player in 1978 (see page 176).

By the mid 1980s, black players had become a regular feature of our game though many clubs, for reasons best known to themselves, had continued to shun their talents. In Scotland black players were unknown and on Merseyside Howard Gayle who played a handful of games for Liverpool, was the only black to have turned out for either of the city's two clubs. But all that changed in the summer of 1987 when Liverpool signed the England and Watford winger, John Barnes.

Even before John Barnes had donned his Liverpool shirt racist slogans appeared on the walls and pitch at Anfield. Much of it was inspired by the National Front which for some years had been whipping up racial hatred on terraces all over the

STAY AWAY YOU SCUM

SOCCER RACE STORM

Carter blasts taunts

By ALEC JOHNSON

EVERTON chairman Philip Carter yesterday disowned the fans who made vicious racist attacks on Liverpool's John Barnes.

Daily Mirror, 31 October 1987

1987

country. The popular football press had hardly played an honourable role in helping to stamp out such intolerance and save for a handful of articles, racism had been allowed to ferment without forceful criticism.

The issue came to a head in October 1987 when Liverpool faced their neighbours Everton in a Littlewoods Cup game at Anfield which witnessed some of the worst abuse seen on an English football ground. The target was Liverpool's John Barnes who was severely barracked by Everton fans, partly because of his extraordinary skills but equally because of his colour. With a live televised league game between the two clubs set to follow five days later, the footballing authorities finally took a firm stance and won the support of the football pages.

'Stay Away You Scum,' was the advice which Philip Carter, the chairman of Everton and President of the Football League, dished out to Evertonians who made vicious racist attacks on Barnes. It was a hard-hitting statement which the popular papers featured prominently. When their joint efforts were put to the test days later, there was a marked improvement although some barracking continued. The whole episode showed that English football still has much to do before it can lose its racist tag, and football writers and broadcasters have as much responsibility as the authorities in stamping out the mindless chants of the terraces.

LEFT: *John Barnes was the victim of vicious racial abuse following his £800,000 transfer to Liverpool. Barnes answered his racist critics by winning a League Championship medal and the Player of the Year award*

1988

WHEN LIVERPOOL striker Ian Rush joined the Italian club Juventus in a £3 million transfer deal, the back-page pundits predicted that the Merseysiders would never be the same – even though they had splashed out the proceeds on John Barnes of Watford and Newcastle's Peter Beardsley. Similarly, when Kevin Keegan left for Hamburg the same headlines had appeared, forecasting the decline and fall of Liverpool. But nobody had considered Liverpool's new signing, Kenny Dalglish.

Within weeks of Rush's departure, however, Liverpool had given notice that he would not be missed as they stormed to the top of the league. Eight months later, still undefeated in the league, they equalled Leeds United's record run of 29 games without loss from the beginning of the season when they drew with Derby County at the Baseball ground. Indeed, their run had been even more impressive than Leeds', having won 22 games and drawn only seven, scoring 67 goals with a mere 13 against. But in their next fixture against neighbours Everton, they lost 1–0 and had to remain content with equalling rather than bettering Leeds' magnificent record. The pundits were forced to eat their words. Three weeks later the applause reached more deafening heights as Liverpool stormed to a thrilling 5–0 win over Nottingham Forest that had every soccer writer reaching for hyperbole. The former England and Preston winger, Tom Finney, called it the finest exhibition of football he had ever witnessed. Two weeks later a 1–0 win over Spurs at Anfield clinched Liverpool's seventeenth league title.

Since 1962 Liverpool have dominated the first division. Under the guidance of Bill Shankly they had won promotion from the second divi-

ABOVE: *John Aldridge, Liverpool's top scorer, with the League Trophy*

BELOW: *The winning squad*

29 KENNY'S KOP KINGS ROAR TO RECORD!

By PETER FITTON

LIVERPOOL, soccer's mightiest conquerors for the past 20 years, marched into the record books last night.

And Kenny Dalglish's invincibles are now ready and prepared to beat history.

Craig Johnston emerged last night from his role as the backstage hand of Anfield with the goal that puts them alongside Leeds' legends with an amazing 29 unbeaten First Division games.

And for the Kop Kings that means one final demanding trial — the ordeal of surviving against their deadliest rivals Everton to beat the famous record.

Come Sunday, they must make the five-minute trip down the road to Goodison Park to show the watching TV nation they still have the skill and nerve against the one side to beat them this season. But, amazingly, this

Sun, 17 March 1988

Liverpool make Finney their latest admirer

By Stuart Jones, Football Correspondent

Tom Finney, entranced as he sat watching Liverpool overwhelm Nottingham Forest 5-0 on Wednesday night, has joined those who believe that Kenny Dalglish's side is the strongest ever to be assembled at Anfield. Not only that, the legendary winger says he has never witnessed a better team.

In his opinion, not the Busby Babes of Manchester United, who perished in Munich, nor Tottenham Hotspur, who won the double 27 years ago, nor even the golden Brazilians, who bestrode the world, would have been a match for Liverpool. "I've never seen skill at that pace," he enthused.

"In all my time as a player and as a spectator, that was the finest exhibition of football I've ever seen. Everybody will have left believing they had seen something that will never be bettered. The execution of the moves was tremendous. They have great individual players and they all support each other.

"The number of times defenders came through to join the attack, it could have been seven or eight quite easily."

Since Liverpool struck the woodwork twice and were denied on at least four occasions by Forest's inspired goalkeeper, his closing words were, if anything, an understatement.

Few of those who were privileged to have been at Anfield would argue with the rest of his appraisal. The night was lit by a show of sustained brilliance, the like of which not even Hansen, their captain, could recall.

Nor was Maurice Roworth, Forest's chairman, indulging in empty flattery when he suggested that Liverpool were "the best team in Europe." All the sadder that his claim (which, on the season's evidence so far at home and abroad, is indisputable) cannot, and may never be, genuinely tested.

Cold-hearted statisticians will doubtless rustle through the record books and prove, to their satisfaction at least, that Liverpool should not be regarded even as the most complete side in English history. They will point, for instance, to Aston Villa's feat of scoring 128 goals in 1931.

They will say that Tottenham won 31 League games in 1961 and that Liverpool themselves conceded a mere 16 goals nine years ago.

The Times, 15 April 1988

RIGHT: *Manager Kenny Dalglish with the Barclays League Trophy*

sion and over the next 26 years proceeded to win a dozen league championships, four European Cups, two UEFA Cups, three FA Cups and four League Cups. They had even equalled the achievement of Huddersfield and Arsenal in clinching the championship in three consecutive seasons, and had established a new record of only conceding 16 goals in a season. Kenny Dalglish had not only helped them to numerous European and domestic triumphs as a player, but in his first season as manager had taken Liverpool to the League and Cup Double. Their achievements were unparalleled. Not only could they rightly boast the title of Britain's most successful club but they could now boast a team of flair and outstanding talent that could match any side soccer had ever produced. A few months are a long time in the back pages.

1988

LIVERPOOL AT 4–1 on were the hottest FA Cup favourites since the War. With their seventeenth league title wrapped up the week before the Final and only two defeats in the league the whole season, there were few who would have bet on Wimbledon to beat the Merseysiders. Wimbledon, after all, was better known for tennis, not football. Eleven years previously they had been a non-league outfit and in 1983 when Liverpool were claiming their fourteenth league title the south London side were still in the fourth division, only reaching the first division in 1986. But the FA Cup is about surprises and, with so many predicting an easy Liverpool victory that would have given them their second League and Cup Double, there was every likelihood of a major upset.

Yet Wimbledon should never have been underrated. Seventh in the league and sixth the previous season, they were certainly consistent. Well-managed by Bobby Gould and with Don Howe cleverly coaching their defence they had proved to be tough opposition for most first division clubs. They were not among the aristocrats of the game but what they lacked in experience and skill they made up for with endeavour. They were not attractive to watch but instead played to their strengths, cutting out the midfield and chasing long balls kicked deep into the opposition's half. The theory was that as long as the ball is in your opponent's half, they cannot put you under pressure. They may have been called unsophisticated, and even at times thuggish, but their style was nevertheless effective.

They had reached Wembley with victories over West Brom, Mansfield, Newcastle, Watford and Luton – a not unformidable task in itself – yet brought to Wembley one of the smallest crowds in Cup Final history. On the Wembley terraces, Wimbledon fans were outnumbered by Liverpool supporters by at least five to one. But despite all the odds they mastered Liverpool as few other teams had managed all season, and came away victorious.

Liverpool might well have gone ahead in the 35th minute when Peter Beardsley shrugged off a fearsome tackle from Andy Thorn and slammed the ball into the net. But instead of signalling a goal, referee Brian Hill awarded Liverpool a free kick. A minute later, with Liverpool still complaining, Wimbledon themselves took a dramatic lead as Lawrie Sanchez sent a glancing header from a Dennis Wise free kick past Bruce Grobbelaar. In the second half Wimbledon's luck again held when goalkeeper and captain Dave Beasant saved magnificently from a John Aldridge penalty. It was the first penalty the normally-sure Liverpool striker had missed all season and the first penalty failure in an FA Cup Final at Wembley. For the remaining 30 minutes Wimbledon's well-drilled defence held steadfast, forcefully snuffing out any assaults by England

GAME, SET AND MATCH TO WIMBLEDON

Underdogs mock odds to sink sad champions

But referee admits: I was wrong to disallow Liverpool's goal

Sunday Express, 15 May 1988

attackers Peter Beardsley and John Barnes.

And so when the final whistle blew big Dave Beasant fittingly became the first goalkeeper ever to lead a side up the Wembley steps to lift the FA Cup. Ironically, the Cup Final was to be the last game Beasant played for the London club. A month later he was transferred to Newcastle United for £750,000.

Unglamorous Wimbledon may not have been the most elegant side to win the Cup, but at least they had given hope to all non-league and fourth division sides that fairy tales can sometimes come true. David had slain Goliath.

BELOW LEFT: *Beasant judges Aldridge's spot kick perfectly*

BELOW: *Laurie Sanchez's glancing header leaves Bruce Grobbelaar stranded*

1989

SATURDAY APRIL 15TH began as a warm spring day but was to end in a black nightmare as 95 Liverpool fans were crushed to death in the most appaling disaster English soccer had ever known. It was FA Cup semi-final day with Liverpool chasing a second league and cup double. Liverpool, the team of the 1980s, looked likely league champions again, and were now just 90 minutes away from another Wembley appearance. They had only to beat Nottingham Forest at Hillsborough.

A few minutes into the game Peter Beardsley rattled the crossbar with a long range shot and an exciting game looked to be in prospect. Two minutes later fans began to pour on to the pitch. It seemed at first that some hooligans had invaded, but instead it was Liverpool fans pleading with their players to tell the police that something awful was happening. It soon became clear that a dreadful accident had occurred. Bodies were being hauled out of the Leppings Lane end of Hillsborough where all the Liverpool fans were congregated. Soon, fans were flooding onto the pitch. Bodies were strewn all over, supporters with makeshift stretchers raced up and down the pitch, there was chaos everywhere. Millions watched in horror on their television sets as the number of casualties began to mount. Just a handful at first, then an hour later it was into double figures. By 5pm there was talk of more than 30 deaths. By that evening the final figure was nudging towards one hundred. 95 fans died that day; another fan died a few years later having never regained consciousness. All 96 had been crushed to death as hundreds of fans had been wrongly ushered into a section at the Leppings Lane end behind the goal. It was a disastrous error, later attributed to the police.

'I thought I was going to die. I was getting short of breath. The weight on me was so great.'

Liverpool Echo, 16 April 1989

'I held a boy in my arms and watched him die . . . he could not have been more than five or six years old'

Liverpool Echo, 16 April 1989

The entire nation was profoundly shocked with almost every family in Liverpool knowing someone who had died. The city of Liverpool was devastated and Liverpool Football Club would never be quite the same again. That week thousands came from all over the country to pay their respects at Anfield, walking

CRUSHED TO DEATH

93 die in soccer horror

THEY were literally crushed to death. At least 93 soccer fans, men and women, young and old, trampled and pushed against railings until their hearts stopped.

Yesterday's FA Cup semi-final between Liverpool and Nottingham Forest turned to disaster six minutes into the game. Many victims were children who had stood at the front to get a good view.

Liverpool fans pushed seemingly uncontrolled into Hillsborough Stadium, Sheffield. "It was like a battlefield," said a stunned policeman. A fan summed up the horror. "It was total terrified chaos. People were screaming in pain."

The carnage of Hillsborough was Britain's worst sports disaster. Last night as the toll of dead — and more than 200 injured — rose, MPs and families of the Liverpool victims asked: How could it have happened?

They demanded to know WHO let hundreds of non-ticket holders into Sheffield's 54,000 capacity ground, crushing hundreds under foot.

A gate steward told a reporter police had urged

Turn to Back Page

Sunday Mirror, 16 April 1989

quietly through the Shankly Gates, then around the ground towards the Kop end which had become a shrine to the memory of those who had died.

An official inquiry was opened, chaired by Lord Justice Taylor. Among its findings was the recommendation to build all-seater stadiums, thereby limiting the possibility of such a tragedy occurring again. The disaster and the subsequent recommendations in the Taylor Report were to have a major impact on English football as work began to convert Victorian stadiums with their terraces into modern all seater grounds. The word Hillsborough had taken on a new meaning, never to be forgotten.

‘ How many more times must we wait and weep on a Saturday afternoon in our great city of sport and sorrow ? ’

Liverpool Echo, 16 April 1989

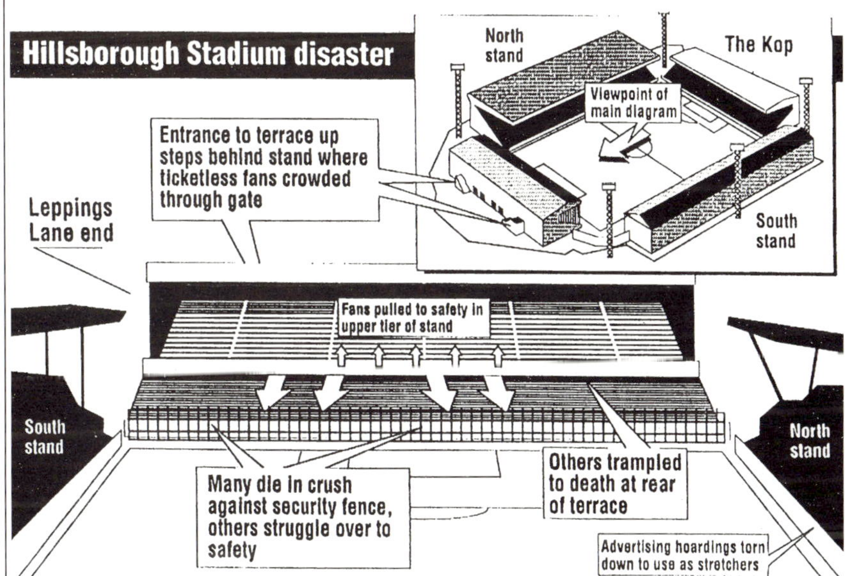

Liverpool Echo, 16 April 1989

BELOW AND FAR LEFT:

Anfield remembers. For days after the tragedy, the Kop paid homage as Liverpool tried to come to terms with all that had happened.

1990

It had been 24 years since that glorious June afternoon when Ramsey's wingless wonders captured the World Cup for England. Since then the national side had failed repeatedly, neither impressing nor inspiring. But in 1990, much to the surprise of everyone, the unfancied men of England came within a whisker of defeating West Germany again and reaching another World Cup final.

England had reached the final stages in Italy without too much trouble, eventually finishing second in their qualifying group behind Sweden. But still nobody gave them much of a chance. Manager Bobby Robson was hardly the most popular manager of his generation, much reviled in the press and on the back-pages. It had been a fairly laboured road to the finals and even in the opening stages England had looked devoid of ideas.

They began brightly enough in their first match, Gary Lineker putting them ahead early on against the Republic of Ireland, but as the match wore on England's game fell apart, eventually hanging on for a 1-1 draw. England's second game also ended in a draw, this time goalless, although on this occasion the opposition, Holland, was more formidable. For the first time England also used a sweeper, playing Derby County's Mark Wright in the role. The critics back home wondered why the manager was still experimenting at such a late stage. England's third game finally brought a victory, 1-0, against outsiders Egypt. Astonishingly England finished top of their group with four points even though they scored a mere two goals.

In the second round England faced Belgium. After 90 minutes it was still goaless but with only seconds on the clock in extra time and penalties looking almost certain, up popped David Platt to volley home Paul Gascoigne's free kick. England barely deserved their win, twice having to thank the woodwork for saving them. But at least they were into the quarter finals where their opponents were the hugely skilful Africans from Cameroon. England led 1-0 at half time, courtesy of David Platt, but in the second half the Cameroons began to push forward snatching a 2-1 lead. England were in disarray and, with just nine minutes remaining, looked to be on their way out of the tournament when Gary Lineker was dramatically upended in the box. The England striker picked himself up, placed the ball and fired home the equaliser. England breathed again and went into extra time looking more positive. With just a minute of the first period of extra time to go Lineker was again fouled in the area and for the second time slammed the resulting penalty beyond the Cameroon keeper.

Although England's presence in the last four owed much to good fortune, there was little doubt that the side had been improving as the tournament progressed. At least they were now scoring goals with Lineker, Gascoigne and Platt looking like world class players while Des Walker and Peter Shilton were as impressive as any players in the tournament.

And so England headed for Turin and a semi-final against West Germany, the most impressive side so far in the competition. The papers dismissed England's chances, yet from the whistle they came out fighting. England clearly had the edge in the first half and although Germany began to look dangerous on the break after the

ABOVE: *Gary Lineker fires England's equaliser past Jurgen Kohler.*

England's Cup final dream ends in tears

Daily Telegraph, 5 July 1990

interval, it still came as something of a surprise when they went into the lead – Brehme's free kick taking a cruel deflection past Shilton. It seemed that England, after so much luck themselves, were about to bow out. But nobody had accounted for Lineker who, with ten minutes to go, fired a glorious left foot shot into the far corner of the net. In extra time Chris Waddle struck a post while the Germans' hit the upright. But there were no more goals and as the final whistle blew the two sides lined up for a dramatic penalty shoot-out. But if England had ridden their luck so far, in the penalty shoot out it finally deserted them as Pearce and Waddle missed their kicks. England were out of the World Cup while Germany would go on to beat Argentina 1-0 in one of the dullest finals in memory. England returned home to a tumultuous reception, having played with

ABOVE: *A tearful Paul Gascoigne salutes the crowd.*
LEFT: *Gary Lineker shows the tension during the penalty shoot out.*

Robson's men pay price of this cruel Russian roulette

By Michael Calvin

THE world shared England's sense of desolation when they played Russian roulette in the Delle Alpi Stadium and discovered a deadly bullet in the chamber.

Just as hearts went out to Roberto Donadoni and Aldo Serena, of Italy, in Naples the previous evening, the plight of Stuart Pearce and Chris Waddle commanded sympathy.

It was no time for rational analysis. There was nothing remotely consoling in England gaining more respect from artificial defeat than a string of victories which attracted persistent criticism.

There was an eerie feeling of *déjà vu* as Waddle had to be helped to his feet and team-mates threw protective arms around the distraught Pearce; but it was not until England's players reached the sanctuary of their dressing room that they realised the enormity of what they had let slip.

"There are tears in there," confirmed Bobby Robson, in the inevitable inquest he handled with dignity and sardonic humour. "You come out and you put on a brave face. It is all you can do.

ITALIA '90

WORLD CUP

best football team. Who, on the evidence of a breezy evening in Turin, can decide the relative merits of England and West Germany?

Who, using Tuesday night's penalty shoot-out as a guide, can claim without the merest hint of unease, that Argentina are necessarily a better balanced side than Italy?

Individual images — the delayed shock on Waddle's face, for instance — are difficult to forget. It is easy to miss the nervous rituals of the players who are obliged to gather in the centre circle, like exhibits in a human zoo.

explained: "We really fancied him and held him back because he usually doesn't miss. He's very upset. These things happen. I feel very sorry for him."

It was an unfortunate way to embroider the folklore of matches against West Germany, which have eaten into the national consciousness. Pearce and Waddle take their place in history, alongside the benevolent Russian linesman of 1966 and the contaminated Coca-Cola which laid Gordon Banks low in 1970.

It will take some days for the England players to appreciate the impact of their best performance of an uneven tournament. There was much talk — as midnight came and went — of heads being held high, of national pride being salvaged.

Having criticised the inconsistency and inherent lack of imagination, one must concede, without reservation, that England's footballers proved their worth.

It was an absorbing, refreshingly cerebral contest that demanded complete concentration and matchless self-control. The exaggerated mutual respect between the teams was revealing.

Daily Telegraph, 5 July 1990

1991

KENNY DALGLISH had been one of the most admired footballers since the War. With a record haul of medals from Celtic and Liverpool, plus a record number of caps and goals for Scotland, he had been appointed player manager at Liverpool on the eve of the Heysel disaster. Many queried whether he would make a good manager but Dalglish confounded the critics by taking Liverpool to three league championships and two FA Cup triumphs. On top of that they had finished runners up in the league twice, had been defeated unexpectedly by Wimbledon in an FA Cup final and had also reached a League Cup final, only to be beaten by Arsenal. What's more, Dalglish's triumphs included a League and Cup double with two other Doubles missed by a whisker.

The Liverpool team that he shaped showed a flair and style not always associated with Liverpool sides of the past. There was none of the emphasis on defence. Instead Dalglish dipped into the transfer market signing players who brought a dash of flair and adventure to Liverpool's football. John Barnes, Peter Beardlsey, John Aldridge and Ray Houghton, all proved entertaining and perceptive signings. Dalglish was well on the way to becoming one of the most successful managers in the game's history when on Friday February 22nd he shocked everyone by suddenly announcing his resignation.

Nobody could believe it, especially the reasons he gave for his decision. He told journalists that he was tired, that the pressures had been too much and he needed a break from the game. There had to be more to it, reckoned the football writers as they searched desperately to unearth some myserious reason behind the Scot's decision. In the event there was no mystery. Dalglish had been playing football at the highest level since the age of seventeen, followed by five years as manager of Britain's top club where the pressures for success were enormous. He had simply found it too

HOWARD KENDALL (Everton): "I'm surprised, though I can understand the reasons he has given. I felt the pressure of the job a few years ago. I needed a break, and took it by going to Spain — a working break. Maybe that is all Kenny needs — a break."

HOWARD WILKINSON (Leeds): "If Kenny Dalglish has resigned because of the pressures of the job, the rest us have no chance. He had the players and financial resources. Every manager feels pressures from time to time and it is simply a matter of whether your are prepared to put up with them or come to the conclusion that the price is too high.

"The longer you stay in the job, the more likely you are to resist the temptation to step aside because we all take satisfaction from seeing our plans come to fruition."

JOZEF VENGLOS (Aston Villa): "Pressure is the big problem. You can't train people to accept the stress that goes with the job. That means it is not easy for wives and children who live with football. Managers work, eat and sleep the game and when they wake up it is still with them."

DON HOWE (QPR chief coach): "I was flabbergasted when I heard. It's one of the most surprising pieces of football news in years, especially after Wednesday night's FA Cup replay with Everton which was a game in a million.

"Kenny will have been mulling over his decision all season. He is not the sort to make rash decisions. He will be greatly missed. He is one of our young, shining lights in management.

"Liverpool will get over his resignation though. They have lost good men before. People said Liverpool would struggle when Bill Shankly and Bob Paisley retired. They never did."

ARTHUR COX (Derby): "I'm not surprised — nothing in football surprises me. Kenny will have his reasons because he has always been a very single-minded man. Whatever they are he has to be respected.

"When you go into management, you find it devours your life and takes everything you've got Perhaps that's what he means by the pressure."

TERRY VENABLES (Tottenham): " am just surprised, very surprised. I have heard on the news he is saying it is because of pressure, and yes, the job can be pressurised. It has its moments. I know no more than anybody else about his reasons. We can only guess. I am sure there will be no shortage of applications for the job."

ALEX FERGUSON (Manchester United): "It comes as a big surprise, a shock. It is very difficult to assess it. I spoke to Kenny only a few days ago and I got no hint of it."

PHIL NEAL (Bolton, a former Liverpool player): 'When you're a manager it's the same whether you're spending £3 million or £30,000 — pressure goes with the job. It's even more so when you're doing the job at the top club in the country."

Daily Telegraph, 23 February 1991

CAREER MILESTONES

March 1951 Kenneth Mathieson Dalglish, son of an engineer, born in Glasgow.

March, 1968: Joined Celtic. Debut 1969; total 204 League appearances (112 goals, 4 titles, 4 Scottish Cups).

Dec 1971: First Scotland cap. Ended with record 102, and his 30 goals equalled Denis Law's record.

Aug 1977: Joined Liverpool (£440,000, British record) to replace Kevin Keegan.

May, 1978: Scored only goal in European Cup final v Bruges at Wembley. Further European medals in 1981 and 84.

April, 1979: Footballer of the Year (also 1983) and PFA Player of the Year.

May, 1979: First League Championship medal. Others in 80, 82, 83, 84, 86, 88, 90 (last three as manager or player-manager).

Dec, 1984: Awarded MBE.

May, 1985: Becomes player-manager when Joe Fagan resigns after Heysel.

May, 1986: Manager of the Year after winning double (also 1988, 1990).

May, 1989: Last League appearance. Total 355, with 118 goals.

Feb, 1991: Quits as manager.

Daily Telegraph, 23 February 1991

ABOVE: *Graeme Souness during his first match as Liverpool manager*

Reluctant King of the Kop

TO THE soccer world, Kenny Dalglish seemed like the perfect manager. In times of tragedy he had offered Liverpool extreme strength. In times of success he had delivered a stream of trophies.

But behind the man who had provided the city with a crutch during the aftermath of the Heysel and Hillsborough disasters, there was an unease with the demands of his profession.

Dalglish was a great player who reluctantly became a great manager. He was never comfortable with the pressures of the job, even during the many moments of triumph.

He cried yesterday — not for the first time — over Liverpool. The most public previous occasion was during the dark days following Hillsborough, when 95 Liverpool fans died.

During that spring of 1989, Dalglish was a rock. He was prominent mourner and a consoling counsellor. Suddenly Dalglish, imported from Glasgow in 1977 knew how much Liverpool — the club and the city — meant to him.

For him to have cut his links with the club must have been the most painful and difficult decision of his footballing life.

At the same time it may have offered him a welcome release from the pressure that had built up around him and which were slowly but surely making his life a misery.

Dalglish was first and foremost a player. He was the man who enjoyed the spotlight of on-the-field glory but afterwards sought to escape into his private world.

He was not really a manager. He admitted last summer that he never felt comfortable in the job. He could not put his hand on his heart and swear he enjoyed the life.

SATURDAY PROFILE

KENNY DALGLISH
BY COLIN GIBSON

Kenny Dalglish... foremost a player, never comfortable as a manager

Daily Telegraph, 23 February 1991

great a burden. He had also gone through the horrors of Heysel and then Hillsborough, where his dignity and leadership had given strength to the club and its grieving fans, but had never left him with enough time of his own to grieve and come to terms with what had happened. So the man who had devoted so many years to Liverpool was gone within the hour. It was as dramatic as that.

Liverpool immediately began the search for a successor but did not have to look too far as Graeme Souness, manager at Glasgow Rangers, indicated his interest. It looked like a perfect marriage, the former Liverpool iron man, now in command at his old club. But it was not to be. Almost three years later Souness would be sacked after Liverpool had flirted with relegation and spent millions in the transfer market with little success. Dalglish meanwhile, after a lengthy period out of the game, joined lowly Blackburn Rovers, and was soon taking them out of the first division to the Premiership title.

1992

> **FREE INSIDE**
> **KICK-OFF TO A NEW SOCCER ERA**
> *Daily Mail, 10 August 1992*

THE IDEA OF A SUPER LEAGUE had been mooted for some years but during 1991 action began to take the place of rhetoric. A year later, as the new season kicked off on August 15th 1992, the old first division became the Premier League.

The Premier League was really about money and television. The satellite broadcaster BSkyB who had paid a phenomenal £304 million for a five year deal involving live coverage of two league games a week, was only interested in matches involving the top clubs. BSkyB were most defintely not interested in any obligation to televise second and third division games. What they wanted was a diet of Liverpool, Manchester United, Tottenham, Arsenal, Leeds and Everton – the clubs that would bring in viewers and subscribers to their channel. No way were the majority of Football League members going to allow that kind of deal.

Not surprisingly it was the top clubs who saw the immediate financial benefit and were quickly tempted by the prospect. Most of these clubs were about to face huge bills from redeveloping their grounds into all-seater stadiums to comply with the Taylor Report. It was going to be expensive and the money would have to come from somewhere.

Eventually all the old first division clubs agreed to break away and form a league of their own where they would have total control over their own affairs. There were some who doubted the wisdom, particularly the smaller clubs in the first division who saw it all as a conspiracy by the rich clubs to become even richer. But in the end they had little option but to go along with the idea. In effect the new set up gave control to the top half dozen rich clubs. Under the old formula, no changes could be implemented in the league unless a majority of clubs in all four leagues agreed. It was a cumber-

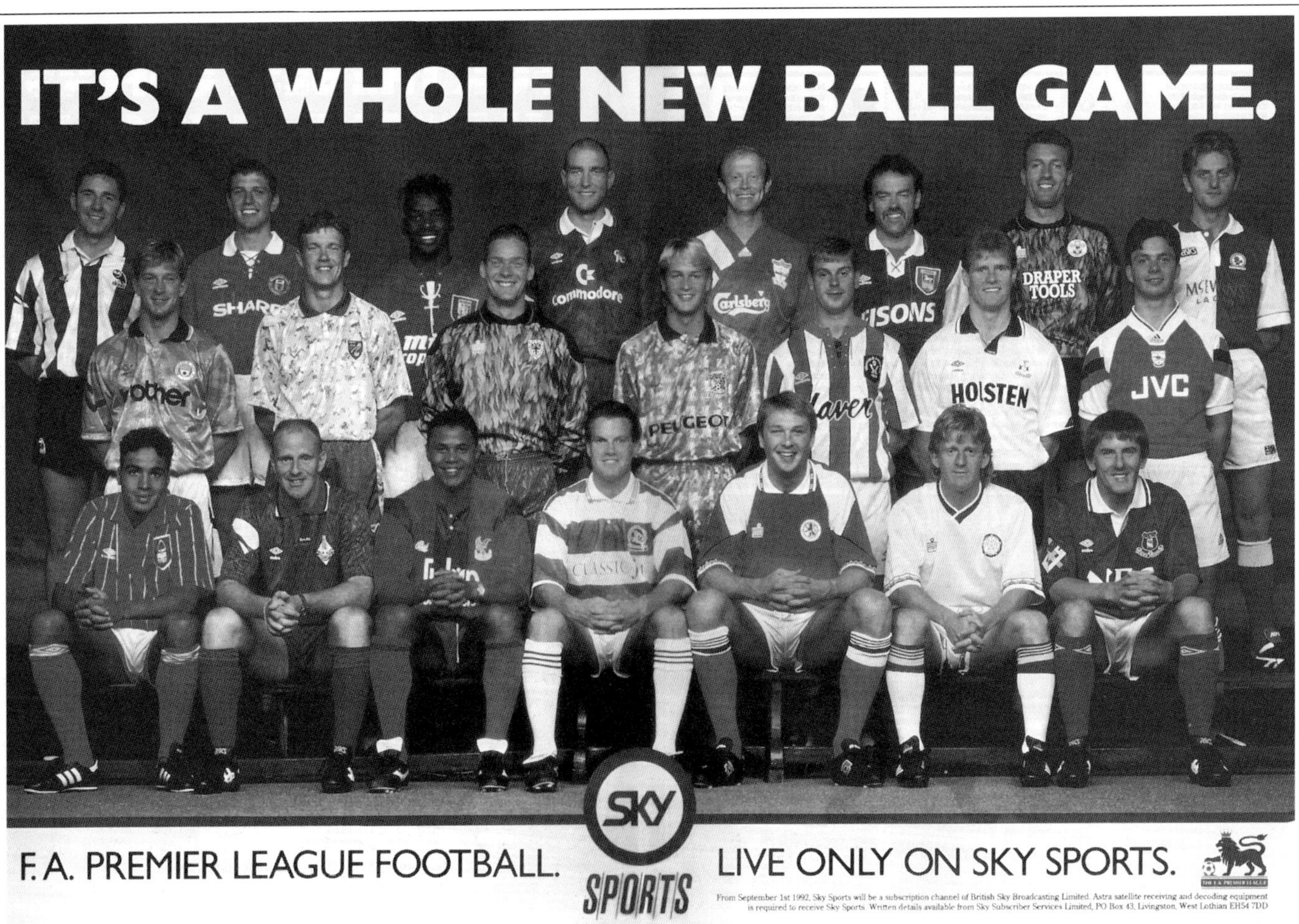

Radio Times, 15 August to 8 September 1992

some process that did not encourage change. Now any changes rested with the 22 clubs of the top division who could decide their own fate.

ABOVE: *The new Premier League was criticised for being a slave to television and money. Here the 'Sky Strikers' entertain the crowd before Arsenal's match against Manchester City at Highbury.*

The first Premier League game to be televised came on the second day of the football season, August 16th when the cameras were live at Nottingham Forest for the visit of Liverpool.

BELOW: *Sir John Quinton and Rick Parry, the pioneers of the Premier League at one of the early news conferences.*

In reality there was little difference. It was still the same number of clubs though with a plan to reduce the league to 20 and eventually 18 teams. The rules were the same with probably the most noticeable change being the bright new green strip worn by referees. A third substitute, a goalkeeper, would also be allowed. The half time interval was also going to be extended to fifteen minutes for the benefit of television while kick off times would also vary to suit television schedules. Instead of all games being played on the traditional Saturday afternoon there were now matches scheduled for late Sunday afternoon and Monday evening so that they could be televised. It caused some confusion and irritated many fans who found that the increase in Sunday and Monday matches meant that they were not

1993

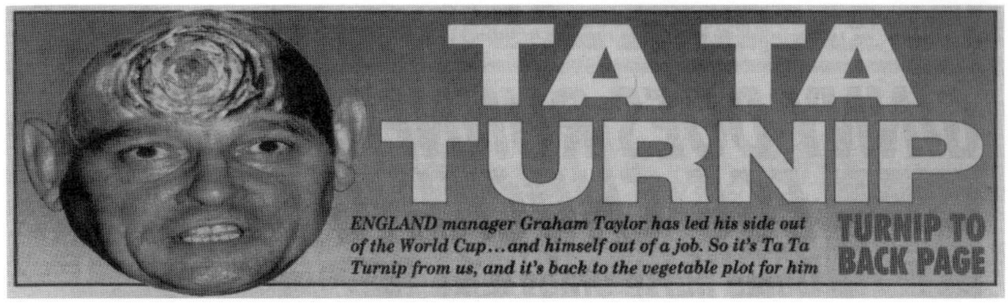
TA TA TURNIP

ENGLAND manager Graham Taylor has led his side out of the World Cup...and himself out of a job. So it's Ta Ta Turnip from us, and it's back to the vegetable plot for him

TURNIP TO BACK PAGE

The Sun, 15 October 1993

GRAHAM TAYLOR'S reign as the England manager came to an abrupt end in November 1993. Six days earlier England had just been defeated by Holland and were out of the 1994 World Cup finals. Taylor was the scourge of Fleet Street, his photo splashed in the unkindest images across every back page. He had little option but to resign. Thankfully he did it quickly, not even waiting to be sacked.

Taylor was never popular with the football writers. He had been a successful manager with Watford, taking them from fourth division obscurity and into the first division, although he would never win any of the major honours as a manager. The nearest Watford had ever come to any distincion was a Cup Final appearance at Wembley when they were defeated by Everton. Then, in 1987, he had surprised everyone by moving down a division to Aston Villa, but again tasted success, taking the club back into the first division.

When Bobby Robson quit the England job in 1990 the name of Graham Taylor was always high on the list of possible successors. There were other contenders, particularly Brian Clough, but the FA shied from taking a gamble on the outspoken and unpredictable Clough. In hindsight they were probably right. There were other names in the frame as well, among them Terry Venables, Joe Royle and Howard Kendall. But in the end the FA decided to play it safe and opt for Taylor.

Taylor began well enough. After a dozen games England were still unbeaten with nine wins behind them. But they were only friendlies. What matters is competition and Taylor's first opportunity came with the 1992 European Championships. England qualified easily enough, even topping their group above the Republic of Ireland and Poland. Hopes were high but in the finals in Denmark they failed abysmally, not even winning one game and scoring just one goal.

For the 1994 World Cup final qualifiers England had been drawn in a group alongside San Marino, Poland, Norway, Holland and Turkey. It was by no means an easy group but with the top two qualifying it was certainly not an impossible challenge. Holland and England were favourites to go through to the finals in the USA but in the event

ABOVE: *Graham Taylor and Lawrie McMenemy after the 2-0 defeat against Holland. Defeat virtually ensured England's exit from the World Cup.*

it was Holland and Norway who stole the glory with the Norwegians surprising everyone by topping the group. England were let down by their poor home record, a 1-1 draw at Wembley with Norway and a 2-2 draw with Holland after being two goals ahead, not helping their cause. Then in the summer of 1993 came a disastrous trip across Europe with a 1-1 draw in Poland and a 2-0 defeat in Norway. Everything now rested on England's trip to Holland but it only ended in a 2-0 defeat and virtual elimination.

By now Taylor was being scorned on all fronts but especially on the backpages. The Sun dubbed him a turnip, the fans even booed him at Wembley but he was determined not to quit until he had completed the job. There was still the faintest of hopes of qualification when England visited San Marino in November 1993 but when England went a goal behind after a few seconds, one of the greatest humilations in soccer history looked to be in the making. In the event England won but it was of little use as Holland also won and joined Norway on the plane to America.

Resignation was inevitable and Taylor did not wait to be pushed. He knew his time was up and he'd also had enough of the jeering and the expectations of the backpages. The newspapers with their instant analysis and cruel headlines had made the job all the harder. After Robson and Taylor it was a wonder anyone would want the job.

Q: Have you been a good England manager?

A: On results...No

GRAHAM TAYLOR'S VERDICT ON HIMSELF

The Sun, 15 October 1993

BELOW: *The pressure starts to tell. The England manager argues with a FIFA offical during the match against Holland.*

1994

UNITED AT THE DOUBLE

Daily Express, 16 May 1994

ONLY THREE TEAMS this century had clinched the League and Cup double – Tottenham, Arsenal and Liverpool – but in 1994 Manchester United became the fourth side to join English football's most elite group. And yet the year had started on as sad a note as possible for United when their former manager Sir Matt Busby died in late Janaury. Not only was the city of Manchester stunned but the entire football world. Busby was a legend and, even though he was 84 and had been ill for some time, his death was still frontpage news. Manchester went into mourning with flags at half mast through-

out the city for the man who had created the modern Manchester United. A few days later his funeral cortege weaved its way past Old Trafford on its final journey, pausing for a few moments outside the stadium that he had helped to build into one of Europe's finest grounds.

Busby had created three outstanding United sides. His first side, just after the war, had been League runners up four times before finally taking the title in 1952 to add to their 1948 FA Cup triumph. A few years later his second great team, the 'Busby Babes', won the championship in successive years as well as reaching the FA Cup final. But then in 1958 they were cruelly destroyed in the terrible air disaster at Munich. For days Busby himself had hovered between life and death but had survived to make an emotional return to Wembley to watch his new side go down to Bolton Wanderers in the FA Cup final. And then there was his third great side – the team that captured two championships in the 1960s and the FA Cup before going on to win the European Cup in 1968.

In May 1993 Busby had been in his usual seat in the directors box at Old Trafford, all smiles, as United lifted the championship, their first since 1967. There could be only one fitting memorial to Busby and that was for the current side to go out and win the Double, the one honour that had escaped him.

United topped the Premiership from virtually the start of the season to the finish. By December the bookmakers were even refusing to take bets as United built up an unassailable lead. Towards the end of the season they faltered slightly, dropping points as the pressures began to mount and the games piled up. United were chasing not just the Double but a Treble as well. In March they reached the Coca-Cola Cup final where they faced Aston Villa at Wembley only to lose 1-3. In the League luck suddenly seemed to desert them when Peter Schmeichel and Eric Cantona were sent off and the sheer num-

What they all said

GEORGE BEST "I cannot pay a bigger compliment to this current Manchester United team than to say that it stands comparison to the great side I played in which won the First Division title in 1967 and the European Cup the following year. In my time if the team had an off day, we could always rely on one of the players to produce something a little bit special and this is one of the secrets of Alex Feruson's team. When you have got players of the quality of Eric Cantona, Mark Hughes, Lee Sharpe, Ryan Giggs and Paul Ince you are always in with a chance

DENIS LAW: "I am delighted not only for the players and the club but for the marvellous fans who have stayed loyal to Manchester United since they last won the League title all those years ago.

"When the Reds slipped up over the last leg of the championship race last season I began to wonder if the title was ever coming back to Old Trafford.

"But the team have made it this season...and made it in style.

BILL FOULKES: "It's been a long time coming but the wait has been worthwhile. This has been a fantastic night for the club and the supporters and I am particularly delighted for Alex Ferguson. United have won the Premier League title by playing soccer as it should be played but it is now that the hard work really starts.

Next season is when Alex will face the big problems when he has the increased demands of the European Cup to add to all the domestic competitions. But he has done a fantastic job and I know he has got the ability to handle everything which will come his way."

KENNY DALGLISH: "Only time will tell what heights Manchester United will reach from now on because you can never be sure how players are going to react to success.

"But United proved throughout the season that they are the fitting champions. They have set a standard which the rest of us must now try to match."

ALEX FERGUSON: "You strive all your life to get a feeling like tonight. I've never experienced anything like it.

"Eric Cantona has illuminated the stadium; he brought imagination to our game that only great players bring. Players respond to that, they were immediately magnetized by him, they couldn't give him the ball quickly enough. He created a flair and chemistry that United followers understand."

Manchester Evening News, 3 May 1994

ber of games began to take its toll in injury and fatigue. But then in the FA Cup semi-final played at Wembley, a goal down to Oldham and with 90 minutes already showing on the clock, Mark Hughes poked a toe at an impossible chance and the ball rocketed into the back of the net. It signalled a change in United's luck. A few days later Oldham were soundly beaten in the replay and United were at Wembley for the fourth time that season. In the league meanwhile their nearest rivals Blackburn suddenly faltered while United pressed ahead with impressive victories over Wimbledon, Manchester City, Leeds, Ipswich and Southampton to reassert their authority and clinch the title.

United's opponents in the FA Cup final were Chelsea, the side that had beaten them twice that season. But there would be no third victory for Chelsea. The Londoners may have held their own for 60 minutes but suddenly, two dramatic penalties within six minutes were slammed into the back of the net by Eric Cantona and the game was all over. Mark Hughes and Brian McClair added United's third and fourth goals to give them a comprehensive 4-0 win. United had won the Double and as they paraded their silverware around Wembley, the crowd fittingly remembered Sir Matt, chanting his name in honour of the Double.

ABOVE: *The celebrations after clinching the double*

FAR LEFT: *Bryan Robson raises the Premiership trophy.*

Finally, it all came together for Ferguson

Hugh McIlvanney sees the United team overcome Chelsea's bright start to keep an appointment with destiny for their club and its manager

FOR a long time at Wembley yesterday, it seemed that Manchester United were intent on refusing the embrace of history. But, though this victory was shaped by two penalties within six minutes in the second half, it would be unfair to suggest that they waited for their destiny to force itself upon them. They had, in fact, taken control before they took the lead and, by the end, there was more than a semblance of majesty about their bearing.

After a first half that saw them falter and slither so abjectly in the north London drizzle that equality at the interval was grossly flattering, they at last began to play like men who believed in their right to join Tottenham, Arsenal and Liverpool as the only teams this century to complete the championship and FA Cup double. Now they share Spurs' record of having won the Cup eight times.

Chelsea — whose last major trophy in English football was secured in this competition, though not on this ground, 24 years ago — were entitled to feel cruelly abused by the scoreline. Through half the match, they were its dominant force, denying the favourites time and space with intelligent industry and a rich, combative spirit that gave them numbers behind the ball whenever required and thrusting runners at the first glimpse of an opening. They paid for all that galloping after half-time but it was thrilling while it lasted.

The chant of "Easy" from the red majority in the stadium at the final whistle was accurate only in relation to the last 20 minutes, which United turned into a stroll towards a coronation.

And even then Chelsea kept striving for a goal to preserve their self-respect. But Schmeichel's leaping, sprawling form was always in the way. The London team were weary by then and their two defeats of United in the Premier League this season were a distant, irrelevant memory. Chelsea must have known when Cantona stroked the second of his two almost identical penalties beyond Kharine's left side in the 67th minute that their cause was lost.

The decision to award that penalty was dubious and they scarcely deserved the torture that came as Alex Ferguson's men belatedly relaxed into the imaginative fluency that has been their natural language through most of the past two years. United's failure in the first three-quarters of an hour to maintain pressure along the flanks (Giggs's tendency to drift inside had been a limiting factor) prevented them from pressing the Chelsea defenders back and creating space in which Cantona could operate effectively. But now they cured themselves of that fault and the Frenchman's skills and ingenuity were able to flourish.

It was never quite possible to see 4-0, the biggest winning margin since United beat Brighton by the same score in a replay 11 years ago, as a legitimate product of their supremacy. Always there was the balancing recollection of what had happened before the interval. As they reeled before Chelsea's superior creativity in that period, United may have drawn confidence from the awareness of just how much of a winner their manager has been over the years. His record is far more remarkable than is generally acknowledged.

While with Aberdeen he accomplished the extraordinary feat of elbowing Rangers and Celtic off centre stage in Scottish football for most of a decade, winning three League championships, four Scottish Cups, one League Cup and the European Cup Winners' Cup. With Manchester United, he has won two successive championships (ending a drought of 26 years), two FA Cups, the League Cup and, again, the Cup Winners' Cup.

Maybe this Wembley occasion was some way short of being the stuff of legend, but it represents another substantial brick in the edifice of achievement associated with the Govan man's name. Of course, it will take the capturing of the European Cup to leave him feeling anything like contented. "We want to do ourselves justice after last year's experience in the European Cup," he said last night with a quiet intensity that left no doubt about the depth of his ambition. But for fellow Scots, he has already performed a major service by obliterating the claim that nobody could be a successful manager in England without coming up through the ranks of the English game.

When United hired him in November 1986, they were recruiting a true football man and one with a bottomless appetite for work and unquenchable drive. Yet there was a time, nearly three years after his arrival, when many were ready to pronounce his managership doomed.

On a day at the end of September 1989, I sat in his spacious, pleasant house out in the tranquil greenery of Cheshire, less than a week after his team had been slaughtered 5-1 by Manchester City, and heard him say: "Believe me, what I have felt in the last week you wouldn't think should happen in football. Every time somebody looks at me, I feel I have betrayed that man. After such a result, you feel as if you have to sneak round corners, feel as if you are some kind of criminal. . .But I mean to be here making a success of things three years from now."

He is there nearly five years on. And it might be fair to say he has made a success of things.

WHAT THEY SAID AT WEMBLEY

☐ **Alex Ferguson on United:** I am very proud of the team. We've lost just six games in 64 matches this season. That's really remarkable consistency. Allied to ability, you need character and resilience — and we have that in abundance.

☐ **Ferguson on Bryan Robson:** It was a tragedy for him that we couldn't have him on the bench today. But Cantona was struggling with sciatica in the back and we really needed McClair's flexibility on the bench.

Bryan knows clearly that I did it in the best interests of Manchester United. But you can't begin to know how it hurt me to have to leave him out.

☐ **Glenn Hoddle on Chelsea:** Peacock's shot against the bar may have been the turning point. Europe will be a consolation for us in a few days' time. But we're losers today and it hurts.

☐ **Mark Hughes on Eric Cantona:** It took a lot of courage for him to take the ball and take those penalties. But there was never any doubt in my mind, nor his, that he'd score.

The Sunday Times, 15 May 1994

1995

Bully Wise stunned by 3-month jail term

Daily Express, 14 March 1995

FOOTBALL / FA insist corruption 'not rife' as police hold three players over bribery allegations

Match-fixing arrests leave new stain on game's image

Daily Telegraph, 15 March 1995

Sacked Graham sues Arsenal

The Mail on Sunday, 21 May 1995

It was the year of sleaze and scandal, a year when football seemed to rarely be off the frontpages, let alone the backpages. Football took a battering as under the table payments, violence on and off the field, drugs, and allegations of match fixing hit the headlines. What's more, it all involved players, clubs and managers at the highest level.

George Graham, the most successful Arsenal manager since Herbert Chapman, a man it seemed of the highest integrity, was fired by Arsenal following a Premier League inquiry into allegations that he had received an illegal payment. The 'bung' was alleged to have been given as payment in the signing of the Danish international John Jensen. Graham's sacking sent shock waves through the business with other top managers also being named by various newspapers. Graham it seemed was merely the tip of the iceberg in a scandal that involved players, agents and managers.

As if the sacking of one of the country's top managers was not enough. There were also allegations of match fixing involving some of the best known names in the game. Heading the list was Bruce Grobbelaar, the Southampton and former Liverpool goalkeeper, who stood accused of taking money to influence the result of a number of games. The Sun newspaper, which exposed the story, alleged that the match fixing had been organised by a Malaysian syndicate.

Investigations, both by the police and the Football Association began immediately with Grobbelaar, one of the most popular goalkeepers in the business, protesting his innocence from the start.

Other players also found themselves in trouble with the law. Eric

BELOW: *Eric Cantona's infamous Kung Fu kick after being sent off against Crystal Palace at Selhurst Park.*

Violence prompts fears about England hosting 1996 European Championship

Riot revives football nightmare

The Guardian, 16 February 1995

Cantona, Manchester United's hugely popular Frenchman, took a Kung Fu kick at a spectator following his dismissal at Crystal Palace. Cantona may have been appallingly provoked but United promptly banned him for the rest of the season, even though they were challenging for the double. A few weeks later the Football Association extended the ban into September and then the Croydon Magistrates court imposed a two week prison sentence on the French captain. Fortunately for Cantona the sentence was then revised on appeal to community service. Nor was Cantona the only player facing jail. Dennis Wise the Chelsea and England midfielder was sentenced to an even longer term in prison following his attack on a taxi driver.

The fans behaved little better either with the Ireland–England international in Dublin halted, as so called England fans launched a barrage of missiles on Irish fans. Fighting broke out, the pitch was invaded and police fought running battles with spectators. In the end the referee was left with little choice but to abandon the match bringing yet more shame on the English game and putting the 1996 European Championships in jeopardy.

Then there were drugs. Arsenal's Paul Merson made a brave confession about being an alcohol and drug abuser. In particular Merson was using cocaine. Arsenal and the FA took firm but lenient action and immediately sent Merson on a rehabilitation course. A few months later he was back in the Arsenal side, having made considerable progress in overcoming his problem. Chris Armstrong of Crystal Palace was also sidelined by his club after a drugs test proved positive. In his case it was marijuana and after a few weeks and a reprimand from the FA, he too was back in action.

It was not a good year. Just when football was beginning to attract a new audience to its super all-seater stadiums, it found itself having to deal with a barrage of negative stories that did little to help the game's new image. The Football Association generally reacted swiftly and sternly, but it was significant that all the allegations had been initiated by the media and not by football itself.

BELOW: *The Southampton crowd show their support for Bruce Grobbelaar, during his first match at The Dell following match-fixing allegations.*

FA PREMIER LEAGUE CHAMPIONS
1994-95

FA CUP WINNERS
1995

PICTURE CREDITS

Aldus Archive: 135; Allsport: 185 bottom (Trevor Jones), 193, 204 both (Simon Buty), 207 (David Cannon); Arsenal F.C.: 38, 49 (Steve Richards); Associated Press: 84, 90, 93, 113 top, 114, 117, 142, 148, 149, 162; Associated Sports Photography: 153, 156, 163; BBC Hulton Picture Library: 15 bottom, 17, 21 top right, 35, 47, 57 top and bottom, 60 left, 61 top, 73, 76, 83, 86-87, 87, 88, 99, 106, 129, 132, 140, 174; Bradford Telegraph & Argus: 160; Colorsport: 11, 16, 17, 23, 29 top left and bottom left, 50, 51, 56, 63 left, 64, 78, 79 left and right, 103, 104 top and bottom, 105, 107 top and bottom, 108, 109, 110, 120, 121 top, 134 all, 137, 138, 164, 166, 176, 177 top, 178 left, 185 top, 189, 194, 197, 203, 205, 206, 208, 209, 210, 211 all, 212, 213, 215, 216, 217, 218, 219, 220, 221; Comprehensive Art Services, Manchester/ Stewart Beckett: 42-43;Express Newspapers: 130; Glasgow Herald and Evening Times: 12, 82, 122, 123, 143; John Harding: 26 centre top, 27 top and right; The Illustrated London News: 15 centre, 18, 19, 22, 24, 30, 31 top and bottom, 33 left, 40 top, bottom left and right, 41, 53, 55, 61 bottom, 69 bottom, 70-71, 71, 72, 77; Joe Laskowski/Swifts Programmes: 44 (Steve Richards); Manchester United F.C.: 32 top, 34; Oxford Newspapers: 191; Photosource/The Keystone Collection: 36, 54, 60 right, 66, 69 top, 75, 85, 91, 112, 127 top and bottom, 136, 141, 144, 159, 171, 192 all; Popperfoto: 28, 52 bottom, 67, 68, 74, 89, 92 top centre, 95 top, 97 top and bottom, 100, 111, 113 top and bottom, 115, 118, 121 bottom, 128 bottom, 131, 133, 139, 146 top and bottom, 150, 151 left, 155, 165, 172 bottom, 173, 190; Press Association: 21 bottom, 65, 125, 161, 200; Professional Footballers Association: 26 top (Alan Seabright), 26 bottom; Solo Syndication, © Mail Newspapers plc: 101; Sport and General: 52 top, 126, 145, 167, 187; Sporting Pictures: 188, 195; Syndication International: 20, 29 right, 95 bottom, 98, 116, 128 top, 147, 151, 152, 154, 157 top and bottom, 175, 182, 184, 196; Bob Thomas: 169, 170, 172 top, 177 bottom, 178 right, 179, 180, 181, 183, 198, 199; Topham Picture Library: 70 top, 81, 186, 201; Wallasey Reference Library: 14; E.W. Wilding, Millwall F.C. Historian: 80.

The publishers wish to thank the following for permission to reproduce copyright material: Associated Newspapers, the *Daily Telegraph*, Express Newspapers, the *Guardian*, the *Independent*, *Liverpool Post* and *Echo*, Mail Newspapers plc, News Group Newspapers, Reuters, Syndication International, Thomson Organisation plc, Thomson Regional Newspapers, Times Newspapers Limited.

While every effort has been made to trace copyright holders, this has proved impossible in some cases and copyright owners are invited to contact the publishers.